Crüe Fest

Guitar TAB Songbook

Mötley Crüe

Crüe Fest

Godsmack

Sixx:A.M.

Theory of a Deadman

Trapt

Papa Roach

Drowning Pool

Buckcherry

Charm City Devils

Alfred

Alfred Music Publishing Co., Inc.
16320 Roscoe Blvd., Suite 100
P.O. Box 10003
Van Nuys, CA 91410-0003
alfred.com

ISBN-10: 0-7390-6137-2
ISBN-13: 978-0-7390-6137-4

Mötley Crüe

CRÜE FEST

Godsmack

Sixx:A.M.

Theory of a Deadman

Trapt

Papa Roach

Drowning Pool

Buckcherry

Charm City Devils

CONTENTS

CRÜE FEST

CRAZY BITCH

Lyrics by JOSH TODD
Music by KEITH NELSON

Moderately ♩ = 98

Intro:

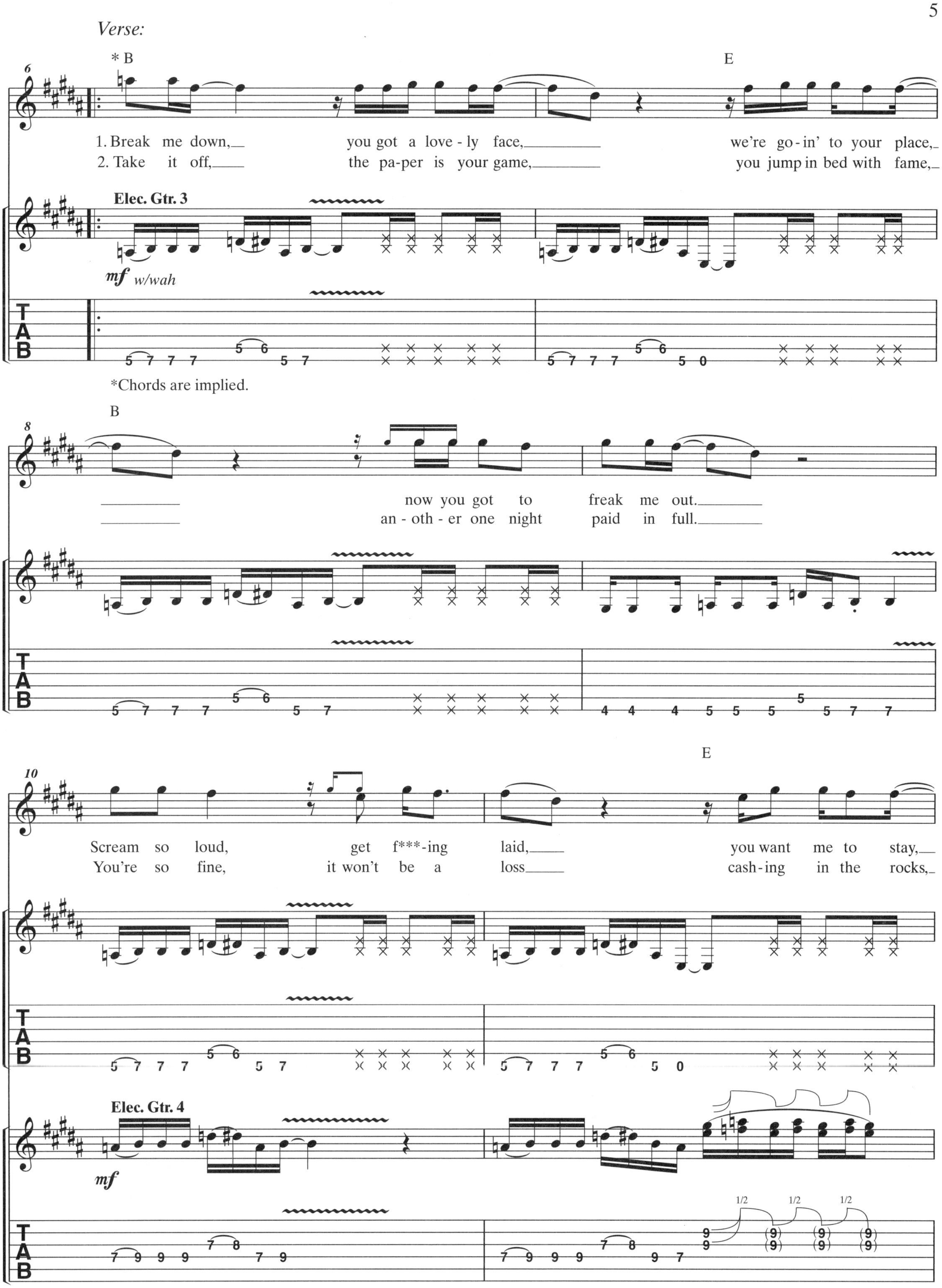
Verse:
* B
E
1. Break me down, you got a love - ly face, we're go - in' to your place,
2. Take it off, the pa-per is your game, you jump in bed with fame,
Elec. Gtr. 3
mf w/wah
*Chords are implied.
B
now you got to freak me out.
an - oth - er one night paid in full.
Scream so loud, get f***-ing laid,
You're so fine, it won't be a loss
E
you want me to stay,
cash-ing in the rocks,
Elec. Gtr. 4
mf
1/2
1/2
1/2

12
B
but I got to make my way.
just to get you face to face.
Elec. Gtr. 1
f
f
TAB
Chorus:
B
7fr.
134211
14
Hey! You're a cra - zy bitch, but you f*** so good I'm on top of it. When I
Elec. Gtrs. 1 & 2
1/2
16
dream I'm do-ing you all night, scratch-es all down my back to keep me right on.

18
Hey! You're a cra - zy bitch, but you f*** so good I'm on top of it. When I
20
dream I'm do - ing you all night,
1.
scratch - es all down my back to keep me right on.
2.
24
scratch - es all down my back to keep me right on.

Guitar Solo:

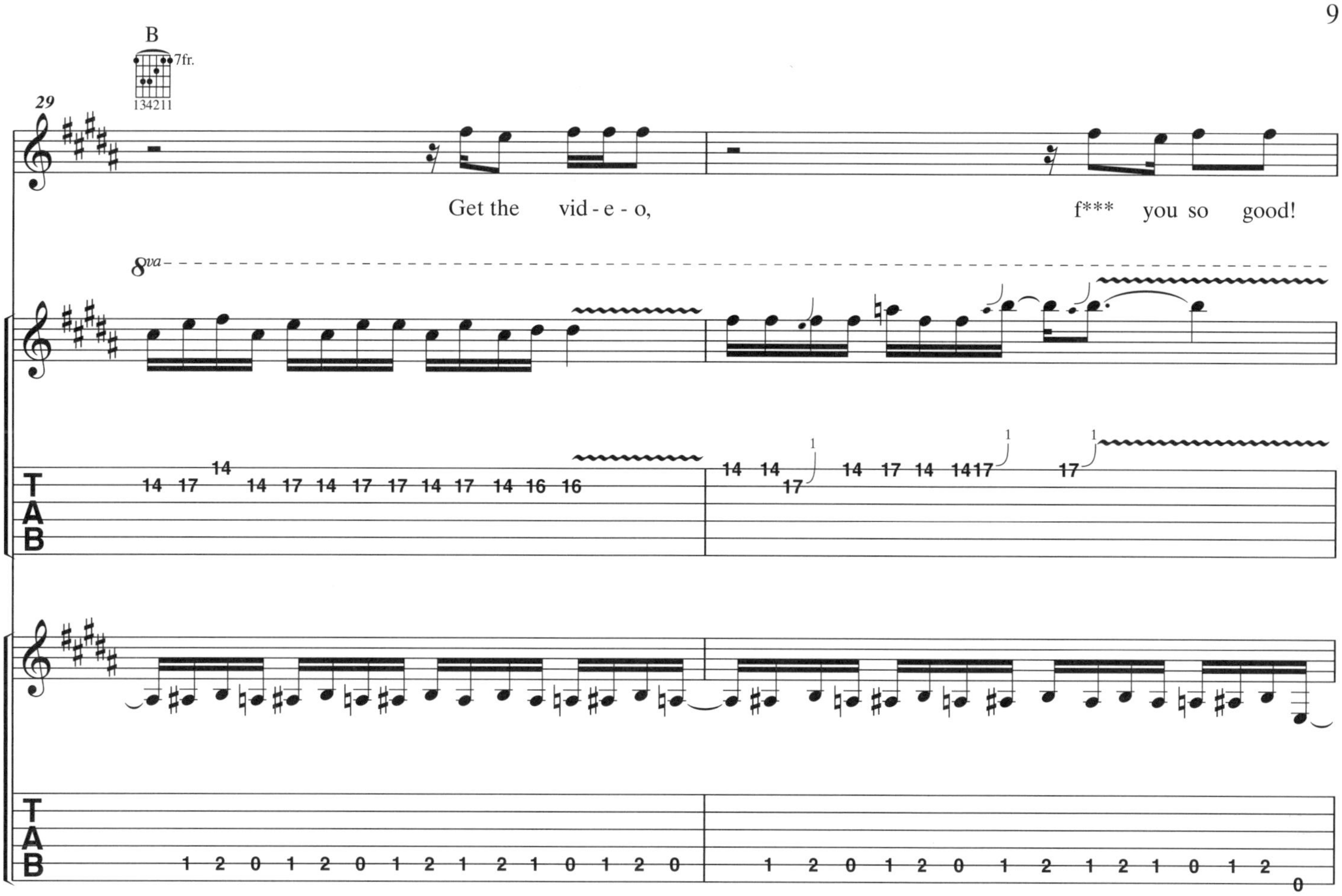
B
7fr.
134211
29
Get the vid - e - o,
f*** you so good!
8va

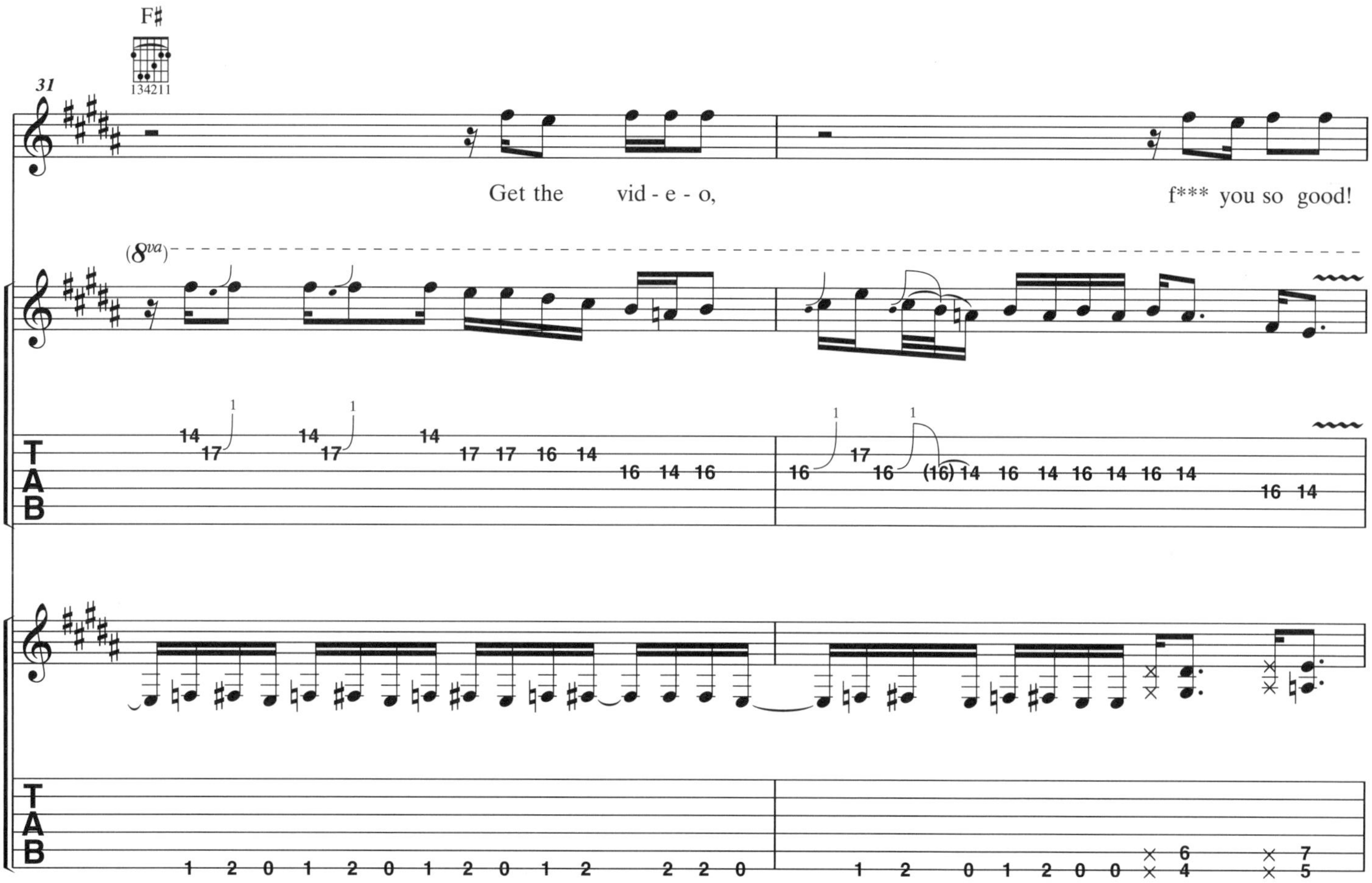
F♯
134211
31
Get the vid - e - o,
f*** you so good!
(8va)

B
7fr.
134211
Cra - zy bitch.
Cra - zy bitch.
Cra - zy
bitch.
(8va)
Elec. Gtr. 4
Chorus:
Hey!
You're a cra - zy bitch, but you f*** so good I'm on top of it. When I
1/2

39
dream I'm do-ing you all night,
scratch-es all down my back to keep me right on.

41
Hey! You're a cra - zy bitch, but you f***
so good I'm on top of it. When I

43
dream I'm do - ing you all night,
scratch-es all down my back to my...
Elec. Gtrs. 1 & 2
Bridge:
D 5fr. 1333
E 7fr. 1333
B 7fr. 134211
45
Ba - by girl,
you want it all.
Rhy. Fig. 1
w/Rhy. Fig. 1 (Elec. Gtrs. 1 & 2) 3 times
47
To be a star, you'll have to go down.
Take it off,
50
no need to talk.
You're cra - zy but I like the way you f*** me.

Chorus:

53
Hey! You're a cra - zy bitch, but you f*** so good I'm on top of it. When I
Elec. Gtr. 1
Elec. Gtr. 2
1/2
55
dream I'm do-ing you all night, scratch-es all down my back to keep me right on.
57
Elec. Gtrs. 1 & 2 cont. simile
Hey! You're a cra - zy bitch, but you f*** so good I'm on top of it. When I

59
dream I'm do - ing you all night, scratch - es all down my back to keep me right on.
61
You keep me right on. You're cra - zy but I
Elec. Gtr. 1
Elec. Gtr. 2
63
like the way you f*** me.

SORRY

Lyrics by JOSH TODD and MARTI FREDERIKSEN
Music by JOSH TODD, KEITH NELSON
and MARTI FREDERIKSEN

Moderately slow ♩ = 72
Intro:
G5
G5(9)
G5
G5(9)
1. Oh,
Acous. Gtr.
mf
hold throughout
Verse:
G5
D5
G5
I had a lot to say, was think - ing of my time a - way,
(2.) I think I'm to blame, it's hard - er to get through the days.
Elec. Gtr. 1
mf
hold throughout

D5
G5
D5
6
I missed you and things were-n't the same.
You get old - er and blame turns to shame.
'Cause ev-'ry - thing in - side,
Bm
Bm/A
G5
9
it nev - er comes out right.
And when I see you cry,

Bm
Bm/A
E
it makes me want to die.
I'm sor - ry I'm bad,
Cont. in slashes
Elec. Gtr. 2
Chorus:
D
A
Bm
F♯
Acous. Gtr.
Cont. rhy. simile
I'm sor - ry I'm blue,
I'm sor - ry a - bout all the things I said to you, and I know
Elec. Gtr. 2
G
Em
Asus
A
I can't take it back.
I love how you kiss,

D A Bm F♯
I love all your sounds, and, ba-by, the way you make my world go 'round, and I just
G Em
1. Asus A
want - ed to say, I'm sor - ry.
Elec. Gtr. 2 & Acous. Gtr.
G5 D5
2. This time
Acous. Gtr.
Elec. Gtr. 1

2.
Bridge:
Asus A Bm D
Acous. Gtr. resume rhy. fig. simile
I'm sor - ry. Ev - 'ry sin - gle day, I
Elec. Gtr. 2 & Acous. Gtr.
Elec. Gtr. 2
A E Bm
think a - bout how we came all this way. The sleep - less nights and the tears you cried, it's
A C
nev - er too late to make it right. Oh,
Chorus:
Asus A D A
Elec. Gtr. 2 & Acous. Gtr.
Acous. Gtr. & Elec. Gtr. 2 resume chorus fig. simile
yeah, sor - ry. I'm sor - ry I'm bad, I'm sor - ry I'm blue, I'm sor - ry a - bout

Bm F♯ G Em
all the things I said to you, and I know I can't take it back.
Asus A D A
I love how you kiss, I love all your sounds, and, ba - by, the
Elec. Gtr. 3
mf
Bm F♯ G Em
way you make my world go 'round, and I just want - ed to say,
A D A
I'm sor - ry.

Bm
F♯
G
Em
I'm sor - ry, ba - by, I'm sor - ry, ba -
Outro:
A
G5
G5(9)
Elec. Gtr. 2 & Acous. Gtr.
- by, yeah, I'm sor - ry.
Acous. Gtr.
G5
G5(9)
G5

ALMOST HOME

Words and Musics by
JOHN ALLEN

*All gtrs. tune down 1/2 step:

⑥ = E♭ ③ = G♭
⑤ = A♭ ② = B♭
④ = D♭ ① = E♭

Moderately slow ♩ = 82
Intro:

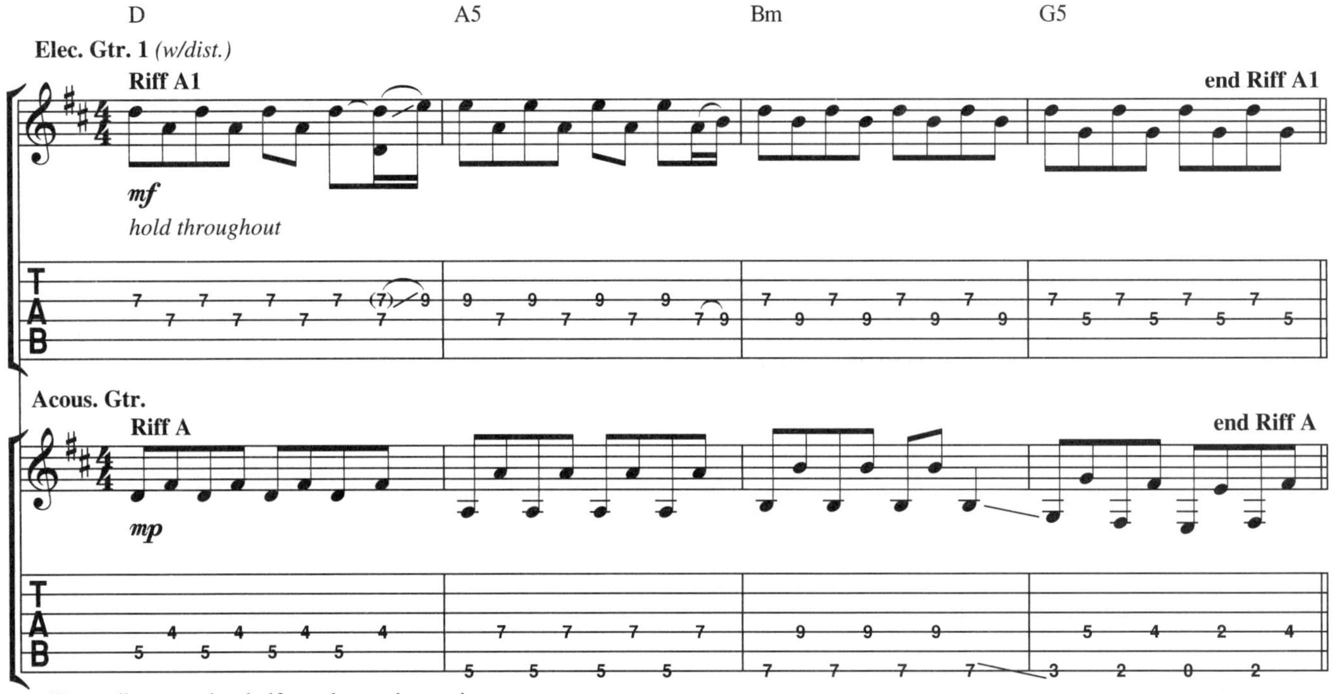

*Recording sounds a half step lower than written.

Verse 1: (0:11)
w/Riffs A *(Acous. Gtr.)* **& A1** *(Elec. Gtr. 1) 3 times*

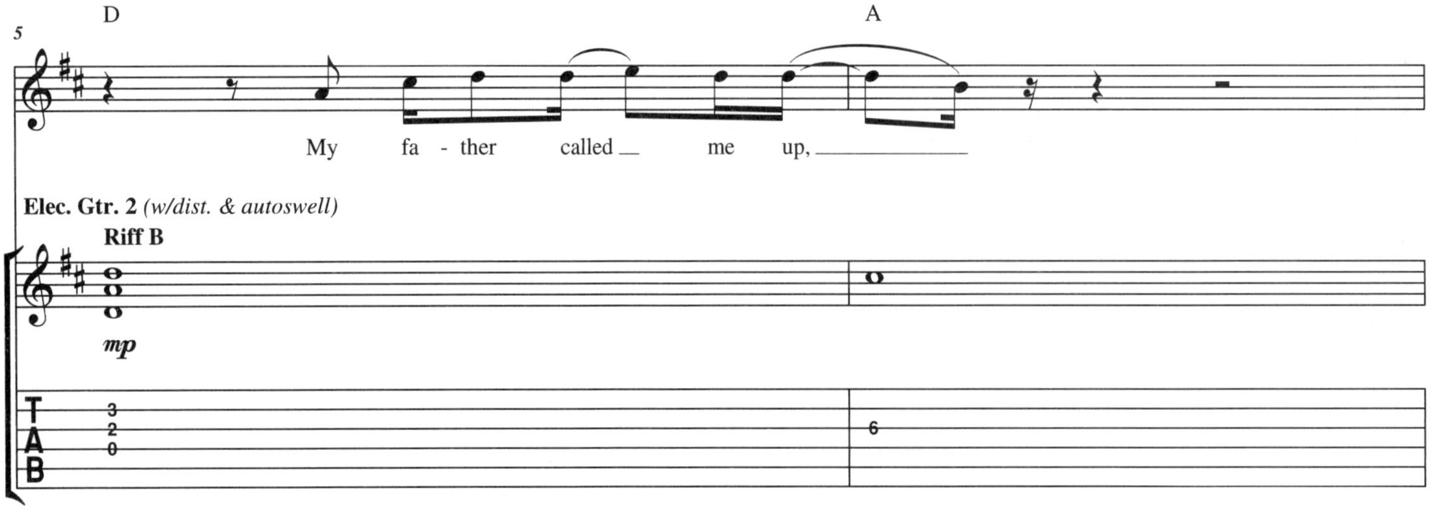

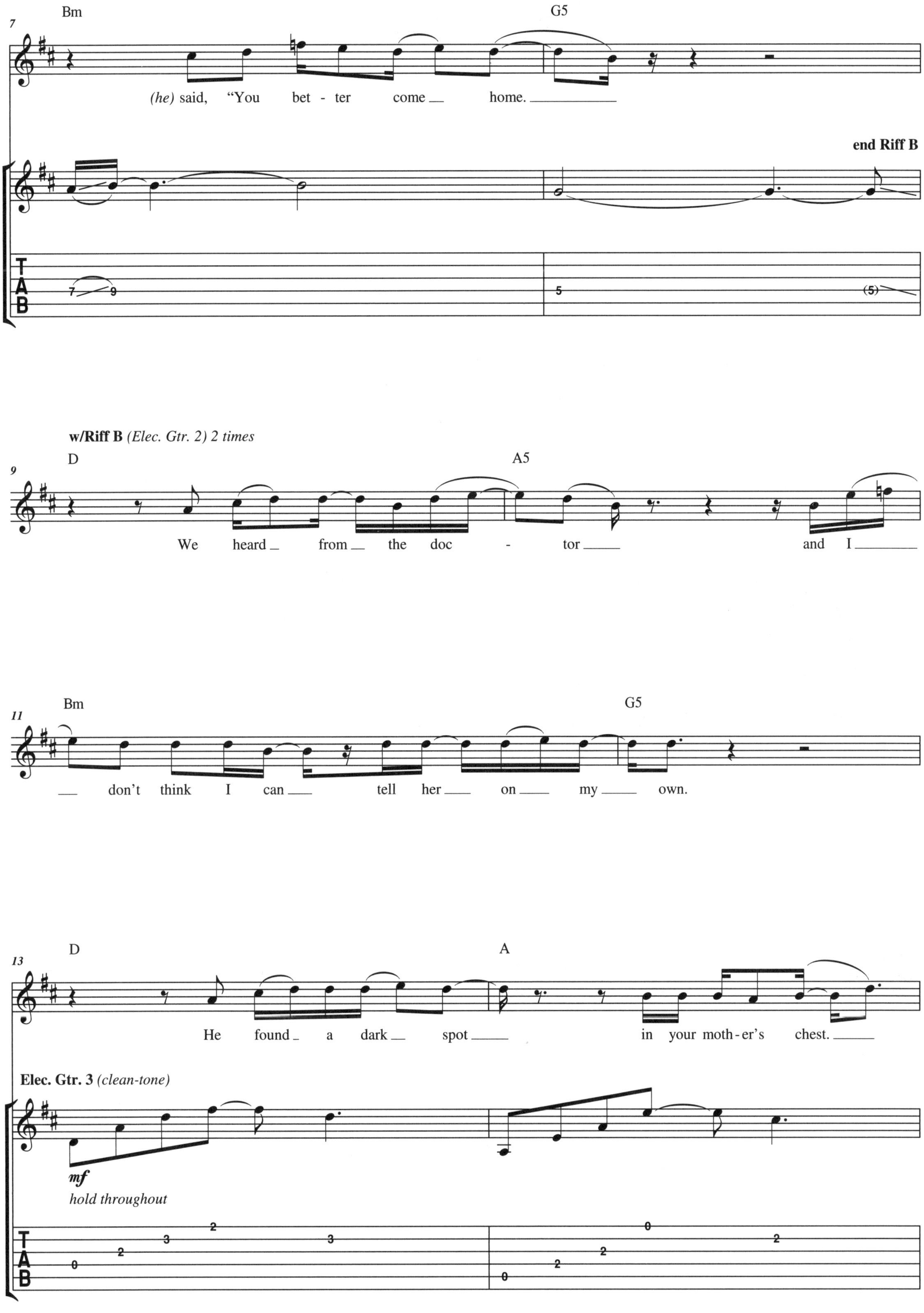
Bm
G5
(he) said, "You bet - ter come home.
end Riff B
7 9
5 (5)
w/Riff B (Elec. Gtr. 2) 2 times
D
A5
We heard from the doc - tor and I
Bm
G5
don't think I can tell her on my own.
D
A
He found a dark spot in your moth-er's chest.
Elec. Gtr. 3 (clean-tone)
mf
hold throughout
0 2 3 2 3
0 2 2 0 2

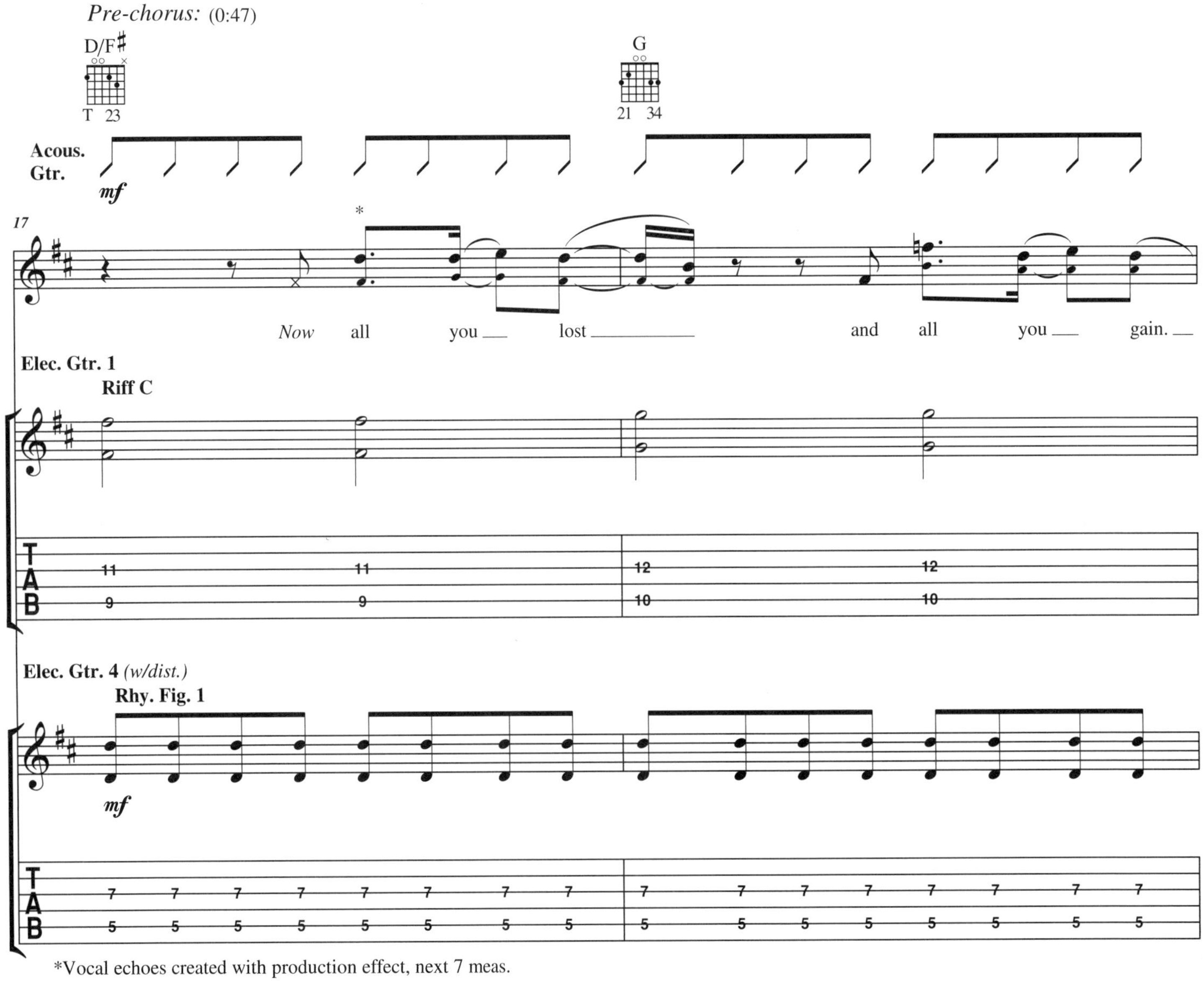

*Vocal echoes created with production effect, next 7 meas.

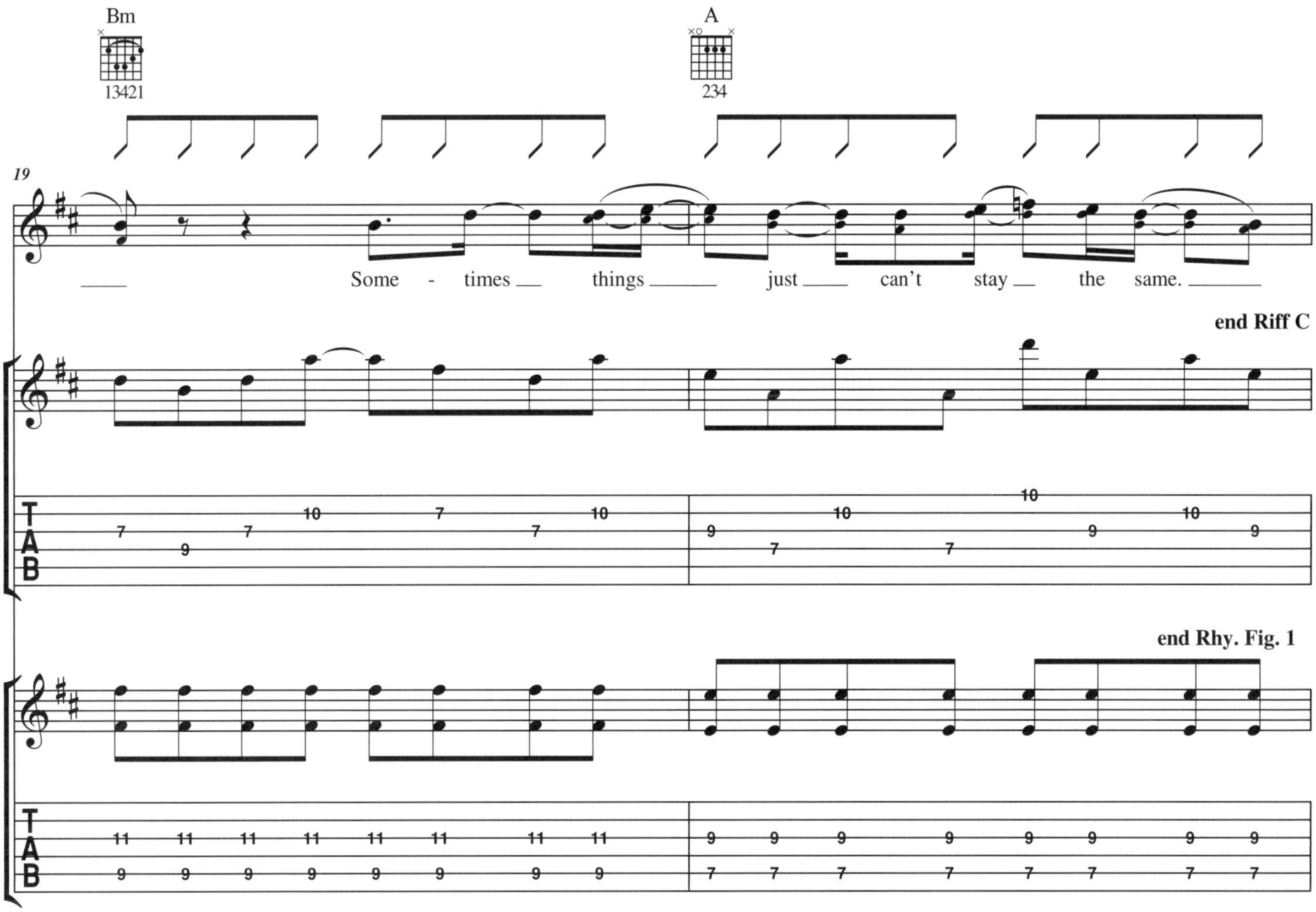
Bm
13421
A
234
19
Some - times things just can't stay the same.
end Riff C
end Rhy. Fig. 1

G
21 34
D/F♯
T 23
Acous. Gtr.
21
Now all you lost and all you gain.
Elec. Gtr. 4

*2nd time, w/vocal echo effect as before.

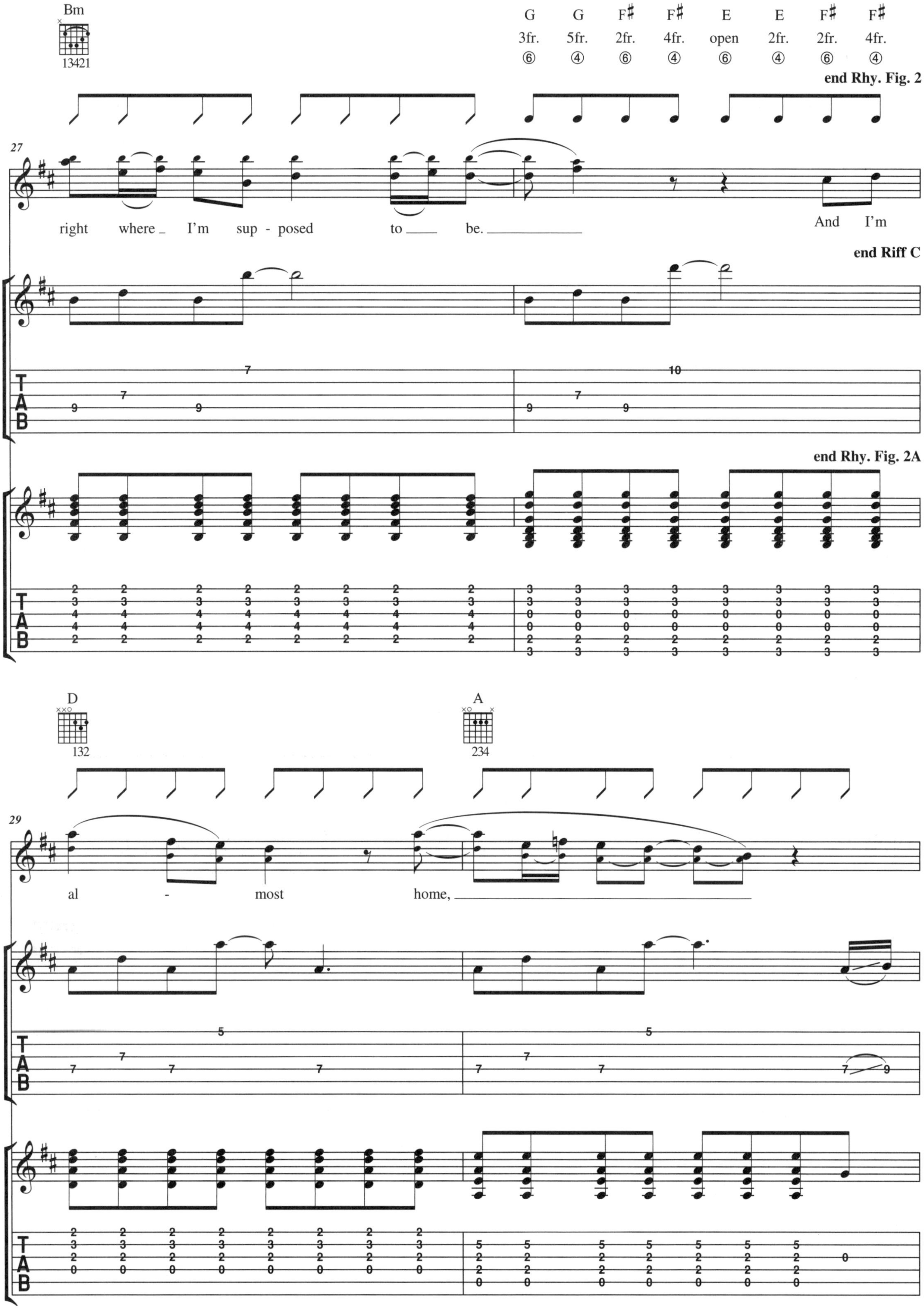
Bm
13421
G G F♯ F♯ E E F♯ F♯
3fr. 5fr. 2fr. 4fr. open 2fr. 2fr. 4fr.
⑥ ④ ⑥ ④ ⑥ ④ ⑥ ④
end Rhy. Fig. 2
27
right where _ I'm sup - posed to ___ be. ___________ And I'm
end Riff C
end Rhy. Fig. 2A
D
132
A
234
29
al - most home, ___________________________

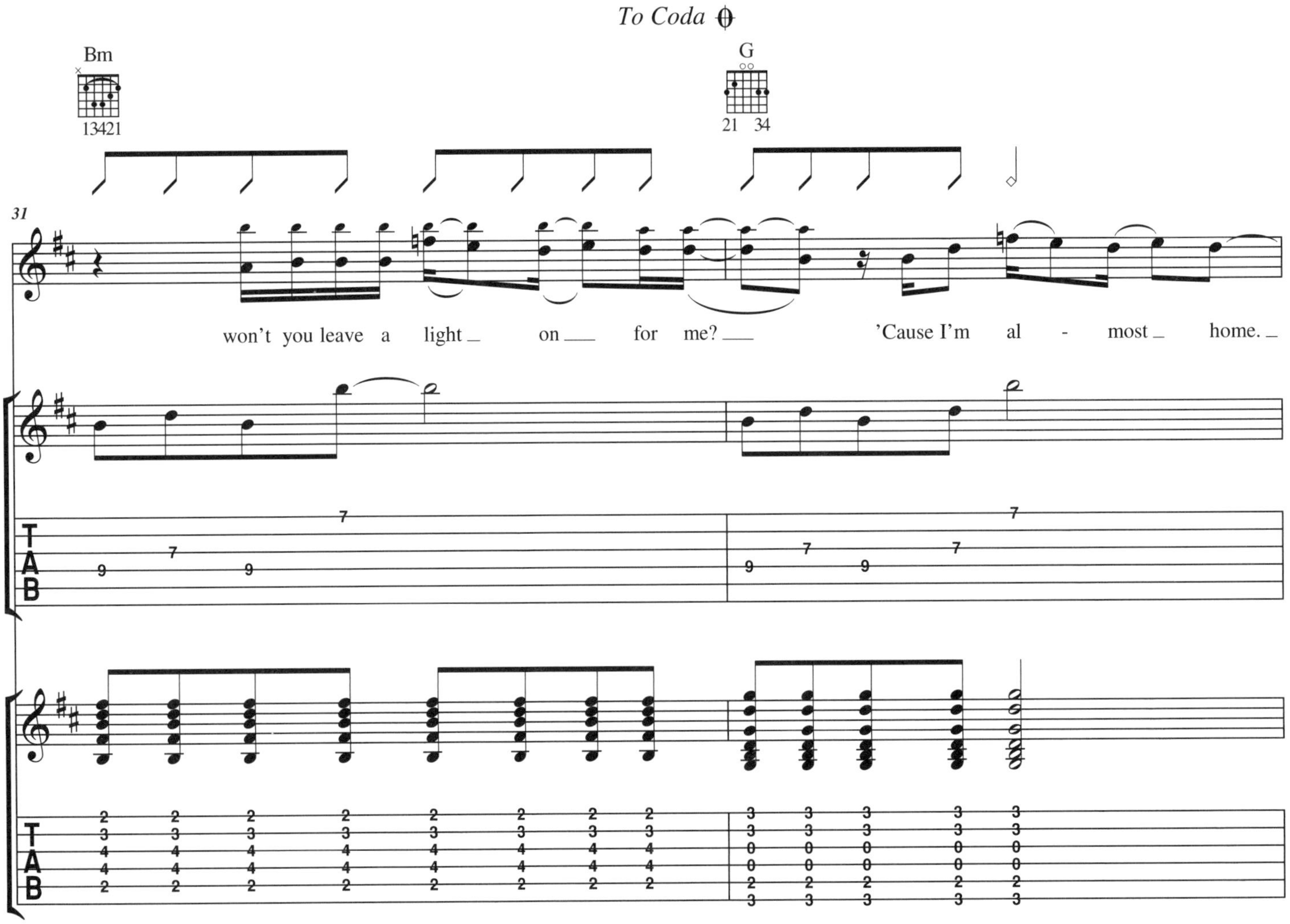
To Coda
Bm
13421
G
21 34
31
won't you leave a light on for me? 'Cause I'm al - most home.
T
A
B

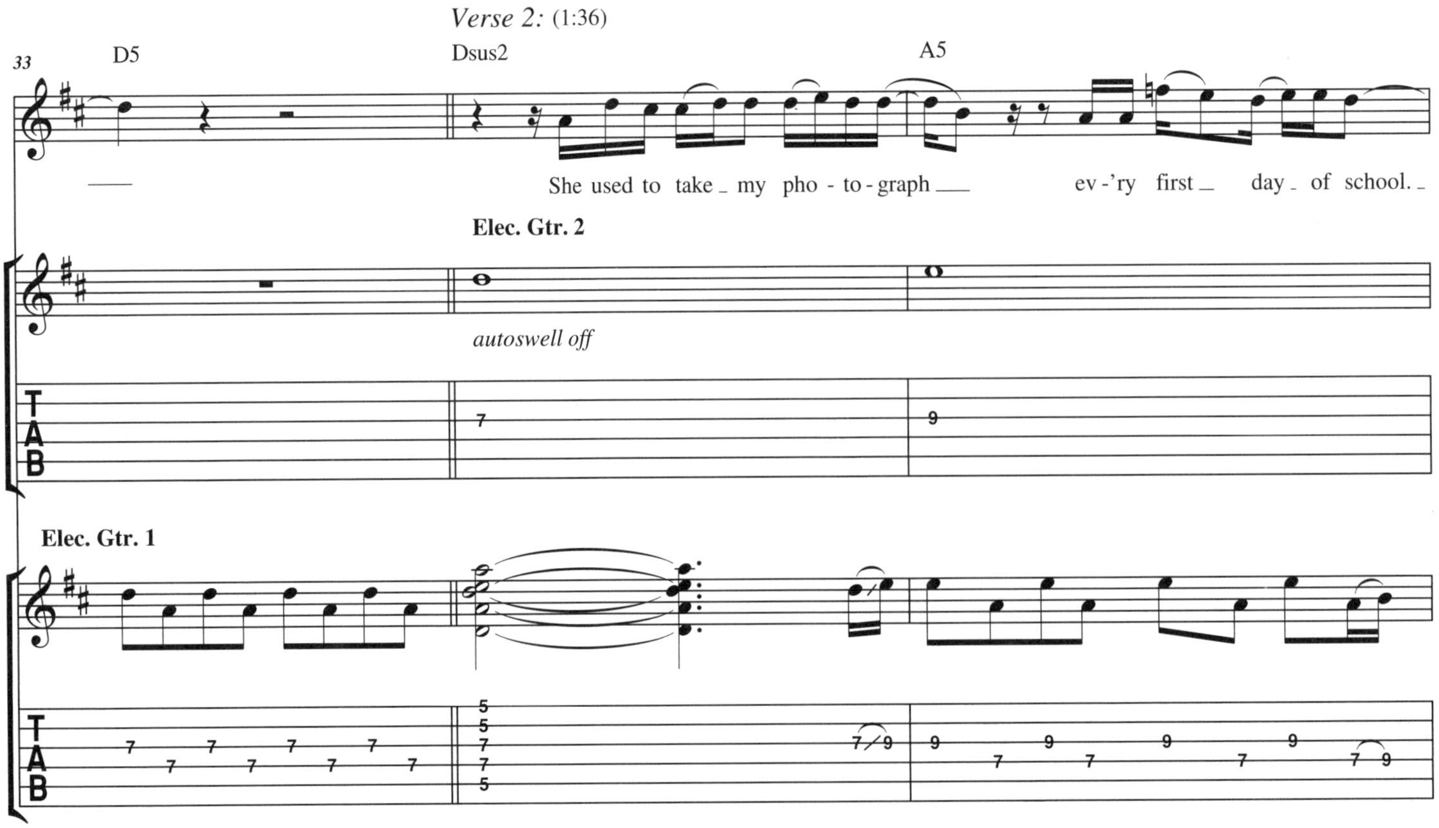
Verse 2: (1:36)
33
D5
Dsus2
A5
She used to take my pho - to - graph ev - 'ry first day of school.
Elec. Gtr. 2
autoswell off
Elec. Gtr. 1
T
A
B

36
Bm
G
Used to teach me how to fight so I would be no - bod - y's fool.
Pre-chorus: (1:48)
w/Riff C (Elec. Gtr. 1) & Rhy. Fig. 1 (Elec. Gtr. 4)
D/F♯
G
Acous. Gtr.
38
Now all I lost and all I gain.
w/Rhy. Fill 1 (Elec. Gtr. 1)
Bm
Asus
A
D.S. 𝄋 al Coda
40
Some - times things just can't stay the same. But I'm
Elec. Gtr. 5

Bridge: (0:23)
w/Riff C (Elec. Gtr. 1) last meas.
G
D/F♯
Em
D/F♯
Coda
Rhy. Fill 2
Acous. Gtr.
42
'Cause I'm al - most home.
Un - der top - field,
Elec. Gtr. 1
Rhy. Fill 2A
Elec. Gtr. 5
G
D/F♯
Em
D/F♯
G
A
44
run - nin' down - hill
un - der the North Point sky.
A - light with Beth - le - hem

Guitar Solo:(2:35)

w/Riff C *(Elec. Gtr. 1)*
w/Rhy. Figs. 2 *(Acous. Gtr.)* **& 2A** *(Elec. Gtr. 5) 1st 3 meas.*

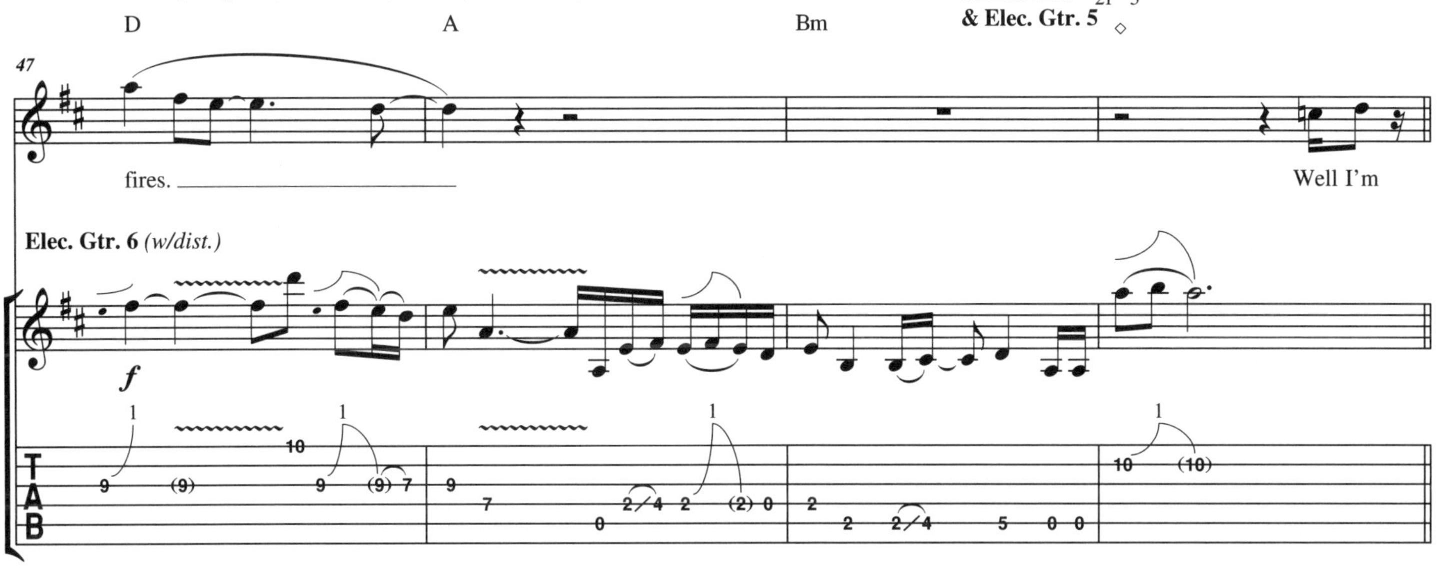

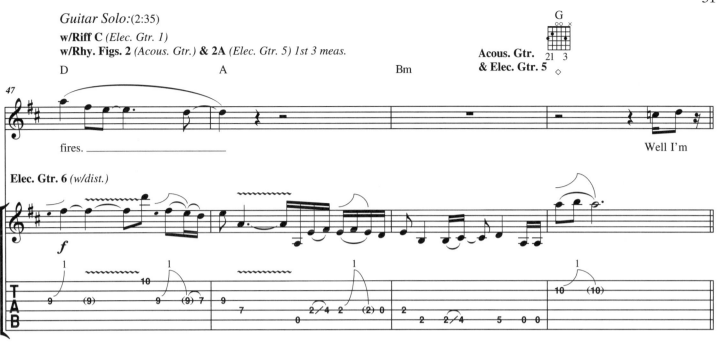

Chorus/Interlude: (2:47)

w/Riff A *(Elec. Gtr. 1) 2 times*

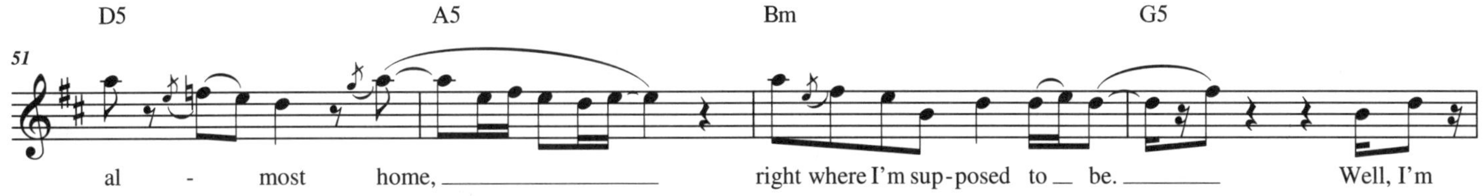

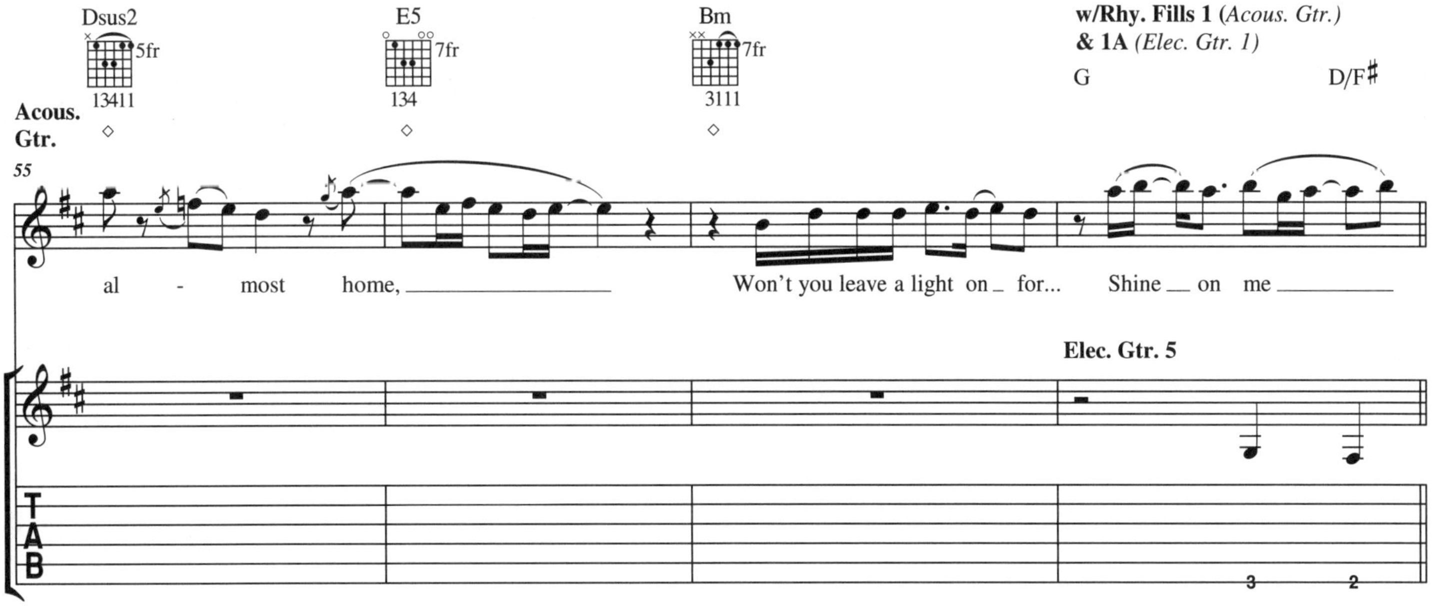

Chorus/Outro:(3:10)
w/Rhy. Figs. 2 (Acous. Gtr.) & 2A (Elec. Gtr. 4) both 1 ¾ times
w/Riff C (Elec. Gtr. 1) 1 ¾ times
D
A
Bm
Al - most home,
right where I'm sup-posed to be.
yeah.
Keep shin - in' on.
*w/vocal echo effect as before.
G5
D
A
And I'm al - most home,
Keep shin - in' on and on.
Home, home.
G
D/F♯
D
Acous. Gtr.
Bm
Be - tween fa - mil - iar sheets 'cause I'm al - most home.
Elec. Gtr. 1
Elec. Gtr. 4

LET'S ROCK-N-ROLL

*Elec. Gtrs. 1, 2, & 4: Tune down 1/2 step:

⑥ = E♭ ③ = G♭
⑤ = A♭ ② = B♭
④ = D♭ ① = E♭

*Elec. Gtr. 3: Drop D tuning, down 1/2 step:

⑥ = D♭

Words and Musics by
JOHN ALLEN

Moderately ♩ = 114
Intro:

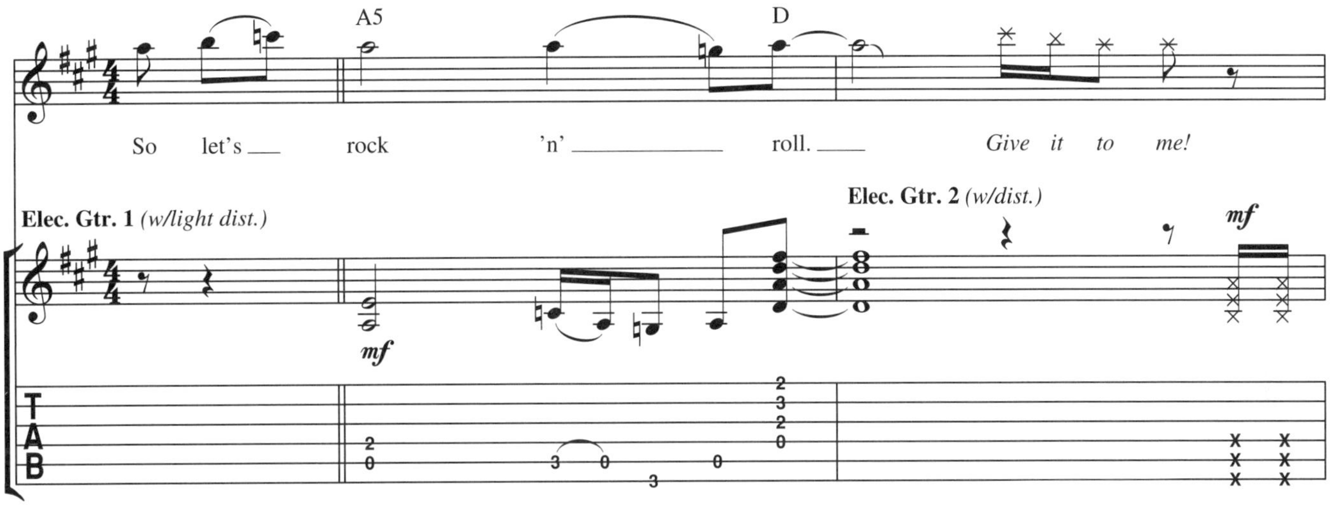

*Recording sounds a half step lower than written.

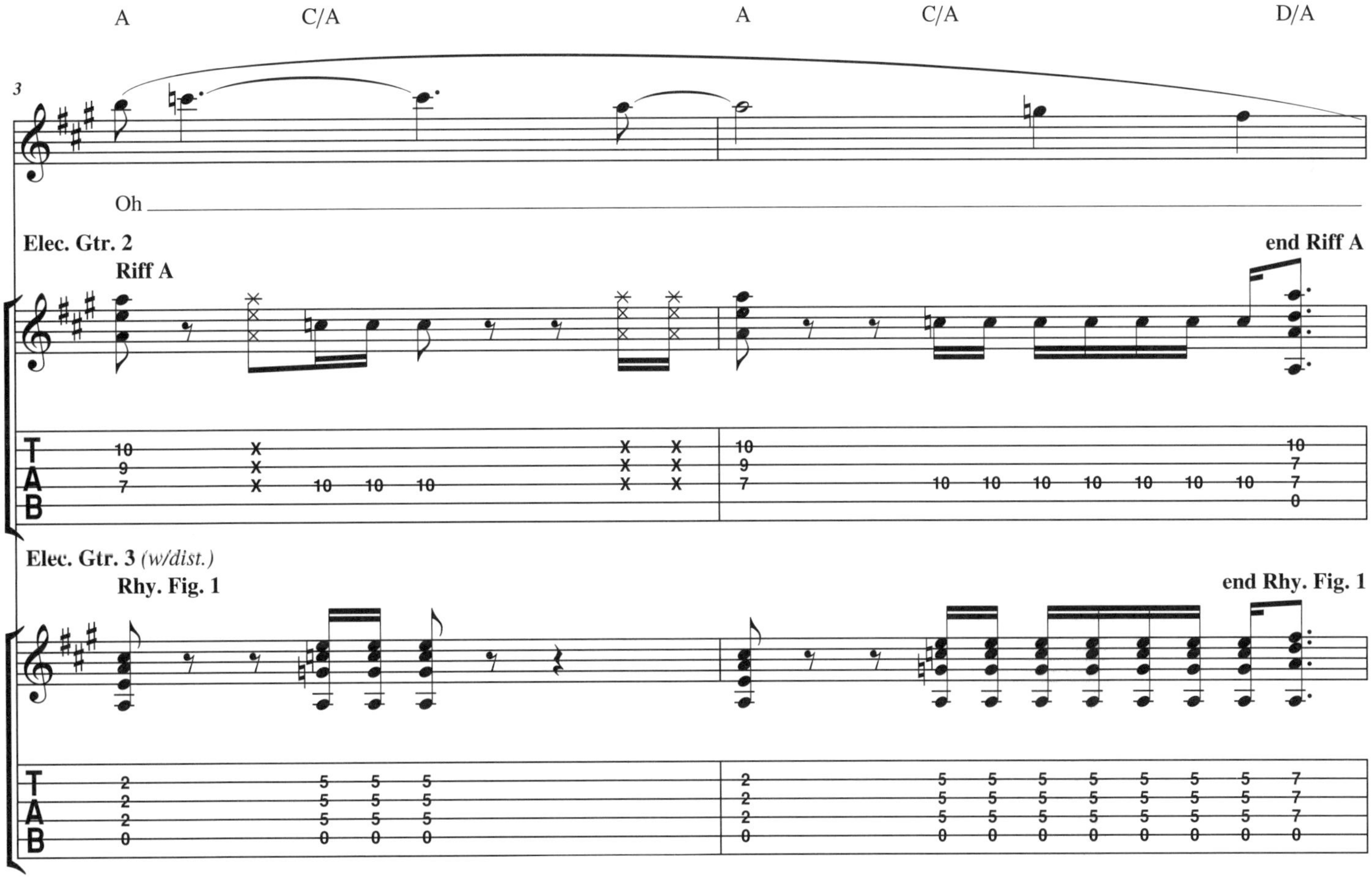

w/Rhy. Fig. 1 (Elec. Gtr. 3) & Riff A (Elec. Gtr. 2)
A C/A A C/A D/A
yeah!
Verse 1: (0:13)
w/Rhy. Fig. 1 (Elec. Gtr. 3) 4 times
A C/A A C/A D/A
Stepped off the train and I told my - self there's no way back.
Elec. Gtr. 2
Riff B
end Riff B
w/Riff A (Elec. Gtr. 2)
w/Riff B (Elec. Gtr. 2)
A C/A A C/A D/A A C/A A C/A D/A
It's in my veins, got a one-way mind on a one-way track. I'll nev-er die and I'm nev-er gon-na stop.
A
Got - ta keep on liv - ing like this is all I got. So let's
Elec. Gtr. 2
1/4
Elec. Gtr. 3
1/4

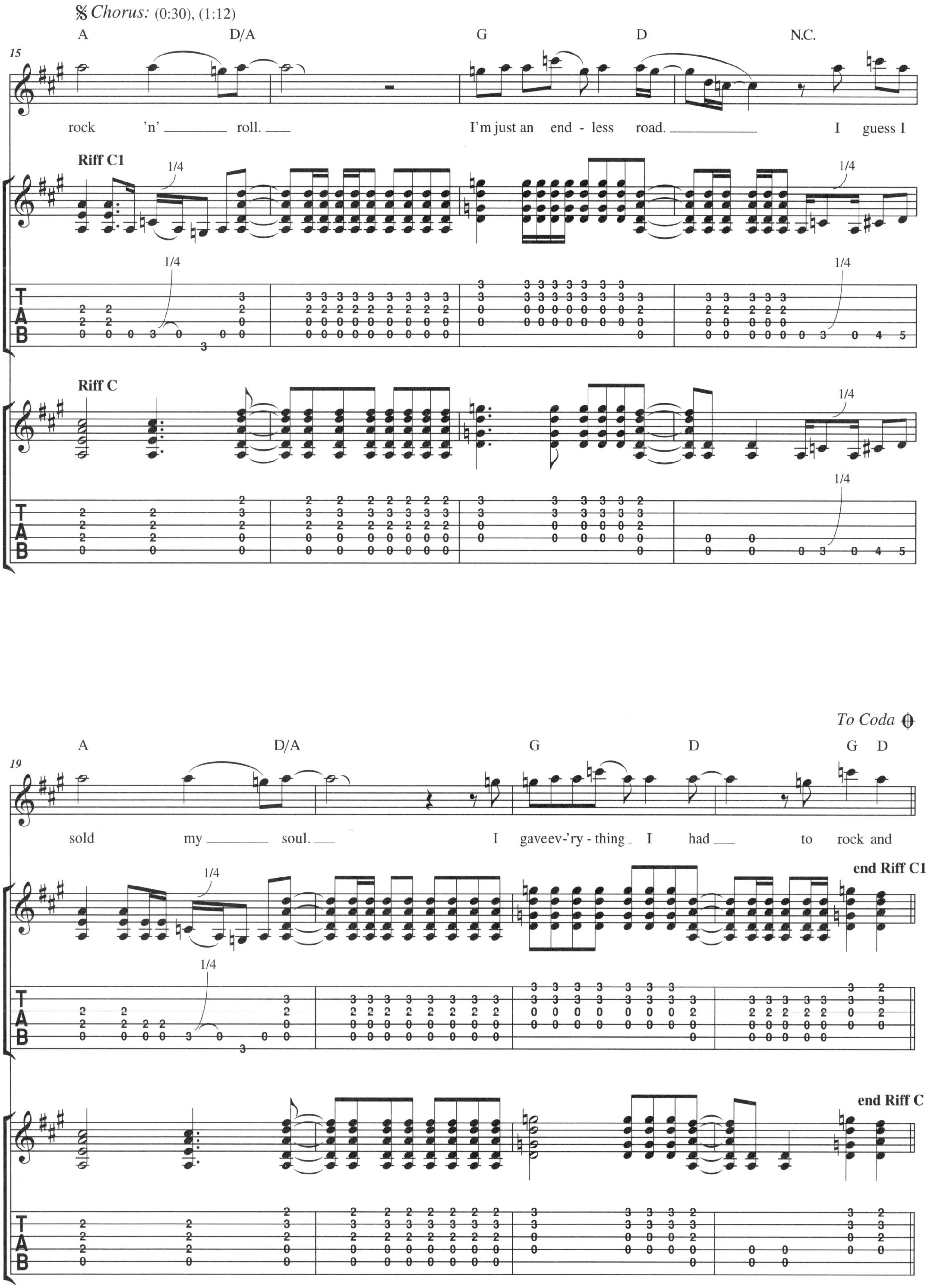

𝄋 Chorus: (0:30), (1:12)
A
D/A
G
D
N.C.
rock 'n' roll.
I'm just an end - less road.
I guess I
Riff C1
1/4
Riff C
To Coda
sold my soul.
I gaveev-'ry-thing I had to rock and
end Riff C1
end Riff C

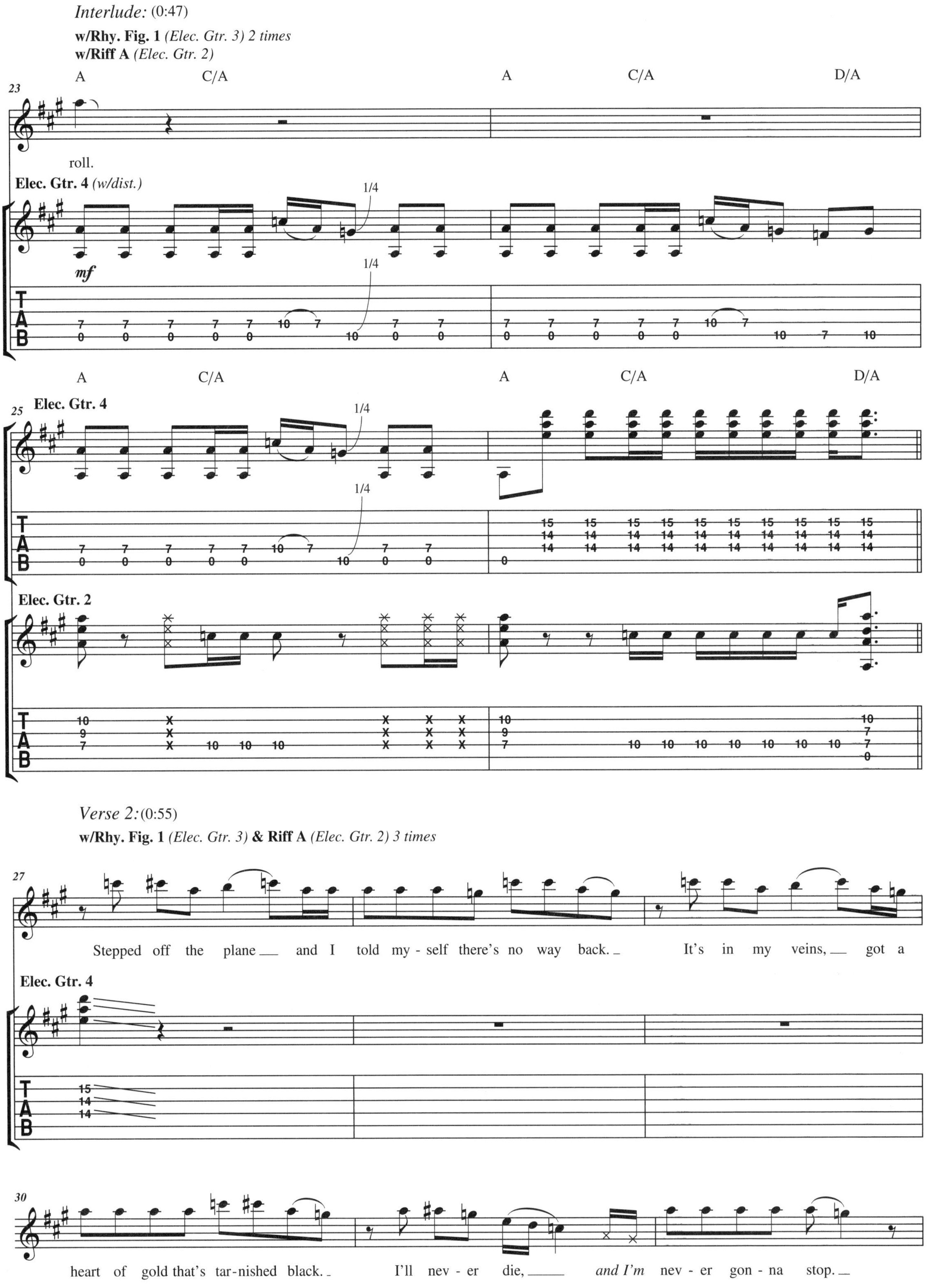
Interlude: (0:47)
w/Rhy. Fig. 1 (Elec. Gtr. 3) 2 times
w/Riff A (Elec. Gtr. 2)
A C/A A C/A D/A
roll.
Elec. Gtr. 4 (w/dist.)
1/4
mf
A C/A A C/A D/A
Elec. Gtr. 4
Elec. Gtr. 2
Verse 2: (0:55)
w/Rhy. Fig. 1 (Elec. Gtr. 3) & Riff A (Elec. Gtr. 2) 3 times
Stepped off the plane and I told my - self there's no way back. It's in my veins, got a
Elec. Gtr. 4
heart of gold that's tar-nished black. I'll nev - er die, and I'm nev - er gon - na stop.

D.S. 𝄋 al Coda
A
E5
N.C.
33
Got - ta keep on liv - ing like this is all I got. So let's
Elec. Gtr. 2
P.M.
Elec. Gtr. 3
1/4
Coda
Bridge: (1:29)
A
D5/A
35
roll. Oh! Rock and
Elec. Gtr. 4
Riff D1
1/4
Elec. Gtr. 2
Elec. Gtr. 3
Riff D

37
A
Asus
roll.
Give it to me!
So let's
end Riff D1
1/4
1/4
end Riff D

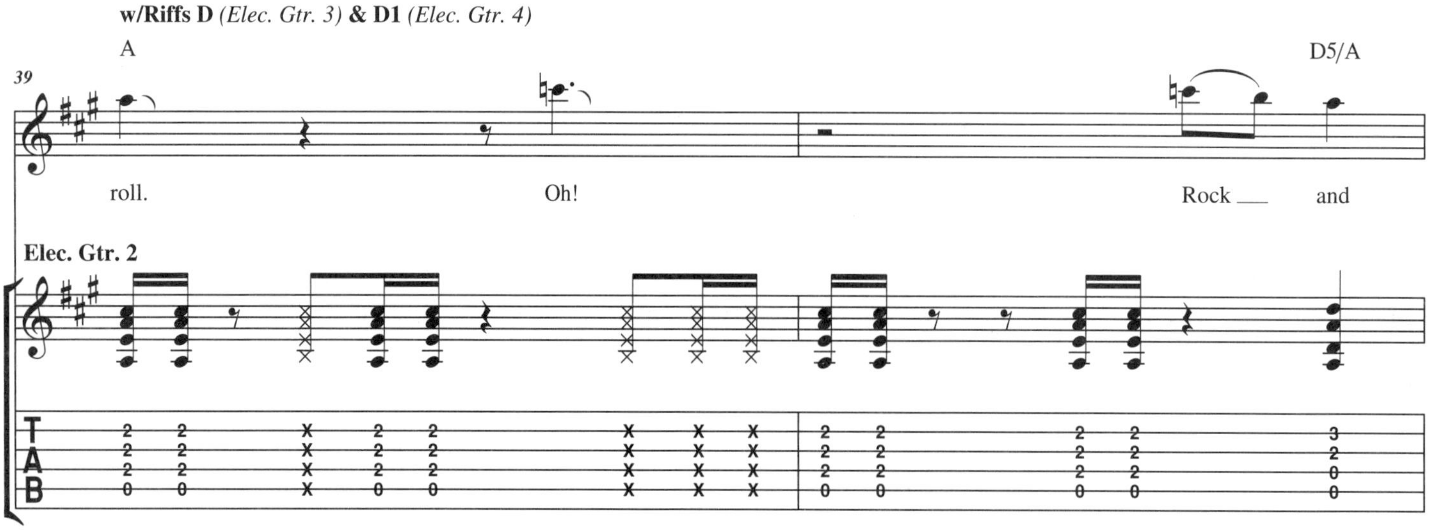
w/Riffs D (Elec. Gtr. 3) & D1 (Elec. Gtr. 4)
A
D5/A
39
roll.
Oh!
Rock ___ and
Elec. Gtr. 2

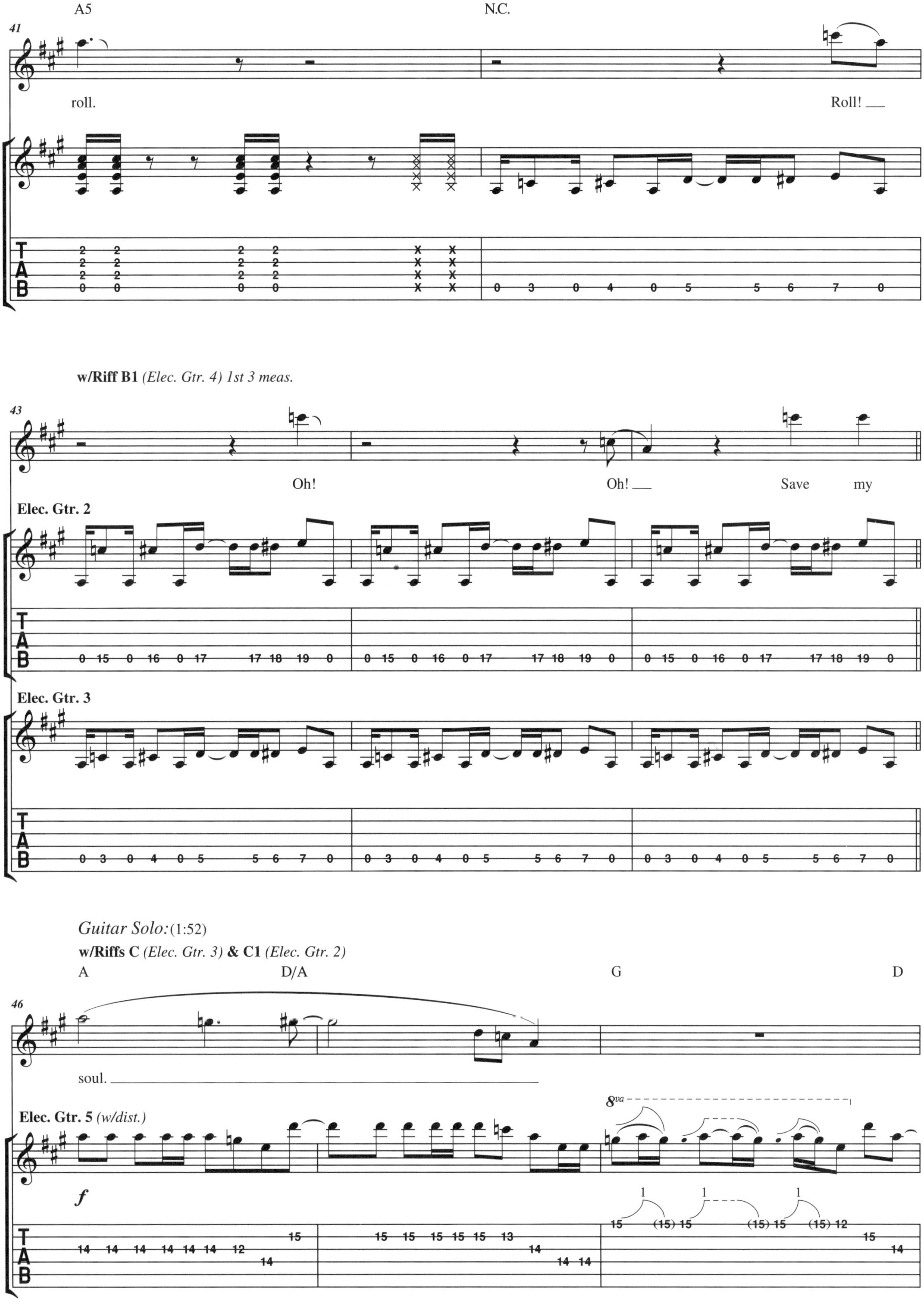
A5
N.C.
41
roll.
Roll!
w/Riff B1 (Elec. Gtr. 4) 1st 3 meas.
43
Oh!
Oh!
Save my
Elec. Gtr. 2
Elec. Gtr. 3
Guitar Solo: (1:52)
w/Riffs C (Elec. Gtr. 3) & C1 (Elec. Gtr. 2)
A
D/A
G
D
46
soul.
Elec. Gtr. 5 (w/dist.)
f
8va

N.C.
A
D/A
1/2
1/2
Chorus: (2:09)
w/Riffs C (Elec. Gtr. 3)
& C1 (Elec. Gtr. 2)
G
D
G D
A
D/A
So let's rock 'n' roll.
8va
G
D
N.C.
I'm just an end - less road. I guess I
(8va)
A
D/A
G
D
G D
sold my soul. I gave ev - 'ry - thing I had to rock 'n'...

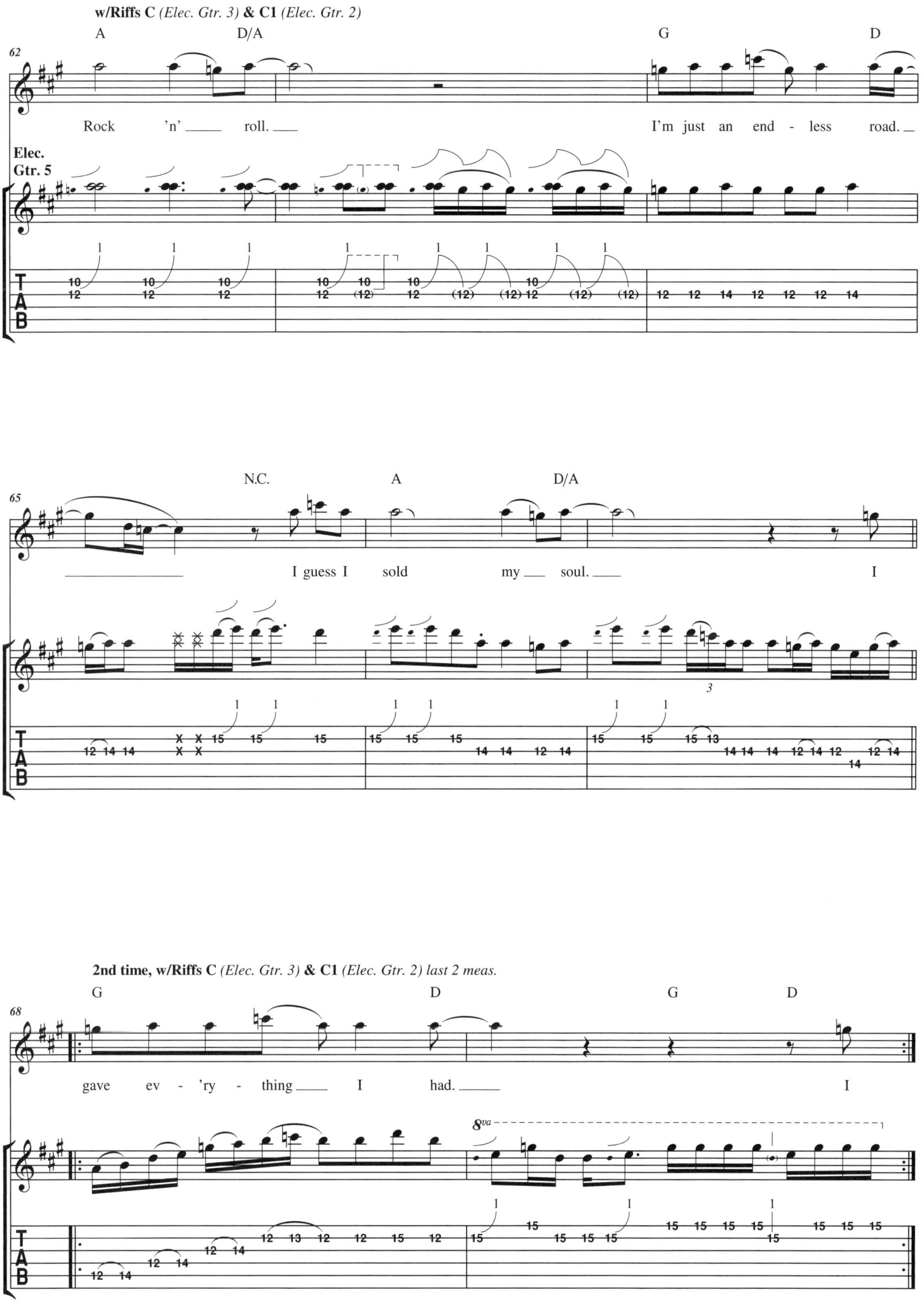
w/Riffs C (Elec. Gtr. 3) & C1 (Elec. Gtr. 2)
A D/A G D
62
Rock 'n' roll. I'm just an end - less road.
Elec. Gtr. 5
N.C. A D/A
65
I guess I sold my soul. I
2nd time, w/Riffs C (Elec. Gtr. 3) & C1 (Elec. Gtr. 2) last 2 meas.
G D G D
68
gave ev - 'ry - thing I had. I
8va

w/Riff C (Elec. Gtr. 3) & C1 (Elec. Gtr. 2) last 2 meas.
G
D
G
D
70
gave ev - 'ry - thing I had to rock 'n'
8va
Outro: (2:51)
w/Rhy. Fig. 1 (Elec. Gtr. 3)
A
C/A
A
C/A
D/A
72
roll. Oh!
Elec. Gtr. 4
1/4
Elec. Gtr. 2
N.C.
74
Oh yeah!

37 STITCHES

*All gtrs. in Drop D, down 1 1/2 steps:
⑥ = B ③ = E
⑤ = F♯ ② = G♯
④ = B ① = C♯

Words and Music by
STEPHEN BENTON, MICHAEL LUCE,
RYAN McCOMBS and CHRISTIAN PIERCE

Moderately slow ♩ = 80

Intro:

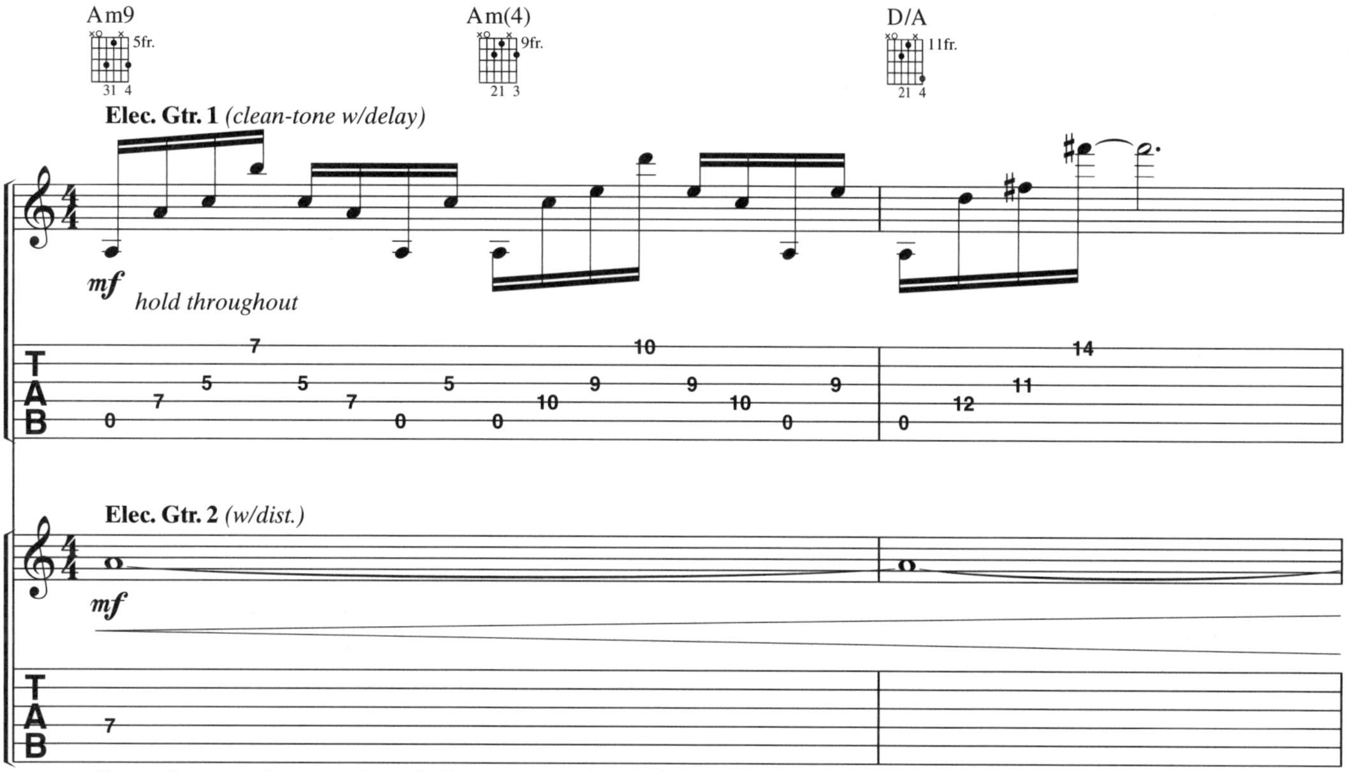

*Recording sounds one and one half steps lower than written.

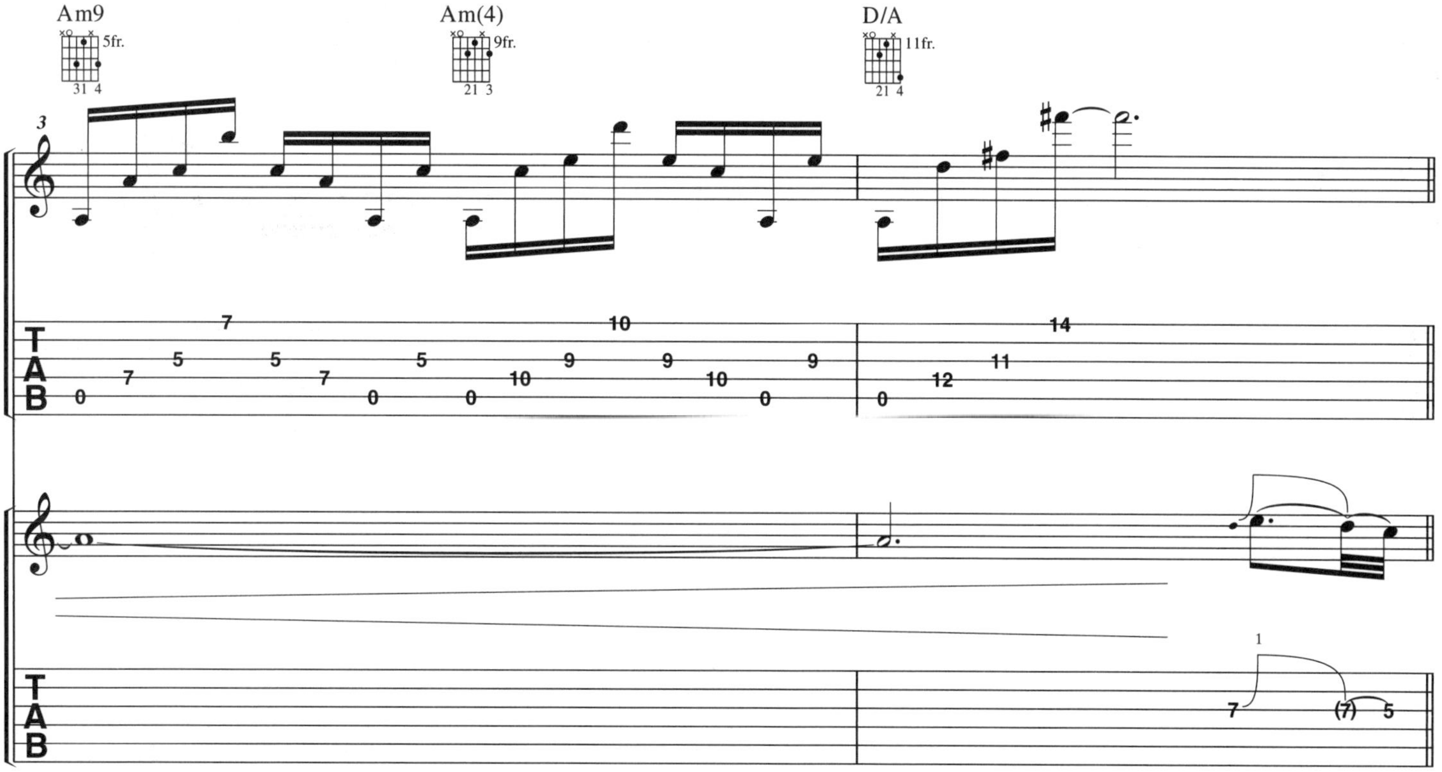

Verses 1 & 2:

A5(9)
Cmaj9
D(4)
5fr.
1. Do you see me sit - tin' here
2. *See additional lyrics*
Elec. Gtr. 1
hold throughout
Elec. Gtr. 2
A5(9)
Cmaj9
D(4)
G5
wait-ing for you to say an - y - thing.
1/2

A5(9) Cmaj9 D(4)
Your head hung low, kick-in' stones down, kick-in' stones down the road to hell now.
A5(9) Cmaj9 D(4)
Wait-ing for you to say an-y-thing, an-y-thing, yeah.
Cont. in slashes
Chorus:
Am C G5(9) D
Elec. Gtr. 1
I know you are the on-ly one, a lit-tle taste of heav-en. And
Elec. Gtr. 2

Am C G5(9) D
Cont. rhy. simile
you know that I am the on - ly one, your bit - ter taste of hell.
Am C G5(9) D
Your eyes scream, the end is creep-in' in, I'll need thir - ty sev - en stitch - es to keep the pain in. And
1.
Am C G5(9) D
I know you are the on - ly one on the dark - est side of the sun.

A5(9)
Cmaj9
D(4)
5fr.
On the dark-est side of the sun.
Elec. Gtr. 2
Elec. Gtr. 1

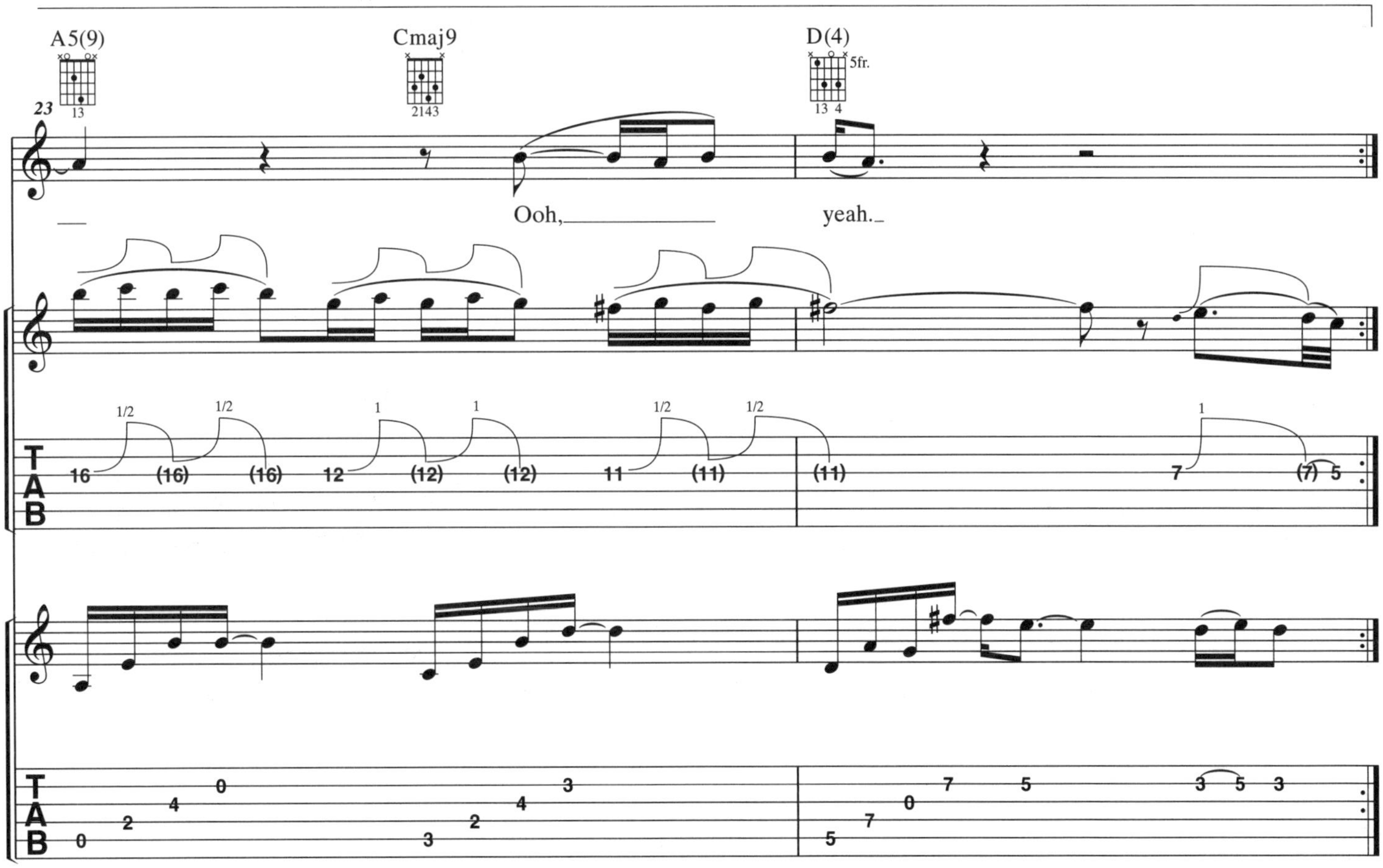
A5(9)
Cmaj9
D(4)
5fr.
Ooh, yeah.

2.
Am C G5(9) D
I know you are the on - ly one on the dark - est side of the sun.
Guitar Solo:
Am C G5(9) D
Elec. Gtr. 1 cont. chorus fig. simile
Elec. Gtr. 2
Am C G5(9) D
Am C G5(9) D

Am
C
G5(9)
D
Verse 3:
Band tacet
Am7
Am9
D/A
Do you see me sit - tin' here,
Elec. Gtr. 1
hold throughout
Am7
Am9
D/A
still wait - ing for you to say an - y - thing?
Am7
Am9
D/A
Your head hung low, kick - in' stones down, kick - in' stones down the road to hell, now.

Am7
Am9
D/A
I'm wait-ing for you, I'm wait-ing for you to just say an - y - thing, yeah.
Elec. Gtr. 2
Chorus:
Am
C
G5(9)
D
Elec. Gtrs. 1 & 3 (w/dist.)
I know you are the on - ly one, a lit - tle taste of heav - en. And
Elec. Gtr. 2
Elec. Gtrs. 1 & 3 cont. simile
you know that I am the on - ly one, your bit - ter taste of hell.

Elec. Gtr. 2 tacet 2 meas.
Am C G5(9) D
3fr. 5fr. 5fr.
231 1333 111341 1333
47
Your eyes scream, the end__ is creep-in' in, I'll need thir-ty sev-en stich-es, thir-ty sev-en stich-es, yeah._
49
I know_ you are the on-ly one___ on the dark-est side__ of the sun._
Elec. Gtr. 2
8va
T
A
B
51
__ I know,_ I know, (On the dark-est side__ of the sun._
53
__) you are__ the one___ on the dark-est side__ of the sun._

Outro:

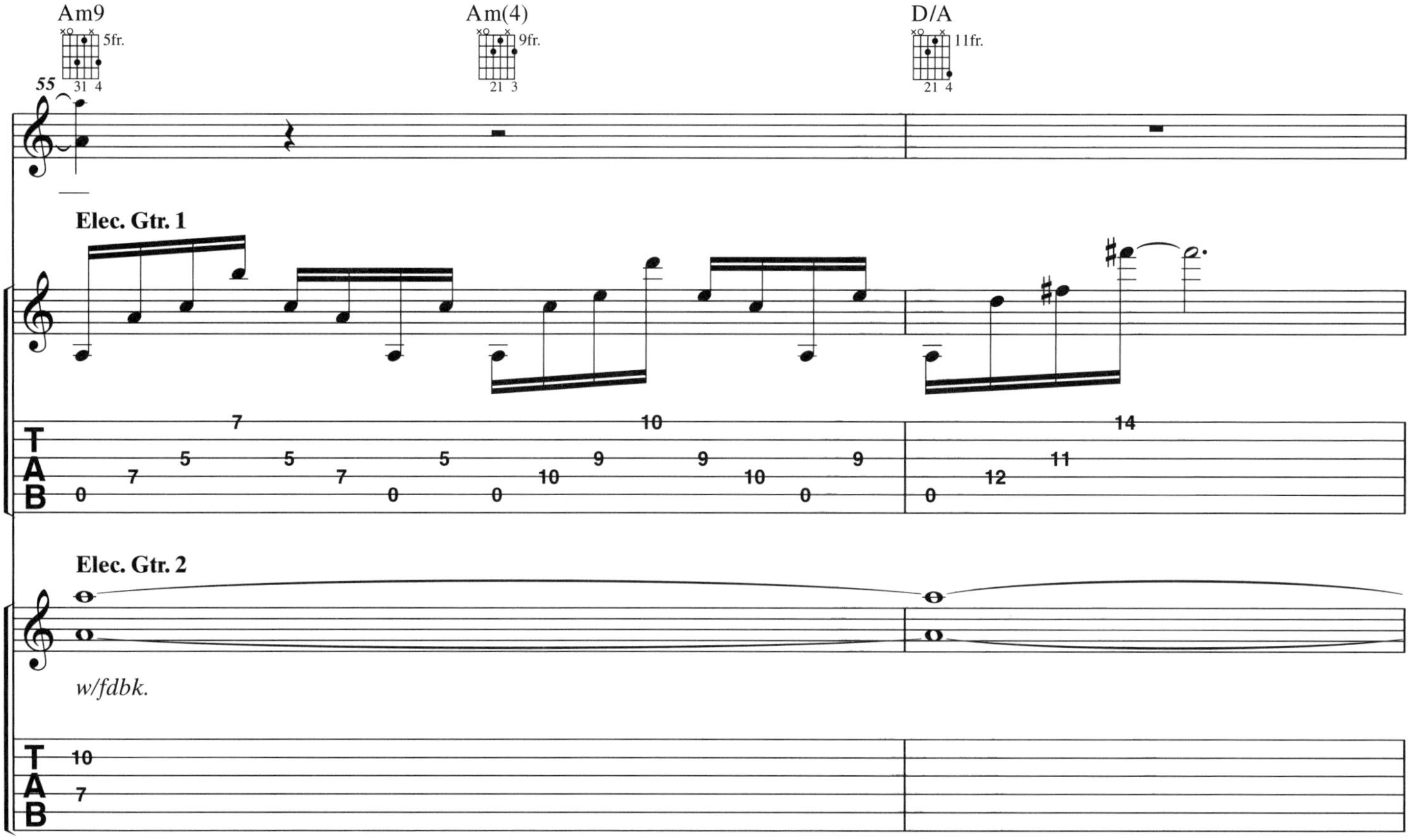

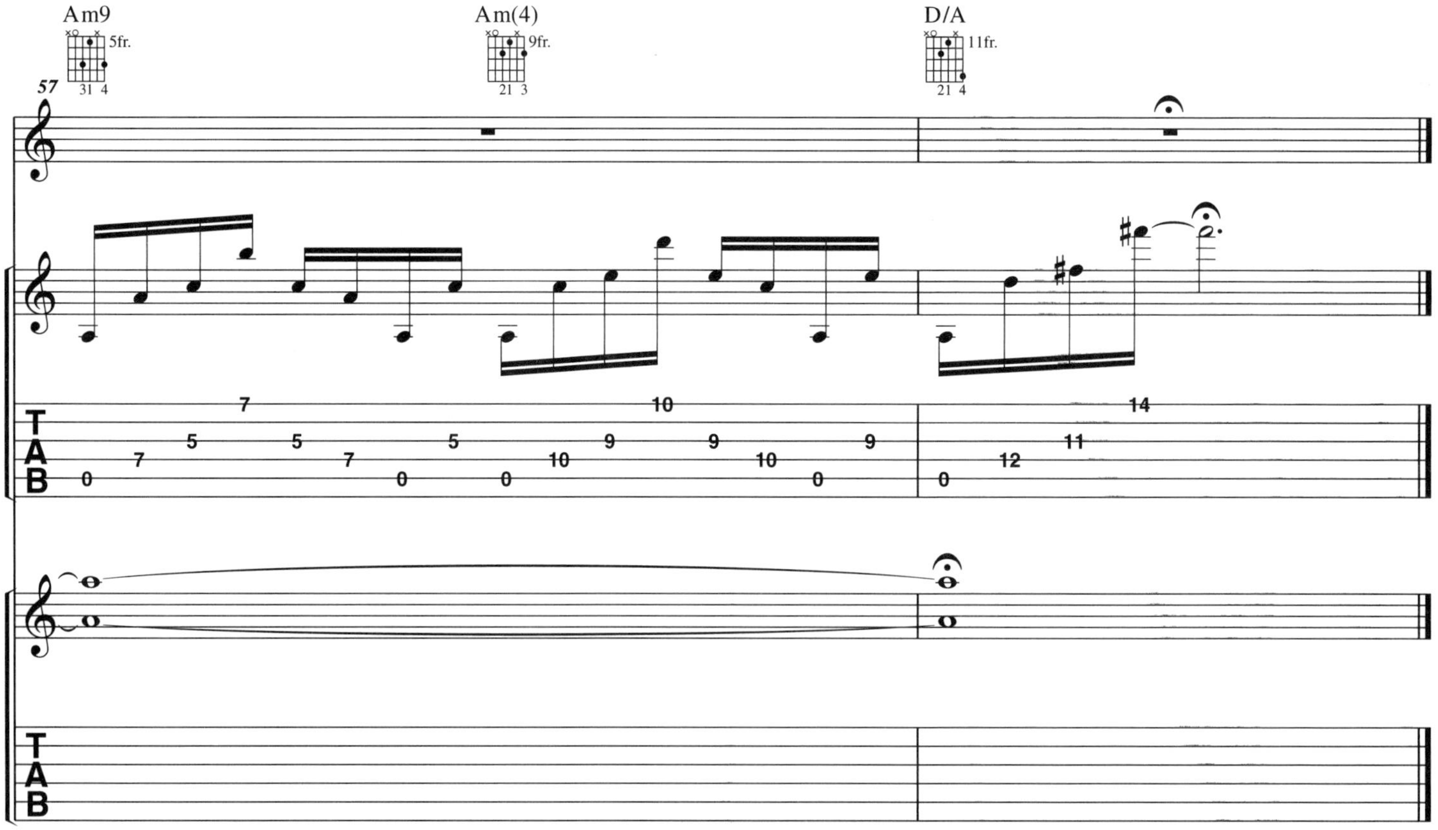

Verse 2:
Followed the piper's sweet whistlin',
Guided down the path by the wrong hand.
Close my eyes for the chance of a better view,
Close my ears so I couldn't hear you.
And I know you are the one.
You know I am the one,
Your bitter taste of hell.
(To Chorus:)

BODIES

*All gtrs. in Drop D, down 1 whole step:

⑥ = C ③ = F
⑤ = G ② = A
④ = C ① = D

Music and Words by
DAVE WILLIAMS, MIKE LUCE,
C. J. PIERCE and STEVIE BENTON

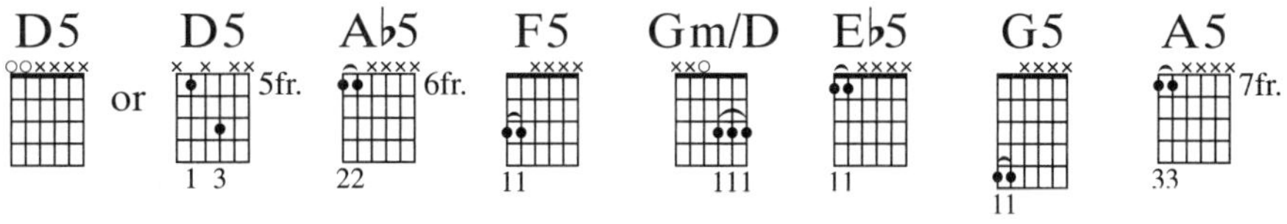

Moderately ♩ = 120

Intro:

*Recording sounds a whole step lower than written.

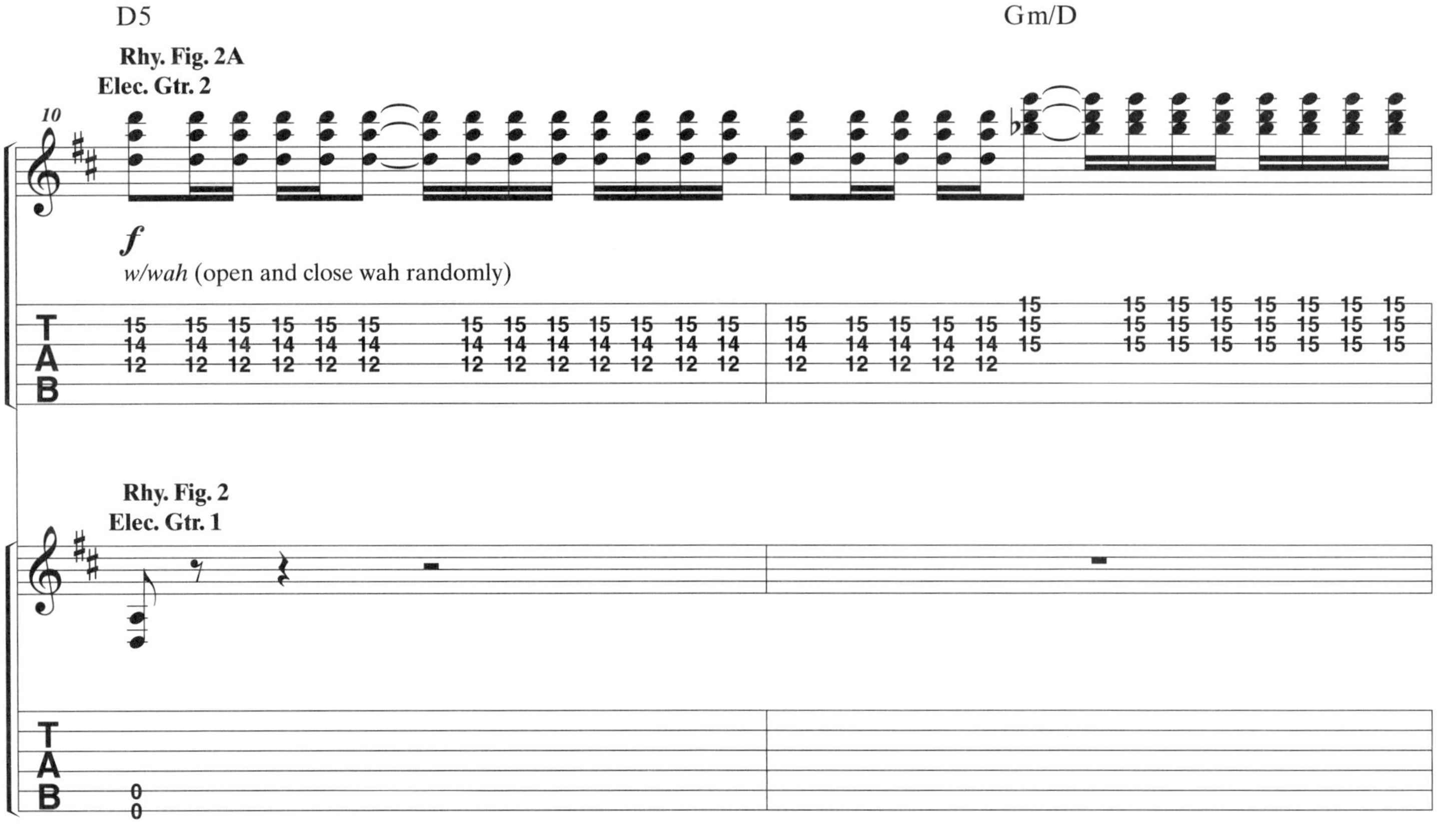
D5
Gm/D
Rhy. Fig. 2A
Elec. Gtr. 2
10
f
w/wah (open and close wah randomly)
Rhy. Fig. 2
Elec. Gtr. 1

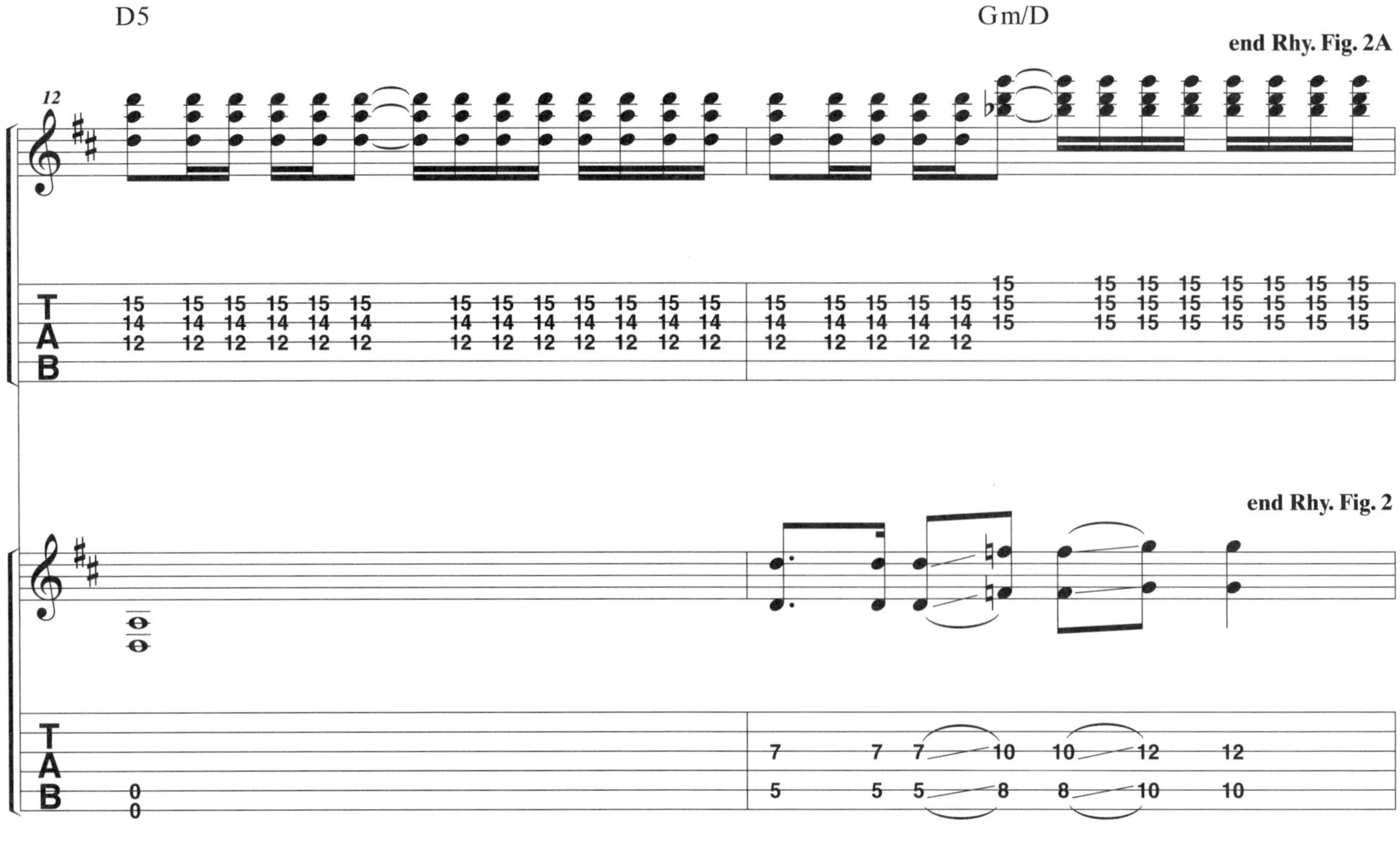
D5
Gm/D
end Rhy. Fig. 2A
12
end Rhy. Fig. 2

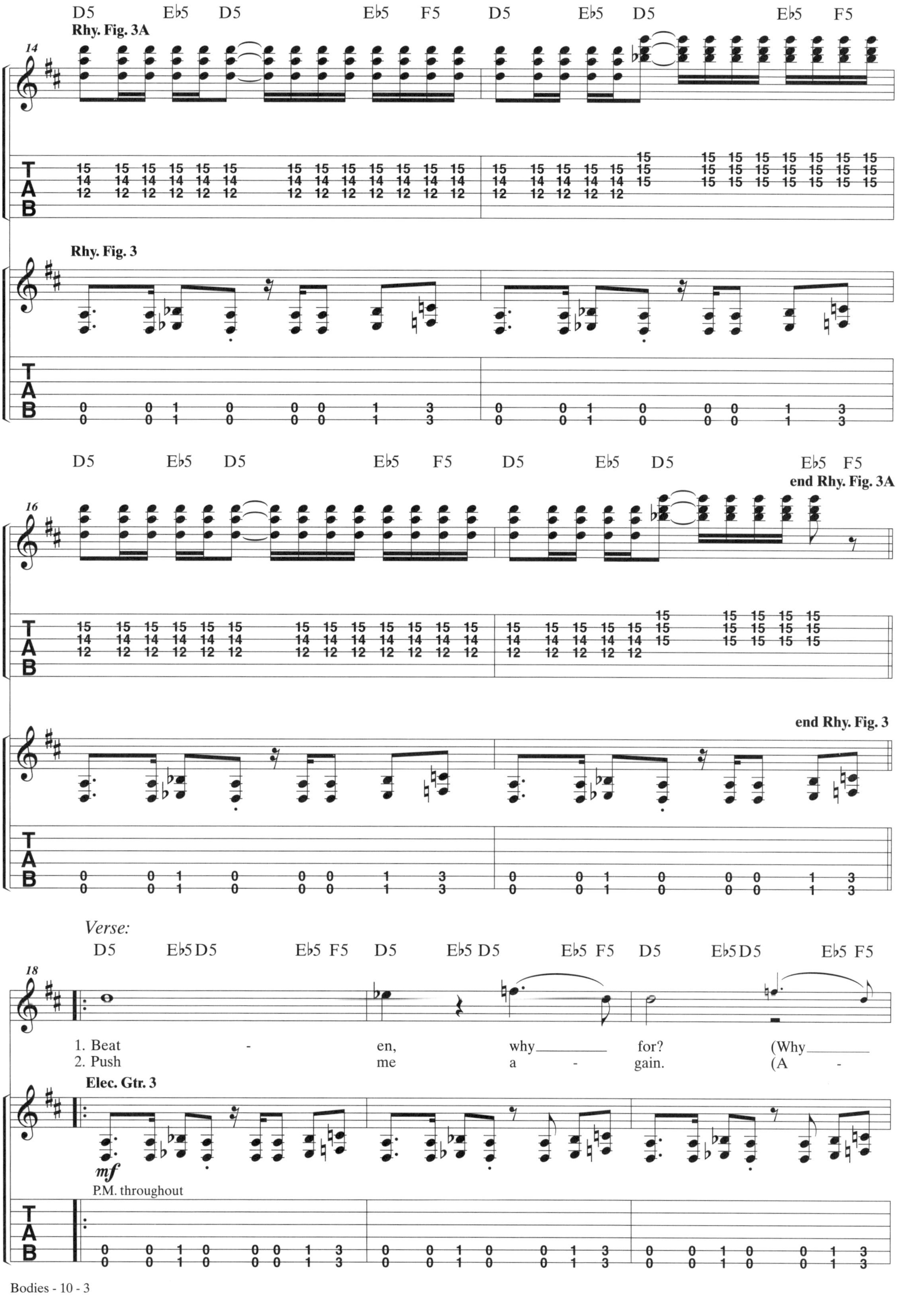
D5 Eb5 D5 Eb5 F5 D5 Eb5 D5 Eb5 F5
Rhy. Fig. 3A
14
Rhy. Fig. 3
D5 Eb5 D5 Eb5 F5 D5 Eb5 D5 Eb5 F5
end Rhy. Fig. 3A
16
end Rhy. Fig. 3
Verse:
D5 Eb5 D5 Eb5 F5 D5 Eb5 D5 Eb5 F5 D5 Eb5 D5 Eb5 F5
18
1. Beat - en, why for? (Why
2. Push me a - gain. (A -
Elec. Gtr. 3
mf
P.M. throughout

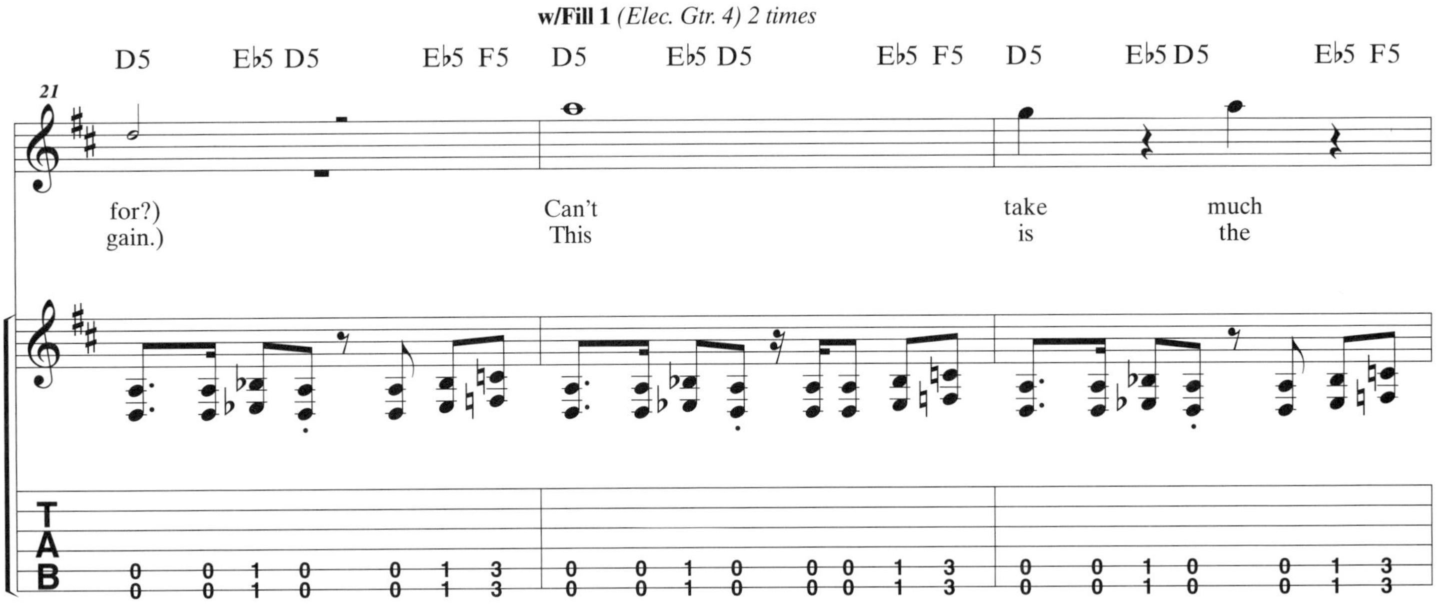
w/Fill 1 (Elec. Gtr. 4) 2 times
D5 E♭5 D5 E♭5 F5 D5 E♭5 D5 E♭5 F5 D5 E♭5 D5 E♭5 F5
21
for?) Can't take much
gain.) This is the
TAB

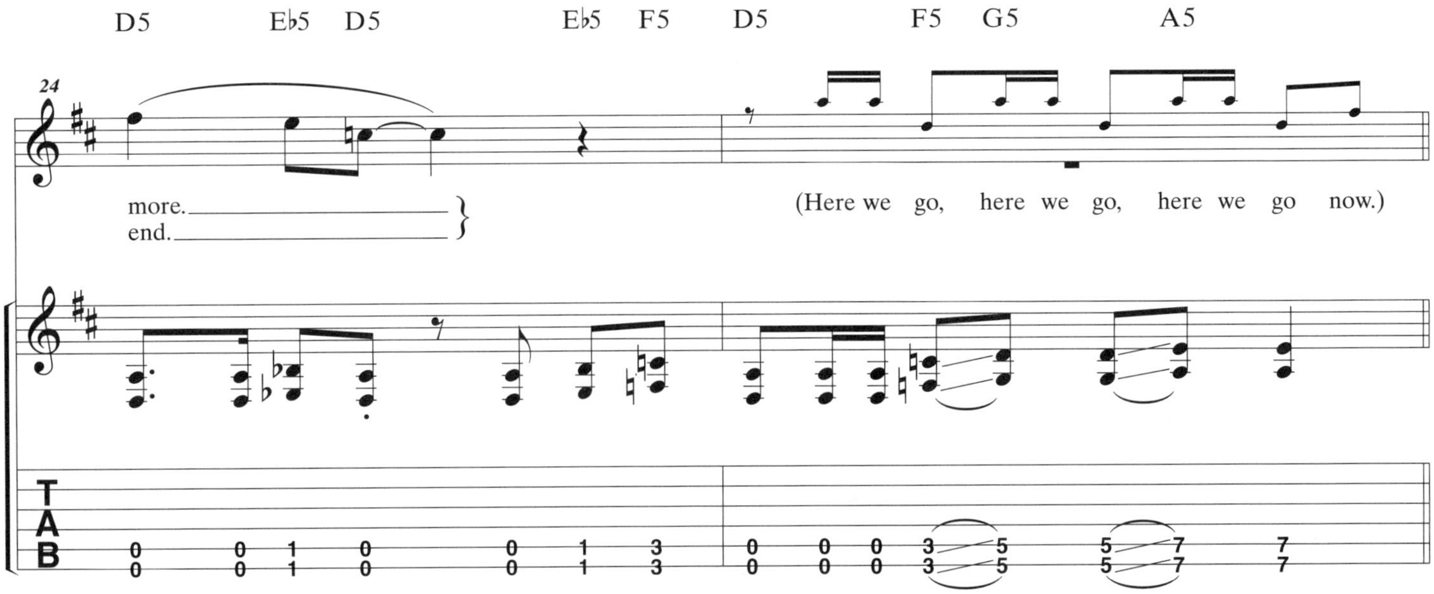
D5 E♭5 D5 E♭5 F5 D5 F5 G5 A5
24
more.
end.
(Here we go, here we go, here we go now.)
TAB

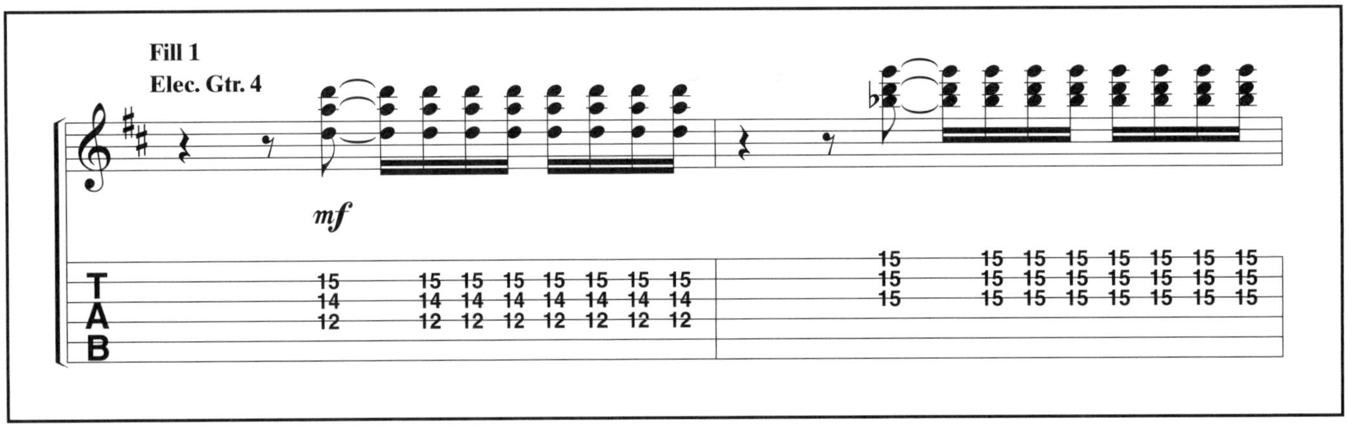
Fill 1
Elec. Gtr. 4
mf
TAB

𝄋 *Pre-chorus:*

Substitute w/Rhy. Fill 1 *(Elec. Gtr. 1) 3rd time only*

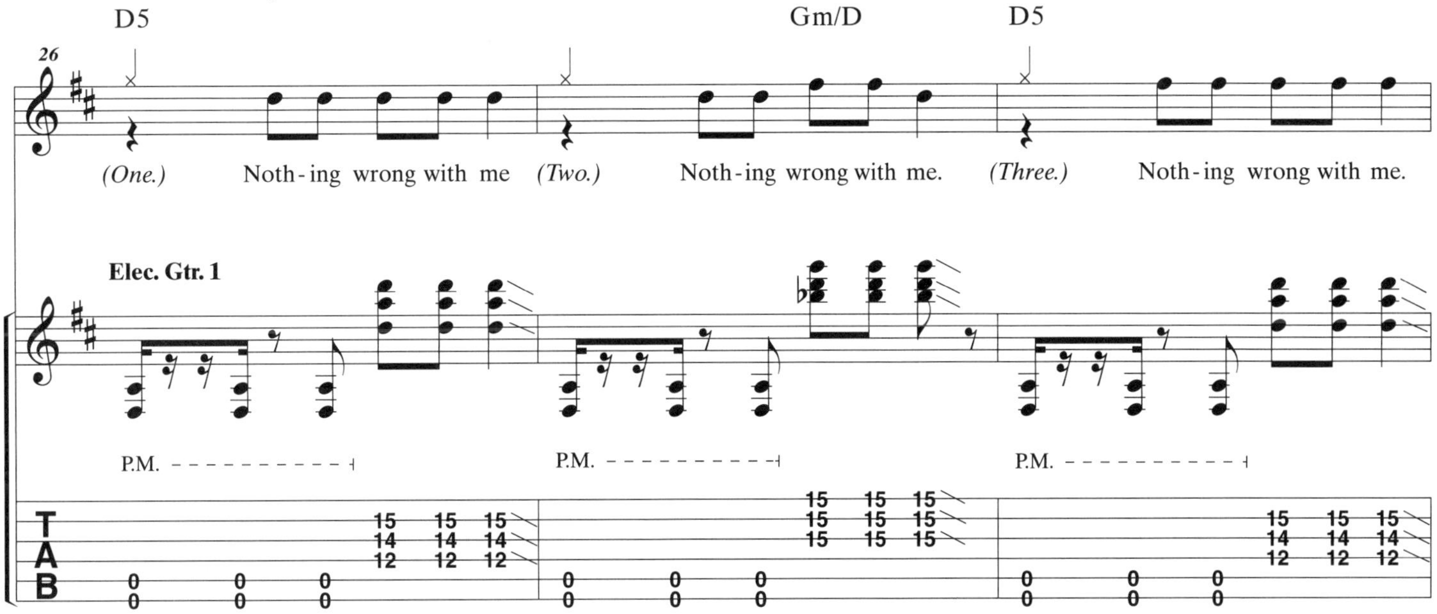

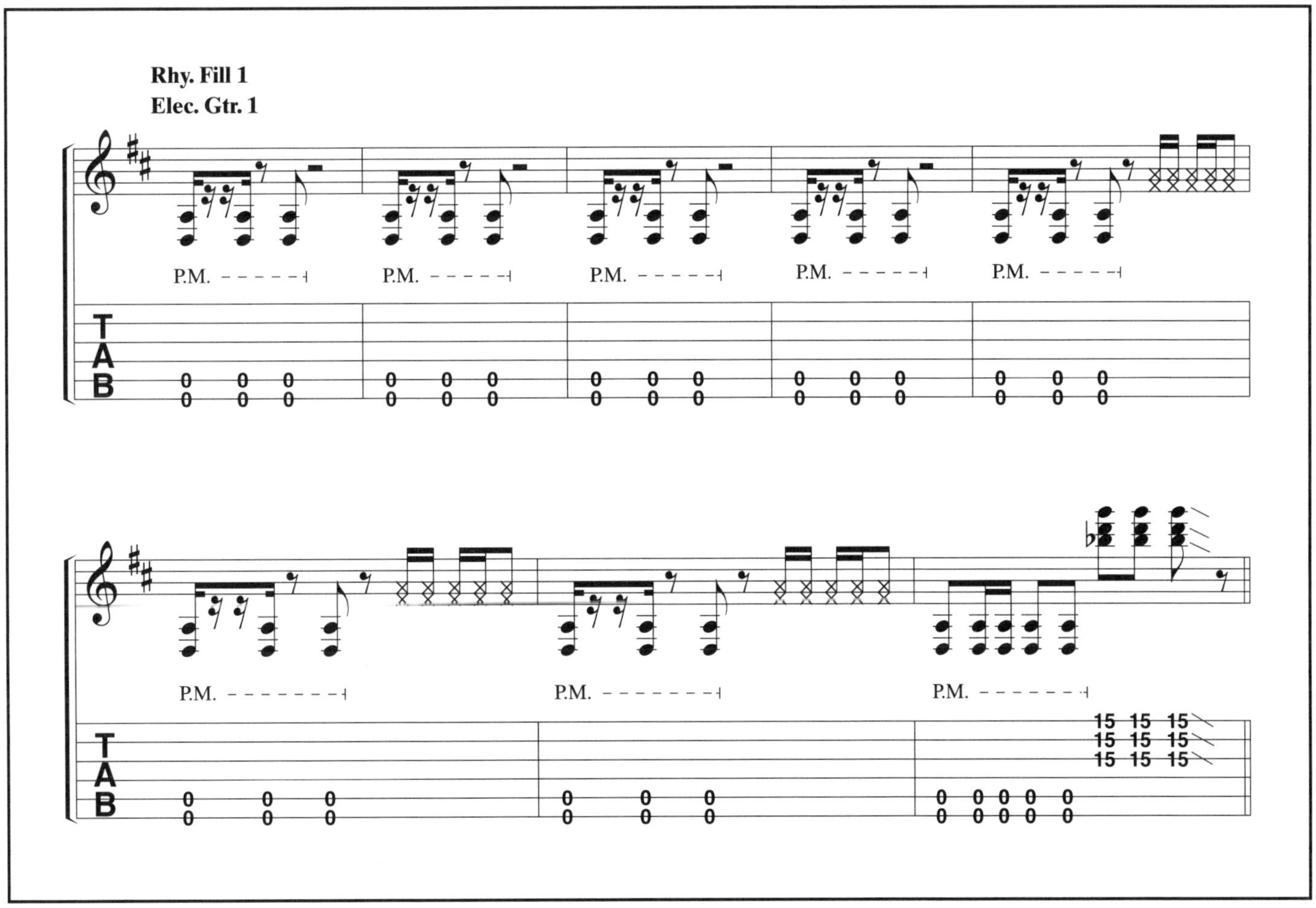

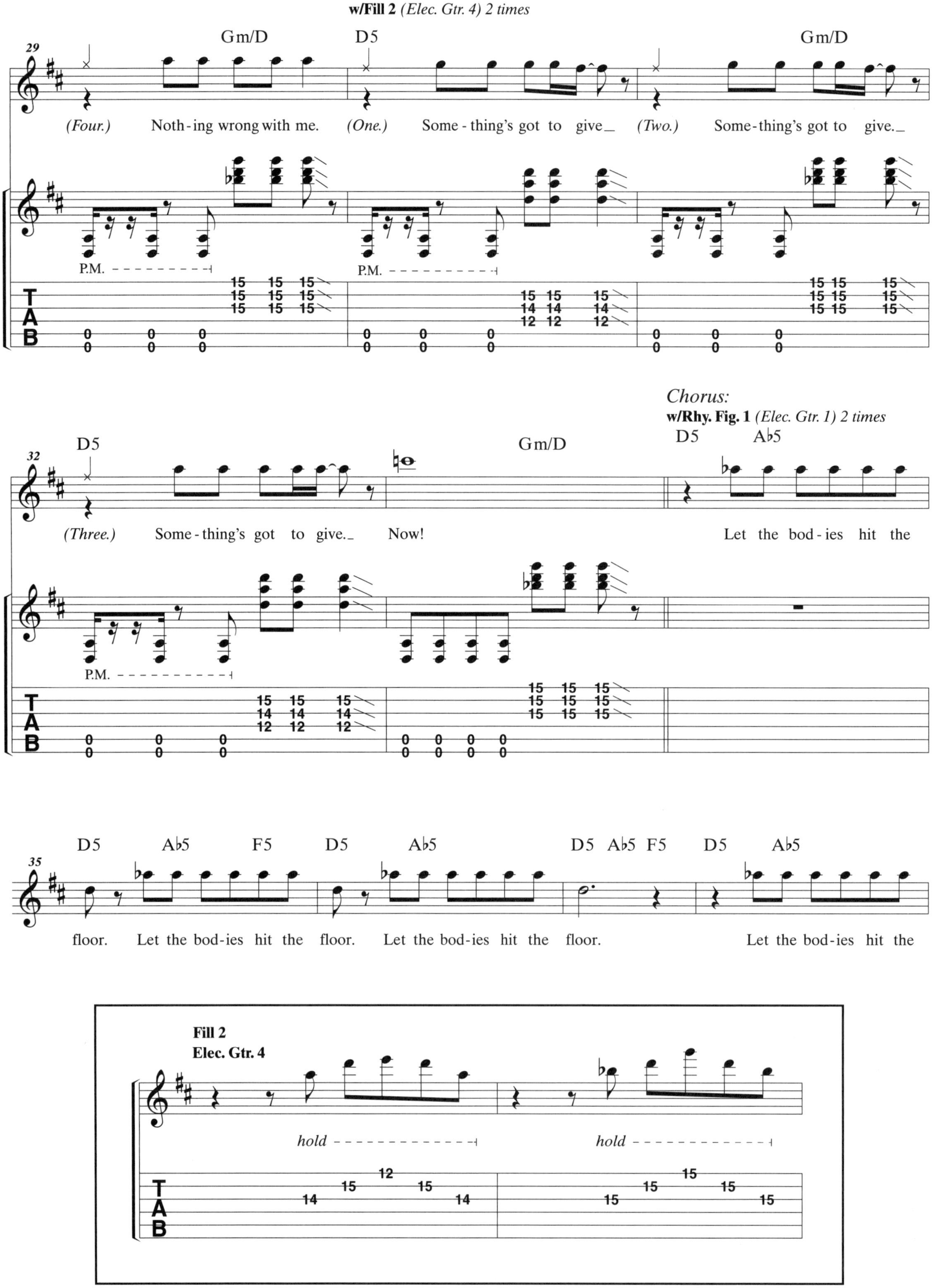
w/Fill 2 (Elec. Gtr. 4) 2 times
Gm/D D5 Gm/D
(Four.) Noth-ing wrong with me. (One.) Some-thing's got to give_ (Two.) Some-thing's got to give._
P.M.
Chorus:
w/Rhy. Fig. 1 (Elec. Gtr. 1) 2 times
D5 Gm/D D5 Ab5
(Three.) Some-thing's got to give._ Now! Let the bod-ies hit the
D5 Ab5 F5 D5 Ab5 D5 Ab5 F5 D5 Ab5
floor. Let the bod-ies hit the floor. Let the bod-ies hit the floor. Let the bod-ies hit the
Fill 2
Elec. Gtr. 4
hold
hold

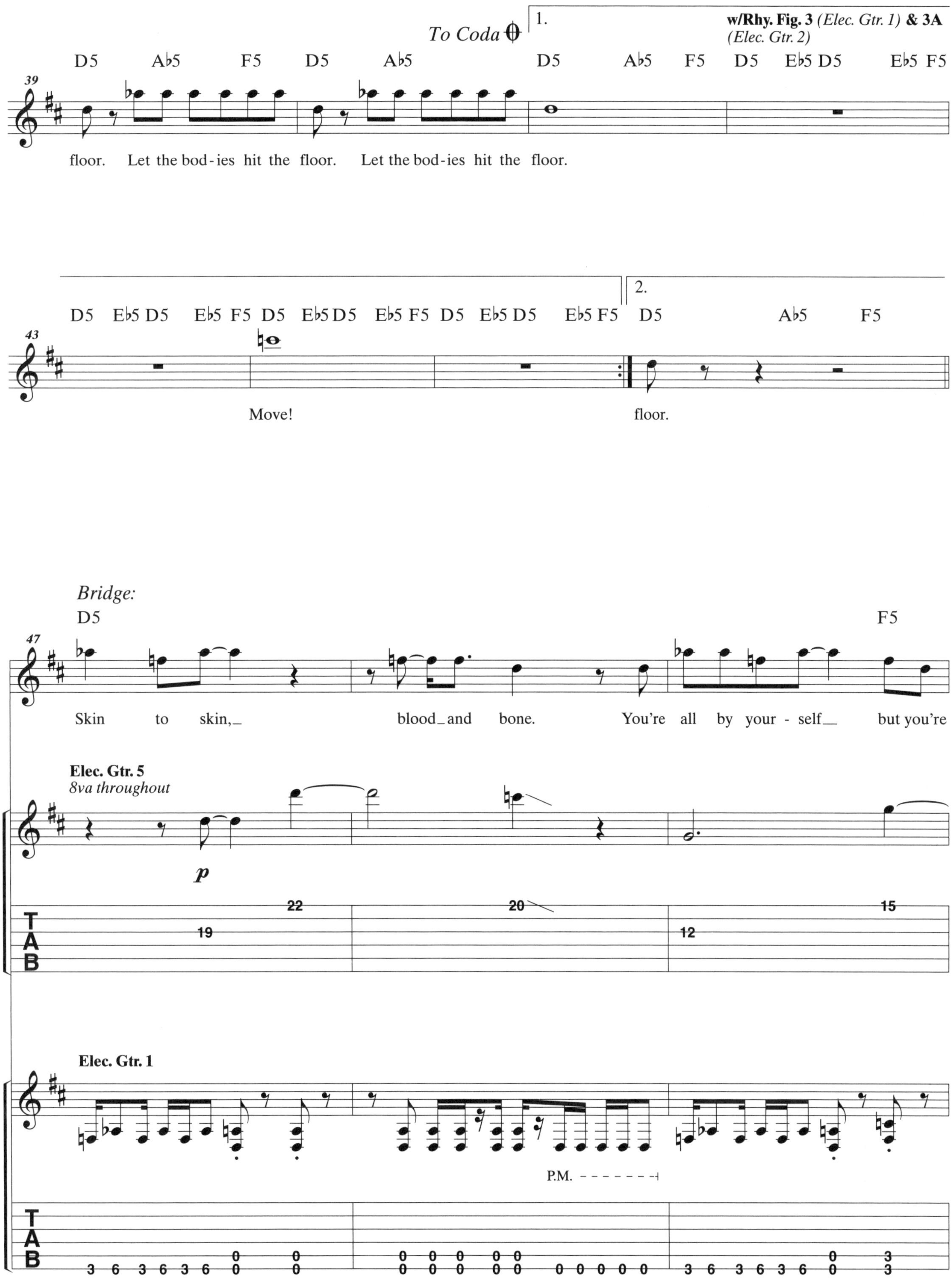
To Coda
1.
w/Rhy. Fig. 3 (Elec. Gtr. 1) & 3A (Elec. Gtr. 2)
D5 A♭5 F5 D5 A♭5 D5 A♭5 F5 D5 E♭5 D5 E♭5 F5
floor. Let the bod-ies hit the floor. Let the bod-ies hit the floor.
D5 E♭5 D5 E♭5 F5 D5 E♭5 D5 E♭5 F5 D5 E♭5 D5 E♭5 F5
2.
D5 A♭5 F5
Move!
floor.
Bridge:
D5 F5
Skin to skin, blood and bone. You're all by your-self but you're
Elec. Gtr. 5
8va throughout
p
22 19 20 15 12
Elec. Gtr. 1
P.M.
3 6 3 6 3 6 0 0 0 0 0 0 0 0 0 0 0 0 0 0 0 0 0 0 0 0 0 3 6 3 6 3 6 0 0 3 3

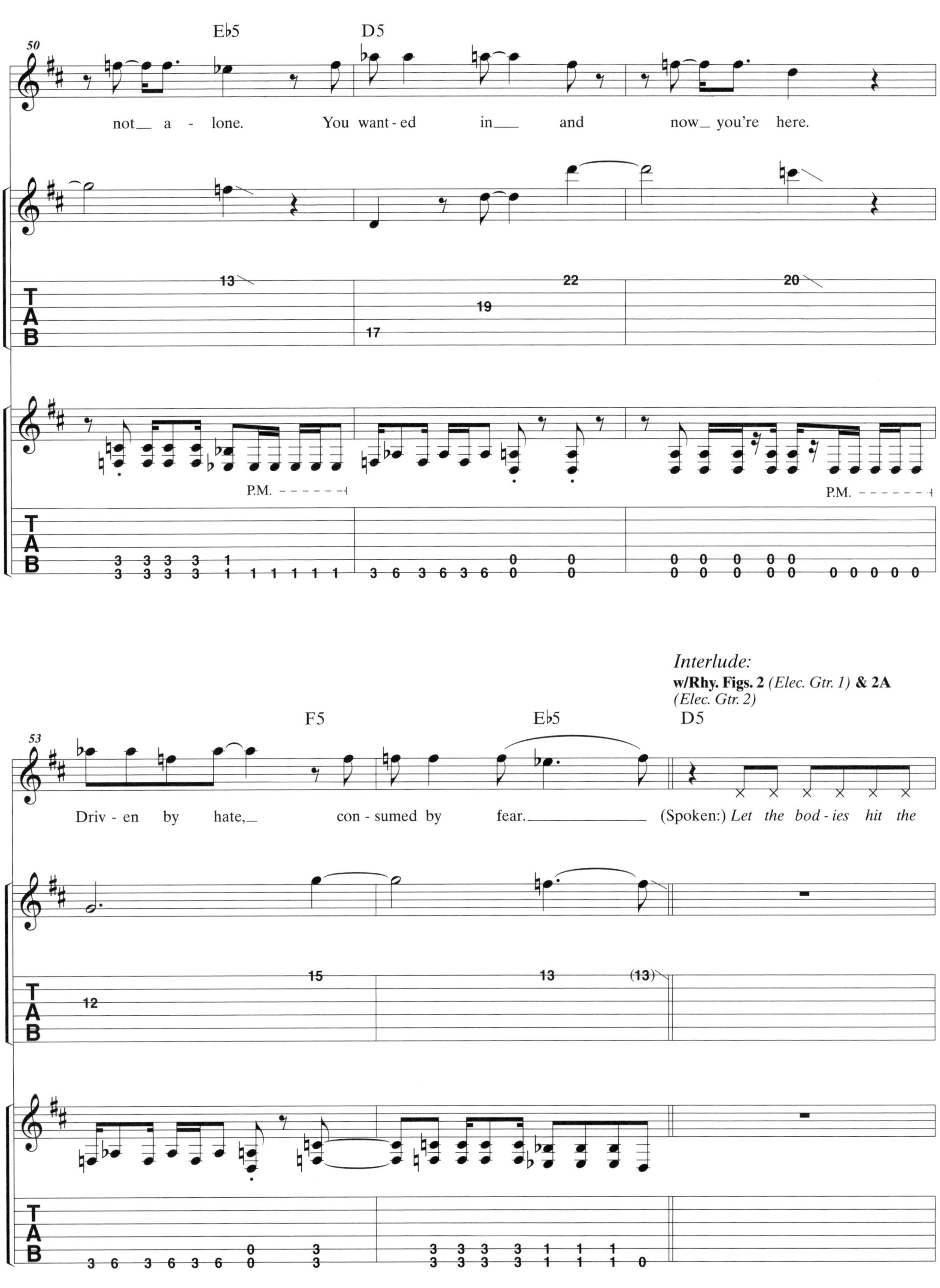
50
E♭5
D5
not_ a - lone. You want - ed in_ and now_ you're here.
P.M.
P.M.
Interlude:
w/Rhy. Figs. 2 (Elec. Gtr. 1) & 2A
(Elec. Gtr. 2)
53
F5
E♭5
D5
Driv - en by hate,_ con - sumed by fear.
(Spoken:) Let the bod - ies hit the

Gm/D D5 Gm/D
floor. Let the bod - ies hit the floor. Let the bod - ies hit the floor. Let the bod - ies hit the
w/Rhy. Figs. 3 (Elec. Gtr. 1) & 3A (Elec. Gtr. 2)
D5 Eb5 D5 Eb5 F5 D5 Eb5 D5 Eb5 F5 D5 Eb5 D5 Eb5 F5 D5 Eb5 D5 Eb5 F5
floor.
D5 Eb5 D5 Eb5 F5 D5 Eb5 D5 Eb5 F5 D5 Eb5 D5 Eb5 F5
Elec. Gtr. 5
8va throughout
Elec. Gtr. 2
Elec. Gtr. 1

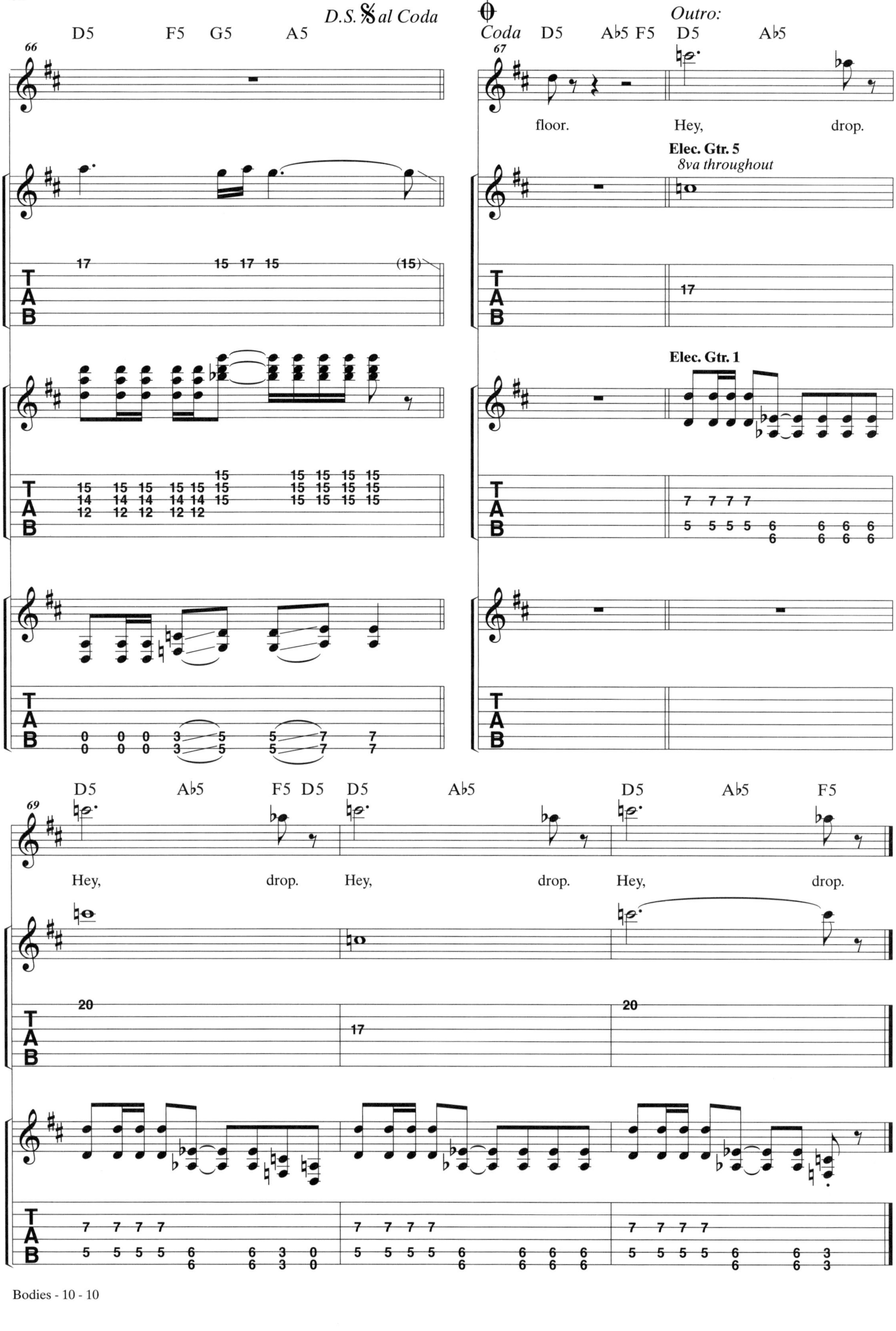
D.S. % al Coda
Coda
Outro:
D5 F5 G5 A5
D5 A♭5 F5 D5 A♭5
floor. Hey, drop.
Elec. Gtr. 5
8va throughout
Elec. Gtr. 1
D5 A♭5 F5 D5 D5 A♭5 D5 A♭5 F5
Hey, drop. Hey, drop. Hey, drop.

AWAKE

*All gtrs. in Drop D, down 1 whole step:

⑥ = C ③ = F
⑤ = G ② = A
④ = C ① = D

Words and Music by
SULLY ERNA

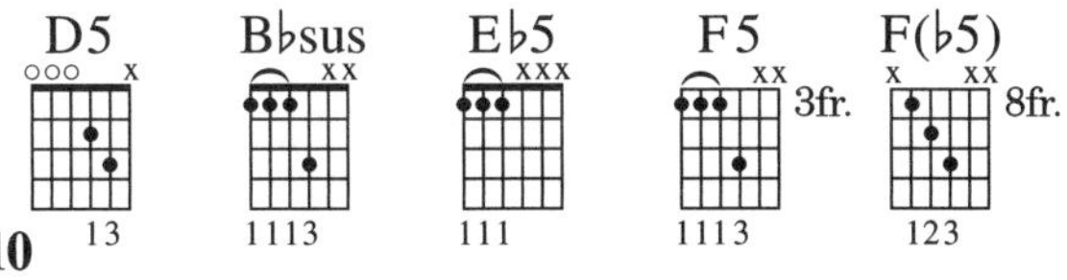

8va
loco
P.M.
harm.
Eb5 D5 Eb5
D5 Eb5 D5 F5 D5 Eb5
1. To Next Strain
(To Verse:)
2.
D5 Eb5 D5 Eb5 F(b5) F(b5)
Verse:
D5
1. Wait an - oth - er min - ute. Can't you see what this
2. Take an - oth - er sec - ond. Turn your back on me and
Rhy. Fig. 2
TAB

Bbsus Eb5
22
pain__ has f*** - in' done to__ me.__ I'm__ a -
make_ be - lieve that you're al - ways hap - py.__ It's safe to
end Rhy. Fig. 2
w/Rhy. Fig. 2 (Gtrs. 1 & 2)
D5
24
live__ and__ still kick - in'. What you__ see, I can see and
say__ you're nev - er e - nough. A big part__ of you has died and
Bbsus Eb5
26
may - be,__ ah, you'll think be - fore you__ speak.__
by the way, ah, I hope you're sat - is - fied.__
I'm__ a -
Chorus:
w/Rhy. Fig. 1 (Gtr. 1) 4 times
Gtr. 2 tacet
D5 Bbsus Eb5 D5
28
live for you.__ I'm__ a - wake__ be -
w/Rhy. Fig. 1A (Gtr. 2) 1st time only
Bbsus Eb5 D5 Bbsus Eb5
31
cause of__ you,__ I'm__ a - live. Told you__ I'm__ a -
1. D.S. 2.
D5 Bbsus Eb5 D5 Bbsus Eb5
34
wake, swal - low - ing you. swal - low - ing you. I'm_ a -

w/Rhy. Fig. 1 (Gtr. 1) 3 times
w/Rhy. Fig. 1A (Gtr. 2) 1st 2 meas. 2 times
37
D5
B♭sus
E♭5
D5
live for you. I'm a - wake be -
w/Rhy. Fig. 1A (Gtr. 2) last 2 meas.
40
B♭sus
E♭5
D5
B♭sus
E♭5
cause of you, I'm a - live. Told you I'm a -
Gtr. 2 tacet
43
D5
wake.
Gtr. 1
T
A
B
Interlude:
Play 4 times
(Play 2 times on single edit)
45
Gtrs. 1 & 2
Rhy. Fig. 3
end Rhy. Fig. 3
P.M.
Bridge:
w/Rhy. Fig. 3 (Gtrs. 1 & 2) 4 times
48
Tear - in' it back, I'm fail - in' me. I'm
50
tak - in' a step back, so I can breathe. Hear the si - lence a - bout to break.
53
Fear re - sis - tance when I'm a - wake. Oh,

56
E♭5
tear - in' it back, I'm fail - in' me. I'm tak - ing a step back, so I can breathe.
Gtrs. 1 & 2
58
D5
P.M.
60
E♭5
Hear the si - lence a - bout to break. Fear re - sis - tance when I'm a - wake.
Rhy. Fig. 4
62
G5
Oo, yeah!
end Rhy. Fig. 4
P.M.

Interlude:
Gtr. 2 tacet
D5
Gtr. 1
64
Gtr. 3 (w/dist.)
66
8va
w/wah
harm.
Gtrs. 1 & 2
8va
loco
harm.
Guitar Solo:
Gtr. 3
w/Rhy. Fig. 3 (Gtrs. 1 & 2) 4 times
68
loco
trem. pick
72
trem. pick

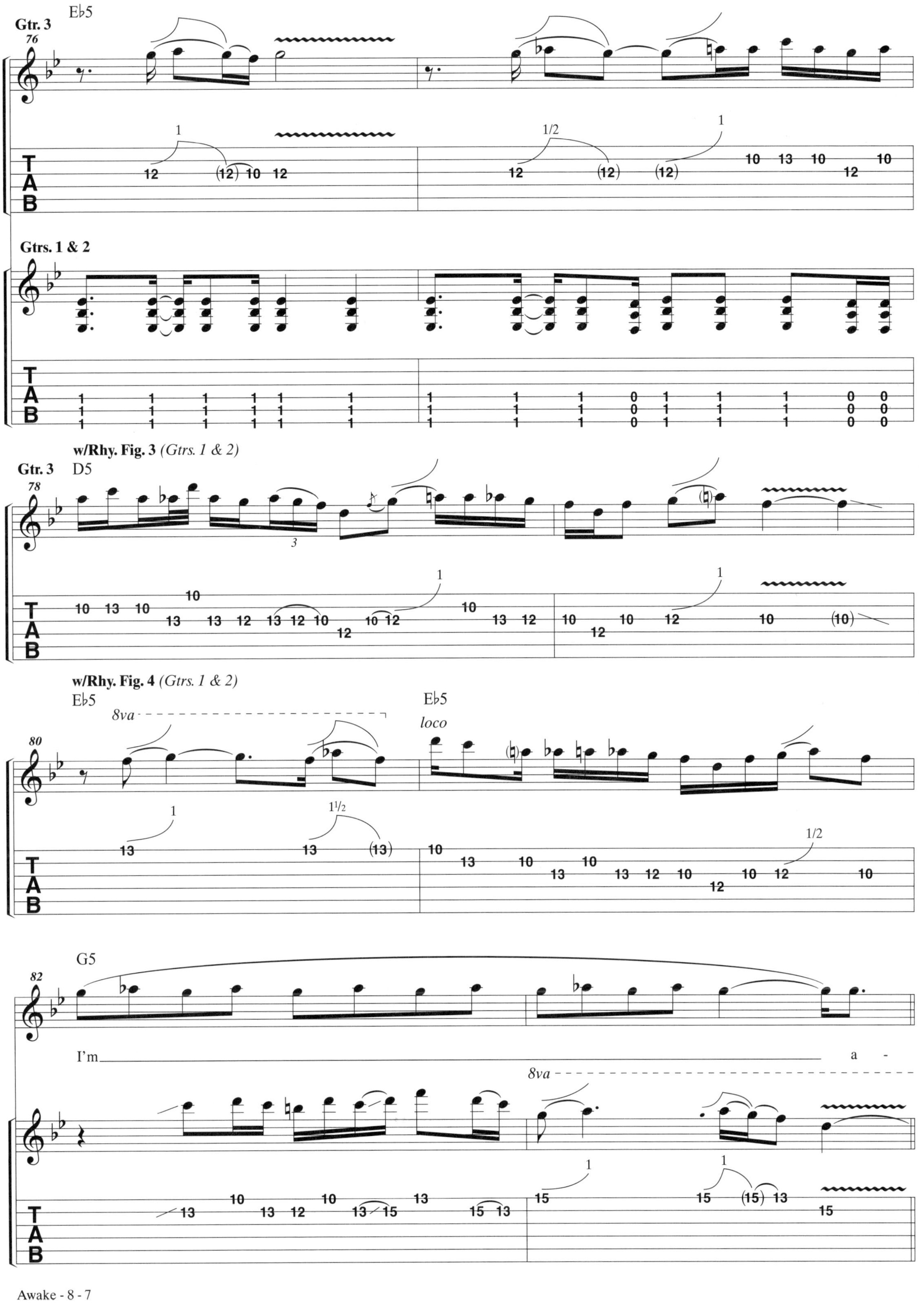
Gtr. 3
E♭5
Gtrs. 1 & 2
w/Rhy. Fig. 3 (Gtrs. 1 & 2)
D5
w/Rhy. Fig. 4 (Gtrs. 1 & 2)
E♭5
8va
loco
G5
I'm
a -

Chorus:
w/Rhy. Fig. 1 (Gtr. 1) 4 times
w/Rhy. Fig. 1A (Gtr. 2) 1st 2 meas., 3 times simile
84
D5 B♭sus E♭5 D5
live for you. I'm a - wake be -
Gtr. 3
8va
(15)
87
B♭sus E♭5 D5 B♭sus E♭5
cause of you, I'm a - live. Told you I'm a -
1.
2.
w/Rhy. Fig. 1A (Gtr. 2) last 2 meas.
90
D5 B♭sus E♭5 B♭sus E♭5
wake, swal - low - ing you, I'm a - swal - low - ing you.
Outro:
Gtrs. 1 & 2
93
D5
P.M.
95

SPEAK

*All gtrs. in Drop D tuning, down 1 step:
⑥ = C ③ = F
⑤ = G ② = A
④ = C ① = D

Words and Music by
SULLY ERNA and TONY ROMBOLA

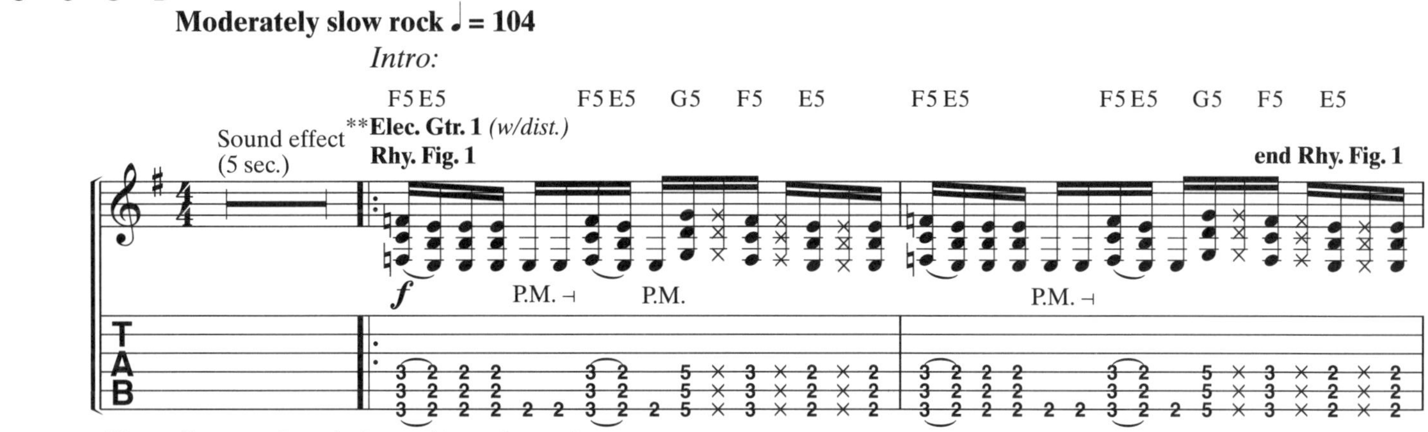

*Recording sounds a whole step lower than written.
**Doubled throughout.

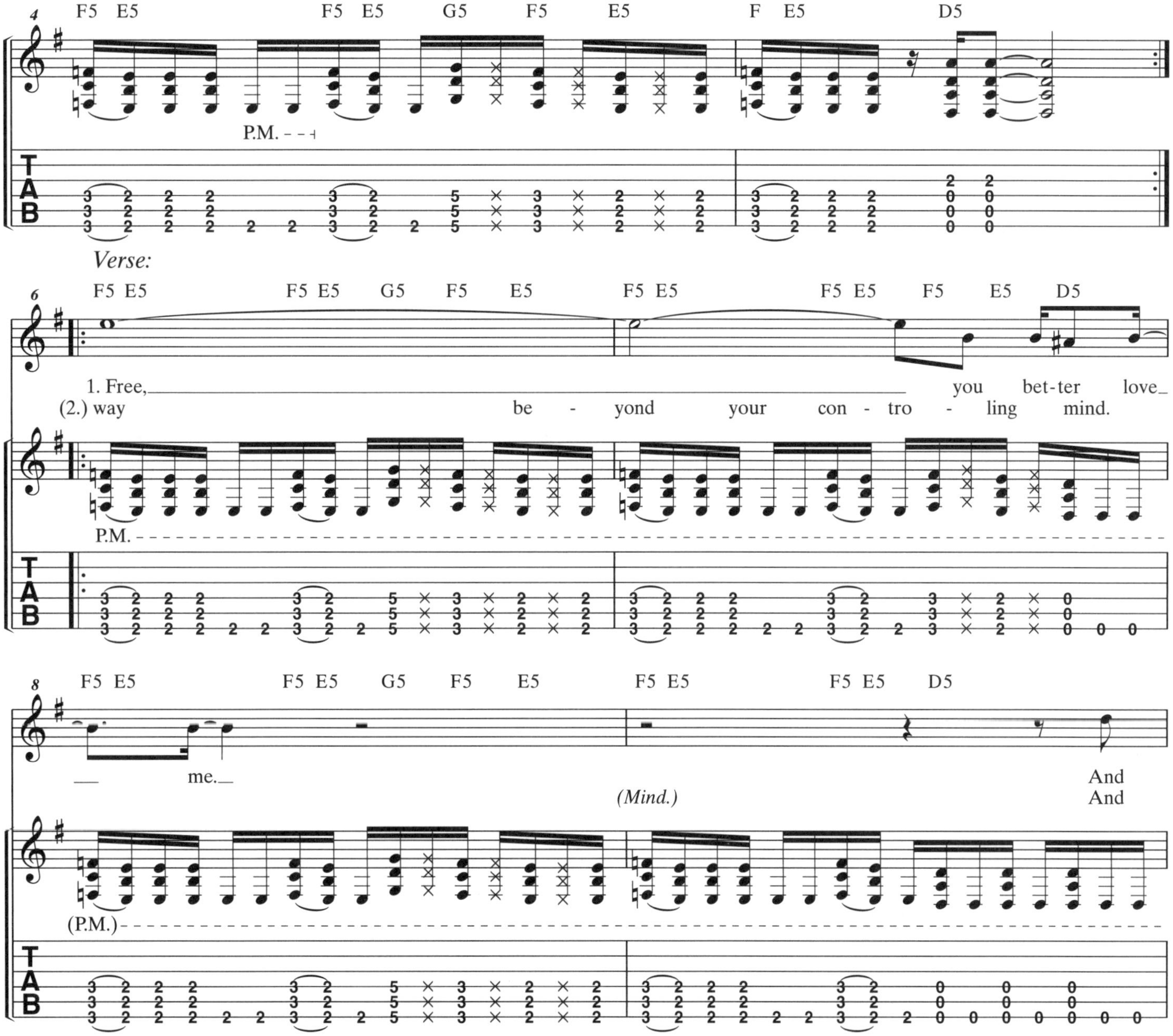

F5 E5 F5 E5 G5 F5 E5 F5 E5 F5 E5 F5 E5 D5
hide, or run a - way
no more be - liev - ing in all your pre -
(P.M.)
*1st time w/echo set for half-note regeneration w/2 repeats.
F5 E5 F5 E5 G5 F5 E5 D5 F5
from all your yes - ter - days.
- cious lies yeah.
(P.M.)
Chorus:
w/Fill 1 (Elec. Gtr. 2) 3rd time only
E5 E(♭6) E5 D5 C5 D5
Speak the truth or make your peace some oth - er way
Rhy. Fig. 2
end Rhy. Fig. 2
Fill 1
Elec. Gtr. 2

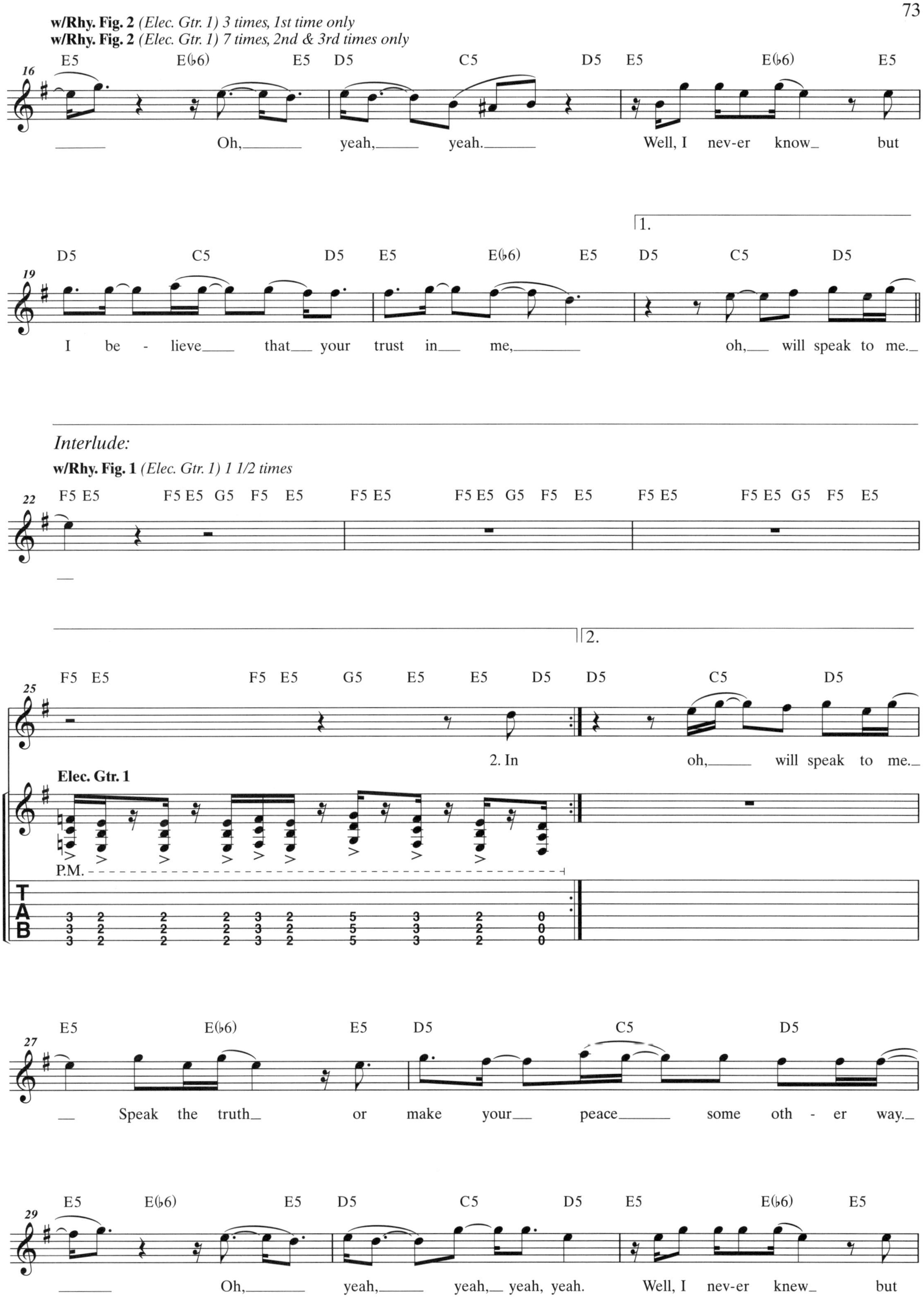
w/Rhy. Fig. 2 (Elec. Gtr. 1) 3 times, 1st time only
w/Rhy. Fig. 2 (Elec. Gtr. 1) 7 times, 2nd & 3rd times only
E5 E(♭6) E5 D5 C5 D5 E5 E(♭6) E5
Oh, yeah, yeah. Well, I nev-er know but
D5 C5 D5 E5 E(♭6) E5
1.
D5 C5 D5
I be - lieve that your trust in me, oh, will speak to me.
Interlude:
w/Rhy. Fig. 1 (Elec. Gtr. 1) 1 1/2 times
F5 E5 F5 E5 G5 F5 E5 F5 E5 F5 E5 G5 F5 E5 F5 E5 F5 E5 G5 F5 E5
F5 E5 F5 E5 G5 E5 E5 D5
2.
D5 C5 D5
2. In oh, will speak to me.
Elec. Gtr. 1
P.M.
T
A
B
E5 E(♭6) E5 D5 C5 D5
Speak the truth or make your peace some oth - er way.
E5 E(♭6) E5 D5 C5 D5 E5 E(♭6) E5
Oh, yeah, yeah, yeah, yeah. Well, I nev-er knew but

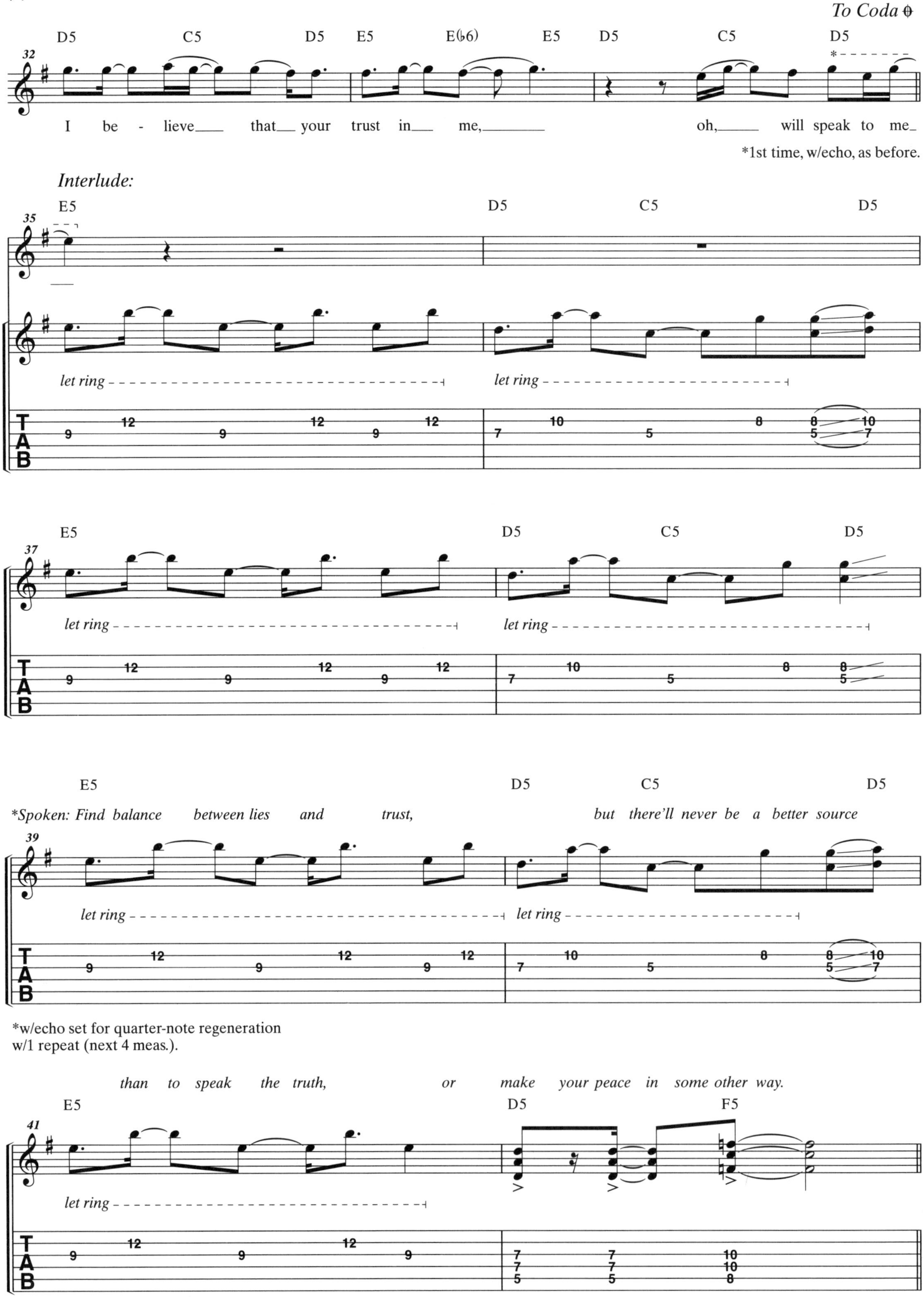
To Coda
D5 C5 D5 E5 E(♭6) E5 D5 C5 D5
I be - lieve that your trust in me, oh, will speak to me
*1st time, w/echo, as before.
Interlude:
E5 D5 C5 D5
let ring
*Spoken: Find balance between lies and trust, but there'll never be a better source
*w/echo set for quarter-note regeneration w/1 repeat (next 4 meas.).
than to speak the truth, or make your peace in some other way.
E5 D5 F5

Guitar Solo:

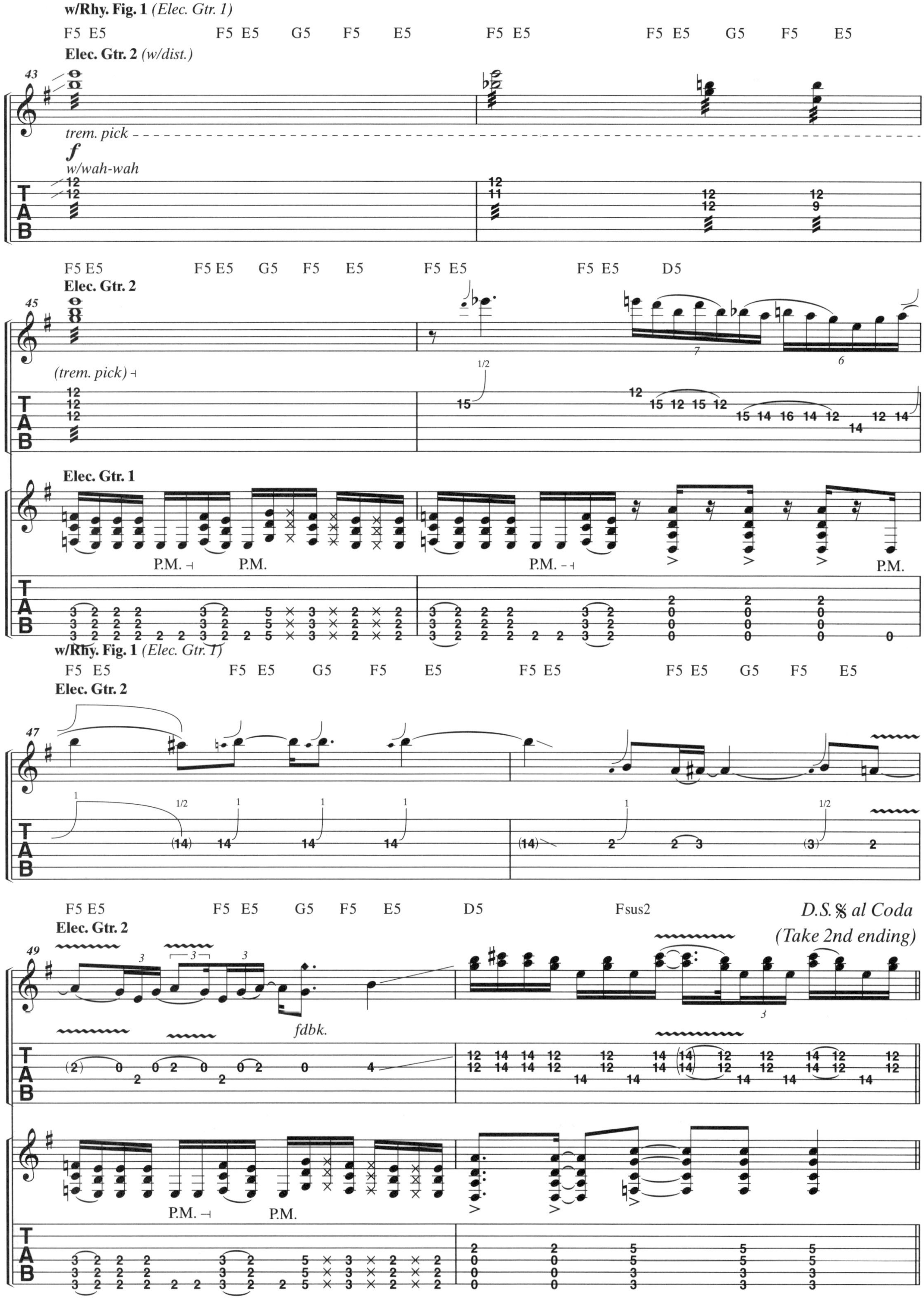
w/Rhy. Fig. 1 (Elec. Gtr. 1)
F5 E5 F5 E5 G5 F5 E5 F5 E5 F5 E5 G5 F5 E5
Elec. Gtr. 2 (w/dist.)
trem. pick
f
w/wah-wah
F5 E5 F5 E5 G5 F5 E5 F5 E5 F5 E5 D5
Elec. Gtr. 2
(trem. pick)
Elec. Gtr. 1
P.M.
w/Rhy. Fig. 1 (Elec. Gtr. 1)
F5 E5 F5 E5 G5 F5 E5 F5 E5 F5 E5 G5 F5 E5
Elec. Gtr. 2
F5 E5 F5 E5 G5 F5 E5 D5 Fsus2
D.S. 𝄋 al Coda
(Take 2nd ending)
fdbk.

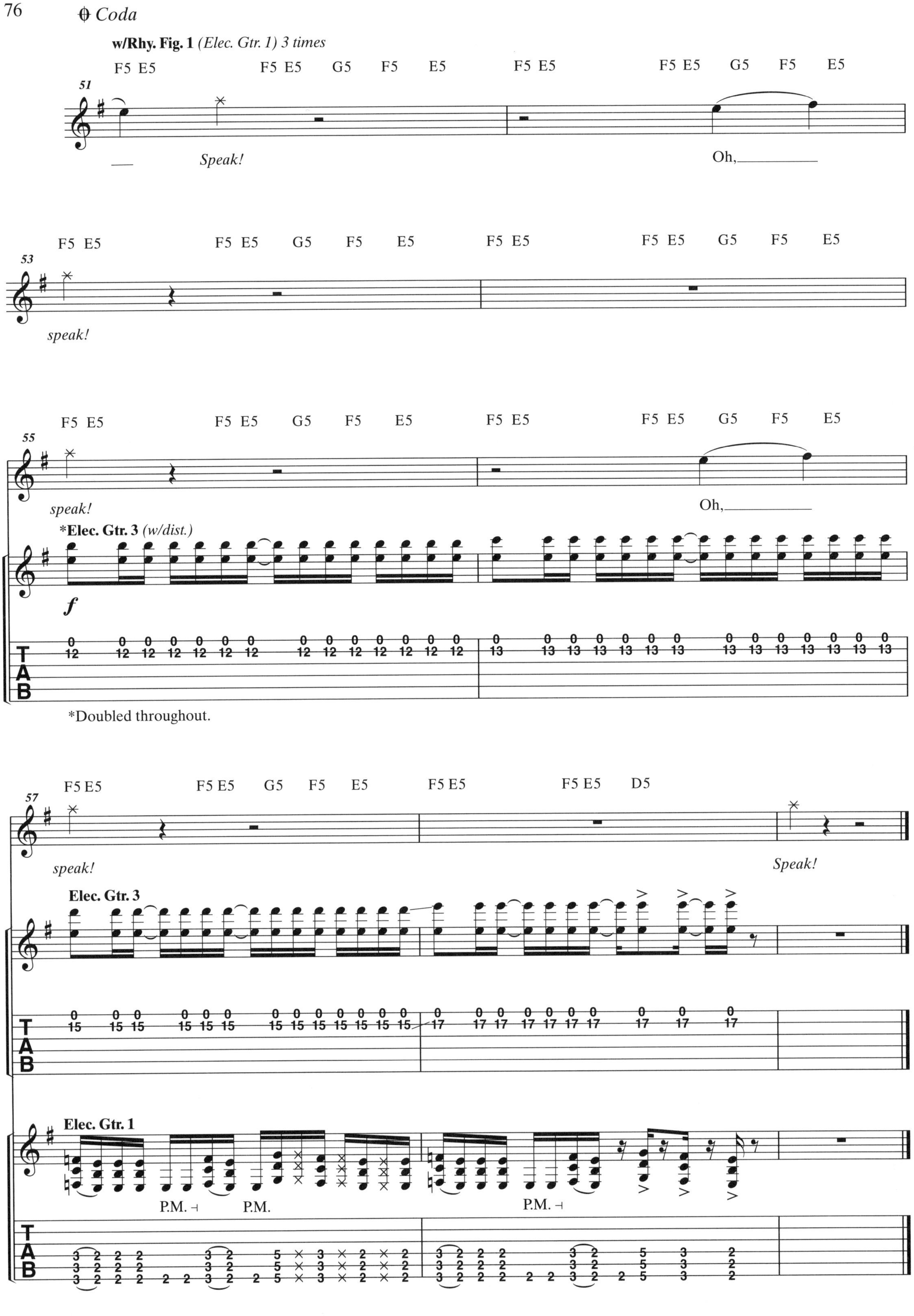
Coda
w/Rhy. Fig. 1 (Elec. Gtr. 1) 3 times
F5 E5 F5 E5 G5 F5 E5 F5 E5 F5 E5 G5 F5 E5
Speak!
Oh,
speak!
speak!
*Elec. Gtr. 3 (w/dist.)
f
TAB
*Doubled throughout.
F5 E5 F5 E5 G5 F5 E5 F5 E5 F5 E5 D5
speak!
Speak!
Elec. Gtr. 3
Elec. Gtr. 1
P.M.
P.M.
P.M.

KICKSTART MY HEART

Words and Music by
NIKKI SIXX

*All gtrs. tune down 1 whole step:

⑥ = D ③ = F
⑤ = G ② = A
④ = C ① = D

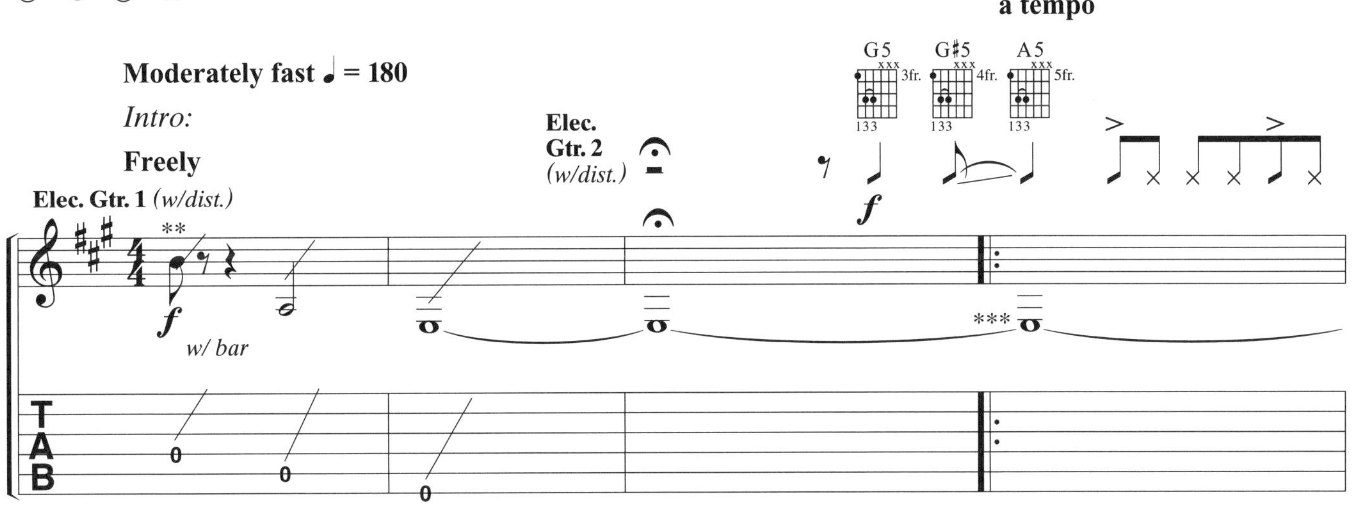

*Recording sounds a whole step lower than written.
**Pre-press vib. and slowly release to pitch.

***Elec. Gtr. 1 tacet on repeat.

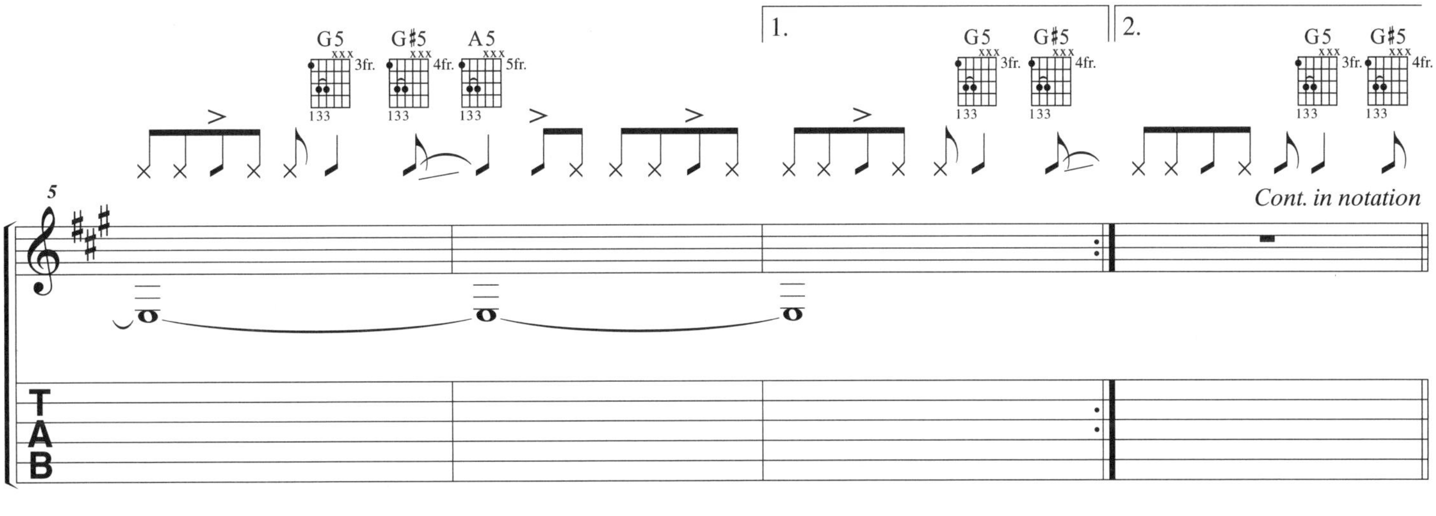

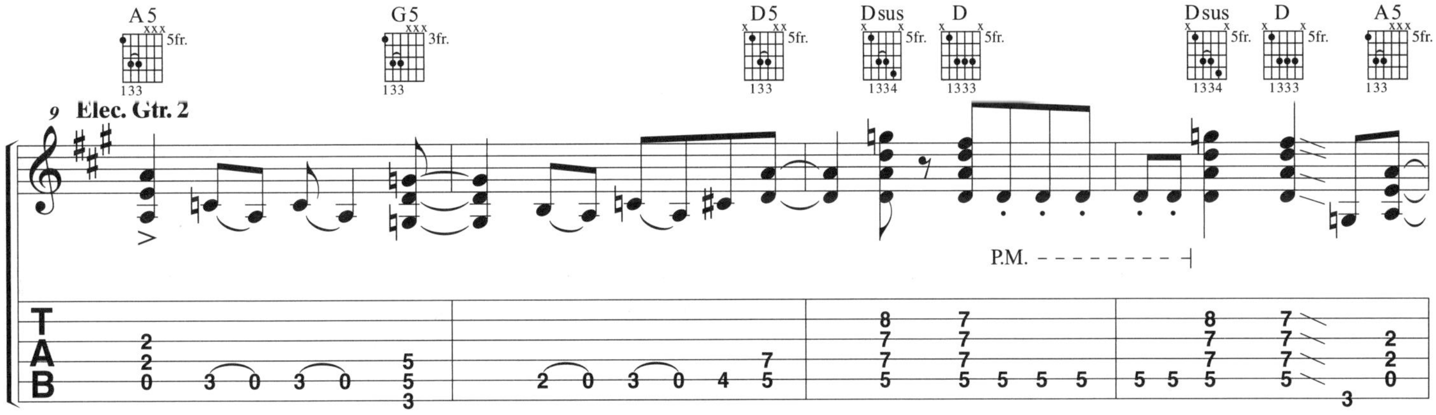

G5 D5 Dsus D D5 A5
G5 D5 G5 G♯5
1. When
Verse:
A5 G5 G♯5 A5
I get high, I get high on speed, top fuel fun - ny car's a
2. Sk y - dive nak - ed from an aer - o - plane or a la - dy with a bod - y from
P.M.
P.M.

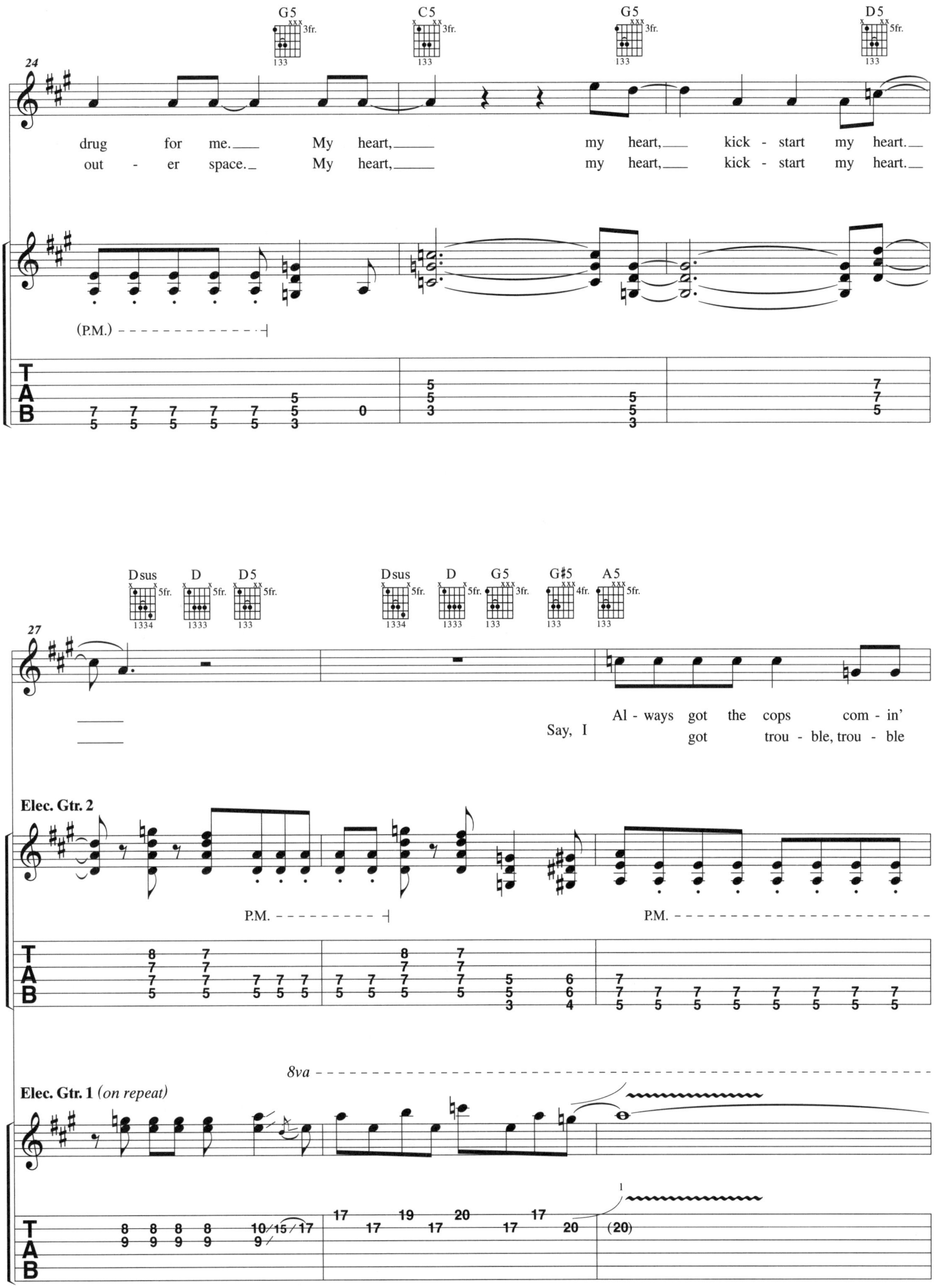
G5 C5 G5 D5
24
drug for me. My heart, my heart, kick - start my heart.
out - er space. My heart, my heart, kick - start my heart.
(P.M.)
Dsus D D5 Dsus D G5 G♯5 A5
27
Al - ways got the cops com - in'
Say, I got trou - ble, trou - ble
Elec. Gtr. 2
P.M.
P.M.
8va
Elec. Gtr. 1 (on repeat)

G5 G♯5 A5 G5
af - ter me, cus - tom built bike do - in' one - o - three.
in my eyes, I'm just look - in' for an - oth - er good time.
My heart,
(P.M.)
P.M.
(8va)
C5 G5 D5 Dsus D D5 Dsus D G5 G♯5
My heart, kick - start my heart.
P.M.
Elec. Gtr. 1
1/2
w/bar
vib. bar dive

Pre-chorus:
A5 G5 G♯5 A5 A5
Ooh, are you ready-y, girls? Ooh, are you ready-y now? Whoa,
Elec. Gtr. 2
Elec. Gtr. 1
w/bar
dive w/bar
Chorus:
G5 D5 Dsus D Dsus D A5
yeah. Kick-start my heart, Give it a start. Whoa,
Elec. Gtr. 1
Rhy. Fig. 1
P.M.
G5 D5 Dsus D D5 A5
yeah. Ba-by, whoa,

G5
D5
Dsus
D
Dsus
D
A5
yeah.
Kick - start my heart, hope it nev - er stops.
Whoa,
P.M.
G5
F5
yeah.
Ba - by,
yeah.
end Rhy. Fig. 1
P.M.
1.
Interlude:
A5
G5
G♯5
P.M.
P.M.

A5
G5
G♯5
A5
P.M.
*Composite arrangement.
G5
G♯5
A5
G5
G♯5
(P.M.)
2.
E5
Elec. Gtr. 1
Elec. Gtr. 2 (clean-tone)
w/echo delay effect
Bridge:
A
G5
D5
A

G5
Dsus
D
A
75
When we
G5
D5
79
start - ed this band
all we need - ed,
need - ed a - was___ a laugh.___
A
G5
Dsus
D
82
___ Years___ gone by, I say___ we've kicked some ass.___
T
A
B

A
G5
D5
Elec. Gtr. 2
Elec. Gtr. 1
When I'm en - raged or hit - tin' the stage,
'dren - a - lin rush - in' through my veins and I say we're still kick - ing
Cont. in slashes
D5
A5
G5
Elec. Gtr. 2
ass. Said ooh, aah, kick -
- start my heart, I hope it nev - er stops. And I think we did
pick scrapes
Chorus:
w/Rhy. Fig. 1 (Elec. Gtr. 2)
all of this to rock. Whoa, yeah.

D5 Dsus D Dsus D A5 G5
Kick - start my heart, give it a start. Whoa, yeah.
Elec. Gtr. 1
vib. bar
w/talk bar
Push down the vib. bar, pick the low E string and gradually release the bar.
D5 Dsus D Dsus D A5 G5
Kick - start my heart, hope it nev - er stops. Whoa, yeah,
D5 Dsus D5 A5
ba - by,
Elec. Gtr. 2
Elec. Gtr. 1

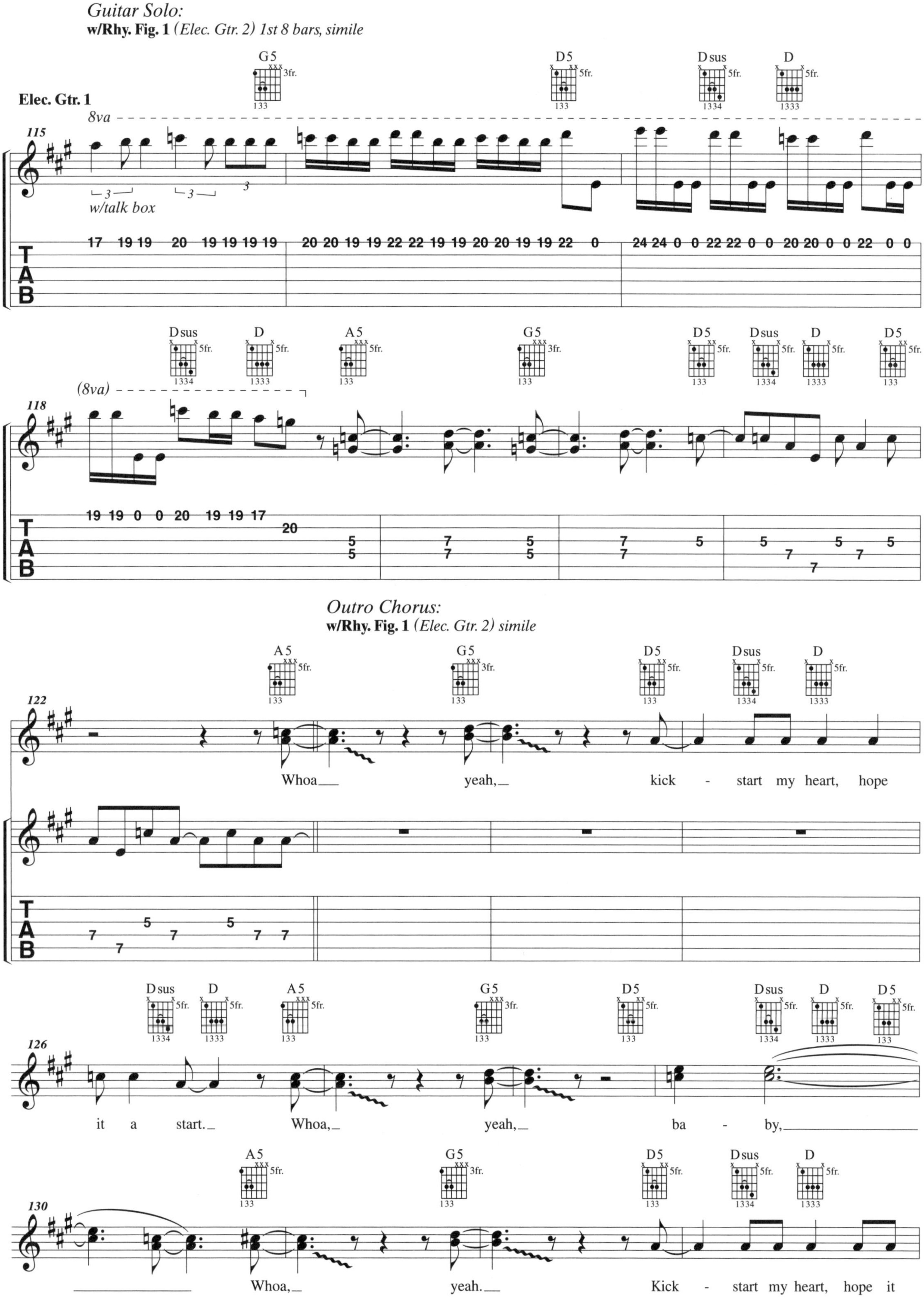
Guitar Solo:
w/Rhy. Fig. 1 (Elec. Gtr. 2) 1st 8 bars, simile
Elec. Gtr. 1
8va
w/talk box
G5 D5 Dsus D
Dsus D A5 G5 D5 Dsus D D5
Outro Chorus:
w/Rhy. Fig. 1 (Elec. Gtr. 2) simile
A5 G5 D5 Dsus D
Whoa yeah, kick - start my heart, hope
Dsus D A5 G5 D5 Dsus D D5
it a start. Whoa, yeah, ba - by,
A5 G5 D5 Dsus D
Whoa, yeah. Kick - start my heart, hope it

Dsus
D
A5
G5
D5
ne - ver stops._ Whoa,_ yeah._ O K, boys,_ let's
Elec. Gtr. 2
Outro:
G5
G♯5
A5
rock the house._
P.M.
pick slide
Cadenza:
Elec. Gtr. 2
trem. pick
Elec. Gtr. 1
w/talk-box

B5
7fr.
133
C5
3fr.
133
8va
D5
10fr.
133
w/bar
A5
5fr.
133
w/talk-box: Kick - start my heart.
dive
Make percussive sounds by rapidly scraping short strokes on the bass strings with the pick.
trem. picking

SAINTS OF LOS ANGELES
(Gang Vocal)

*All Gtrs. in Drop D, down one whole step:
⑥ = C ③ = F
⑤ = G ② = A
④ = C ① = D

Words and Music by
JAMES MICHAEL, NIKKI SIXX,
D.J. ASHBA and MARTI FREDERIKSEN

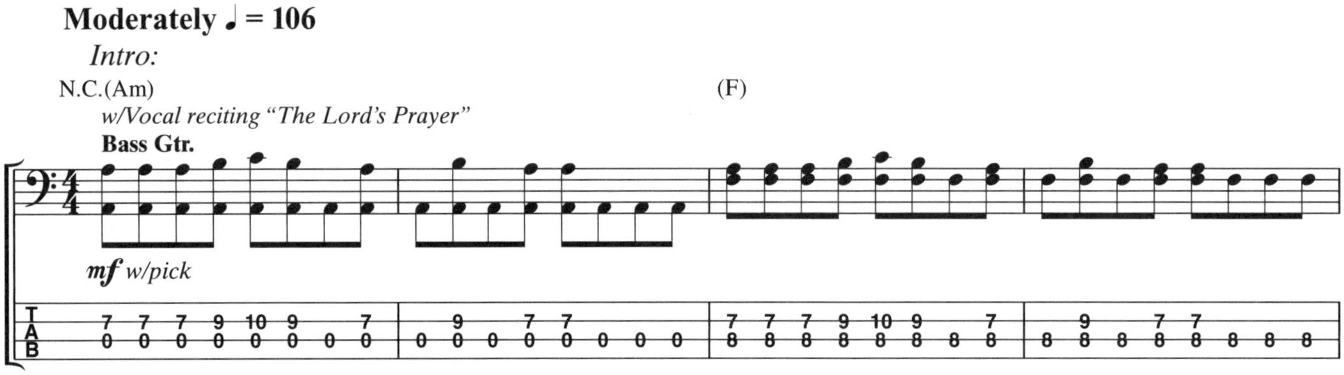

*Recording sounds a whole step lower than written.

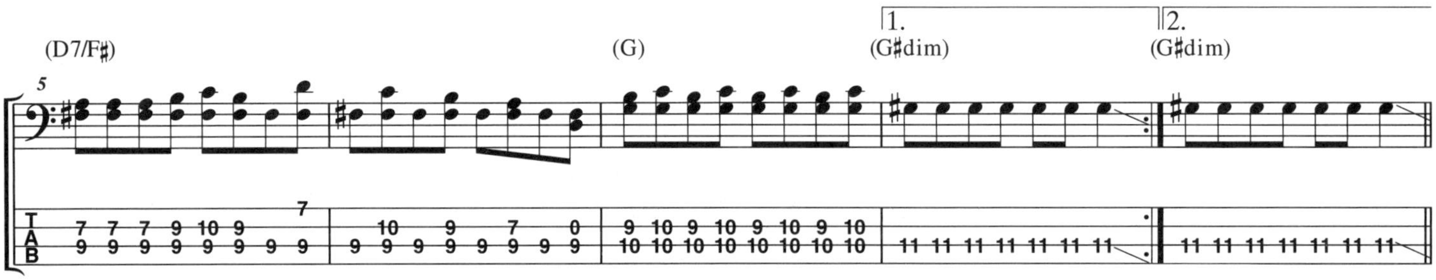

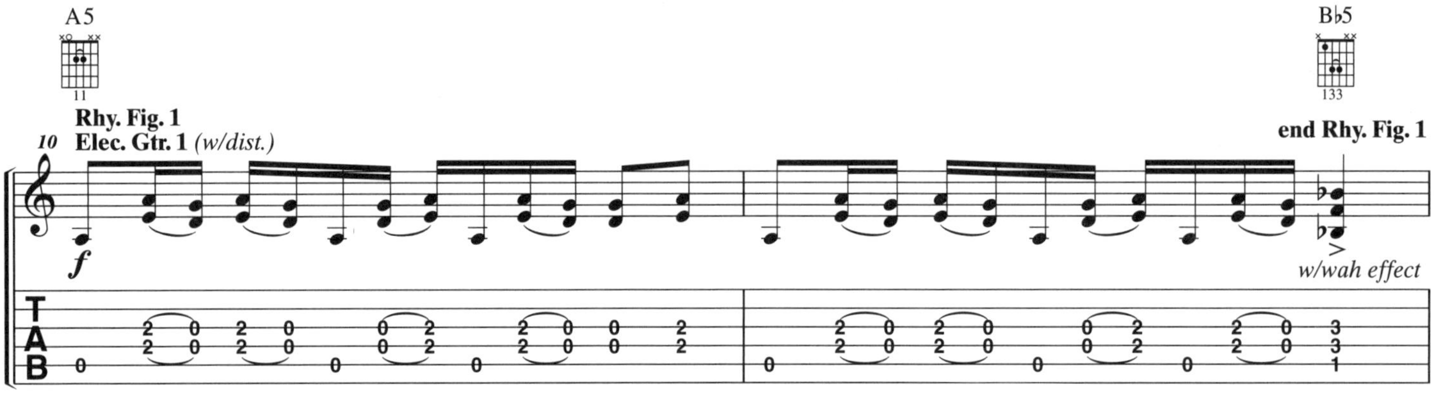

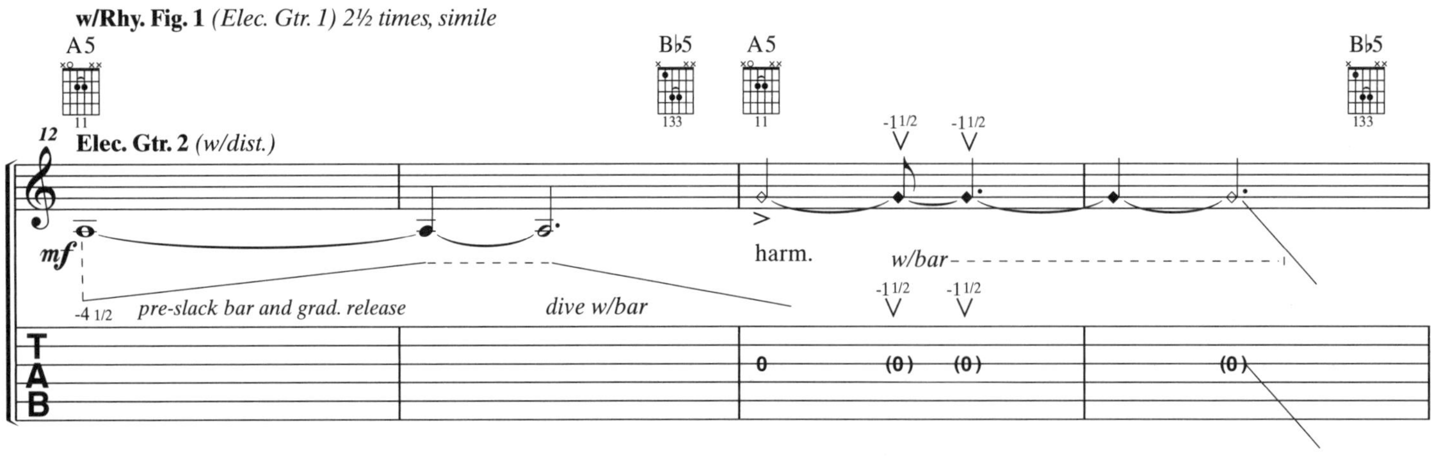

A5
(G5)
1/2
Elec. Gtr. 1
1/2
Verse:
A5
B♭5
1. To - night there's gon - na be a fight. So, if you need a place to go, got a
2. Red - line, trip - ping on a land mine, sip - ping at the Trou - ba - dour.
Rhy. Fig. 2
mf
w/wah effect
P.M. single notes
C5
3fr.
G5
3fr.
B♭5
two room slum, a mat - tress and a gun and the cops don't nev - er show. So,
Girl's passed out nak - ed in the back lounge, ev - 'ry - bod - y's gon - na score. She's
end Rhy. Fig. 2

w/Rhy. Fig. 2 (Elec. Gtr. 1) simile
1.
A5
B♭5
come right in 'cause ev - 'ry - bod - y sins; wel-come to the scene of the crime. You
all jacked up, she's down on her luck. You
To Next Strain
(To Pre-chorus:)
C5
G5
B♭5
want it, be-lieve it, you got it if you need it. The dev - il is a friend of mine.
Elec. Gtr. 2
harm.
dive w/bar
2.
Pre-chorus:
A5
E5
want it, you need it, the dev - il's gon - na feed it.
Oh, if you think it's cra -
Don't you say it's cra -
Elec. Gtr. 1
C/E
E6
- zy, you ain't seen a thing. Just wait un - til we're
- zy, you don't know a thing. Just wait un - til we're

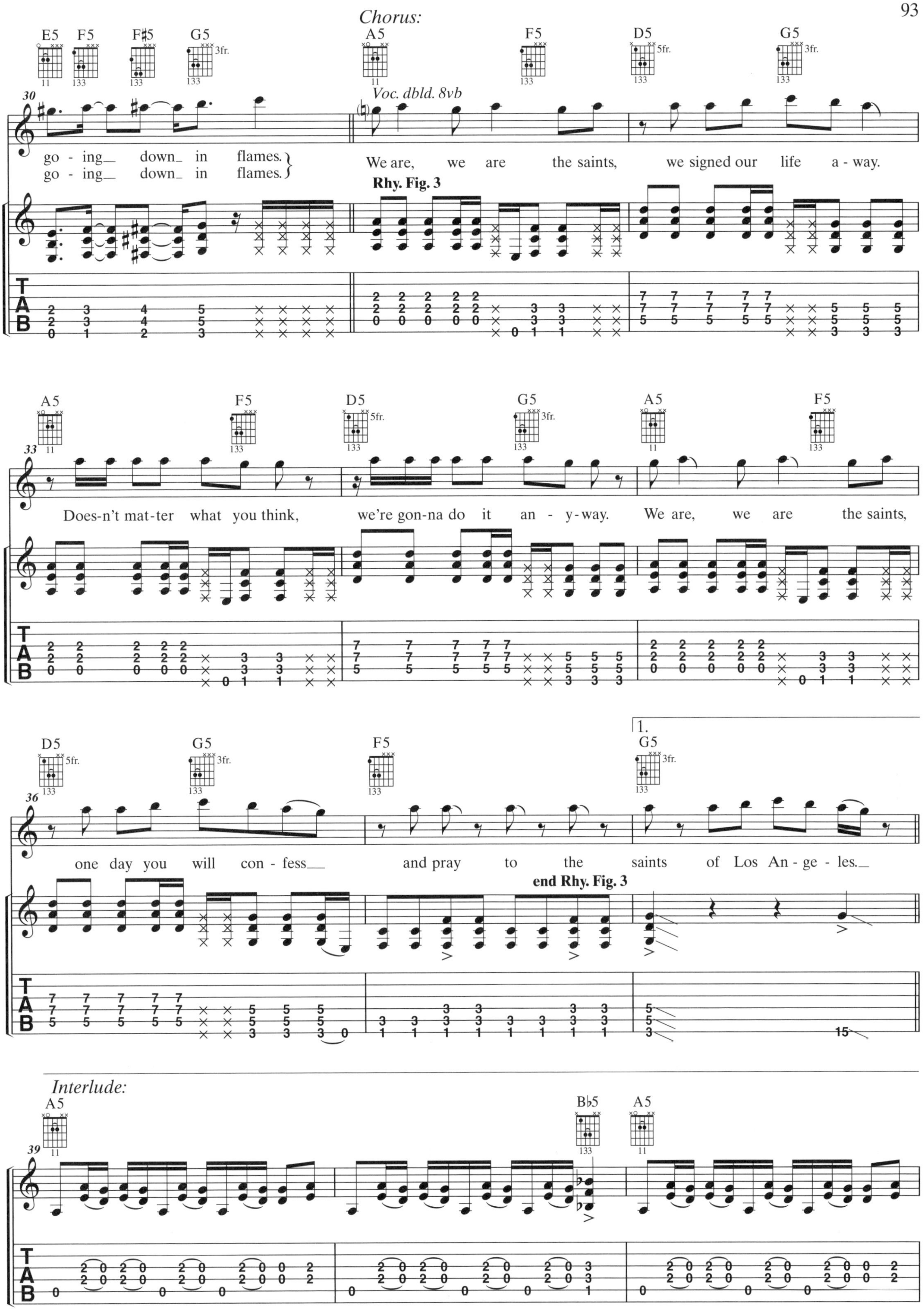
Chorus:
E5 F5 F♯5 G5 3fr.
A5 F5 D5 5fr. G5 3fr.
Voc. dbld. 8vb
go - ing__ down_ in flames.
go - ing__ down_ in flames.
We are, we are the saints, we signed our life a - way.
Rhy. Fig. 3
A5 F5 D5 5fr. G5 3fr. A5 F5
Does-n't mat-ter what you think, we're gon-na do it an - y - way. We are, we are the saints,
D5 5fr. G5 3fr. F5
1.
G5 3fr.
one day you will con - fess__ and pray to the saints of Los An - ge - les._
end Rhy. Fig. 3
Interlude:
A5 B♭5 A5

2.
(G5)
G5
saints of Los An - ge - les.
Elec. Gtr. 2
dive w/bar
A.H.
harm.
dive w/bar
Elec. Gtr. 1
Guitar Solo:
w/Rhy. Fig. 3 (Elec. Gtr. 1) 1st 6 meas., simile
A5
D5
G5
A5
harm.
D5
G5
A5
D5
G5
P.H.

E5 G5 E5 B♭5
Elec. Gtr. 2
Rhy. Fig. 4
Elec. Gtr. 1
end Rhy. Fig. 4
P.M. single notes
w/Rhy. Fig. 1 (Elec. Gtr. 4) 2½ times, simile
E5 G5 E5 B♭5 E5 G5
Give it up, give it up.
Give it up, give it up.
Give it up, give it up.
w/bar
P.M.
E5 B♭5 E5 G5
Give it up, give it up.
Give it up, give it up!
(P.M.)
harm.

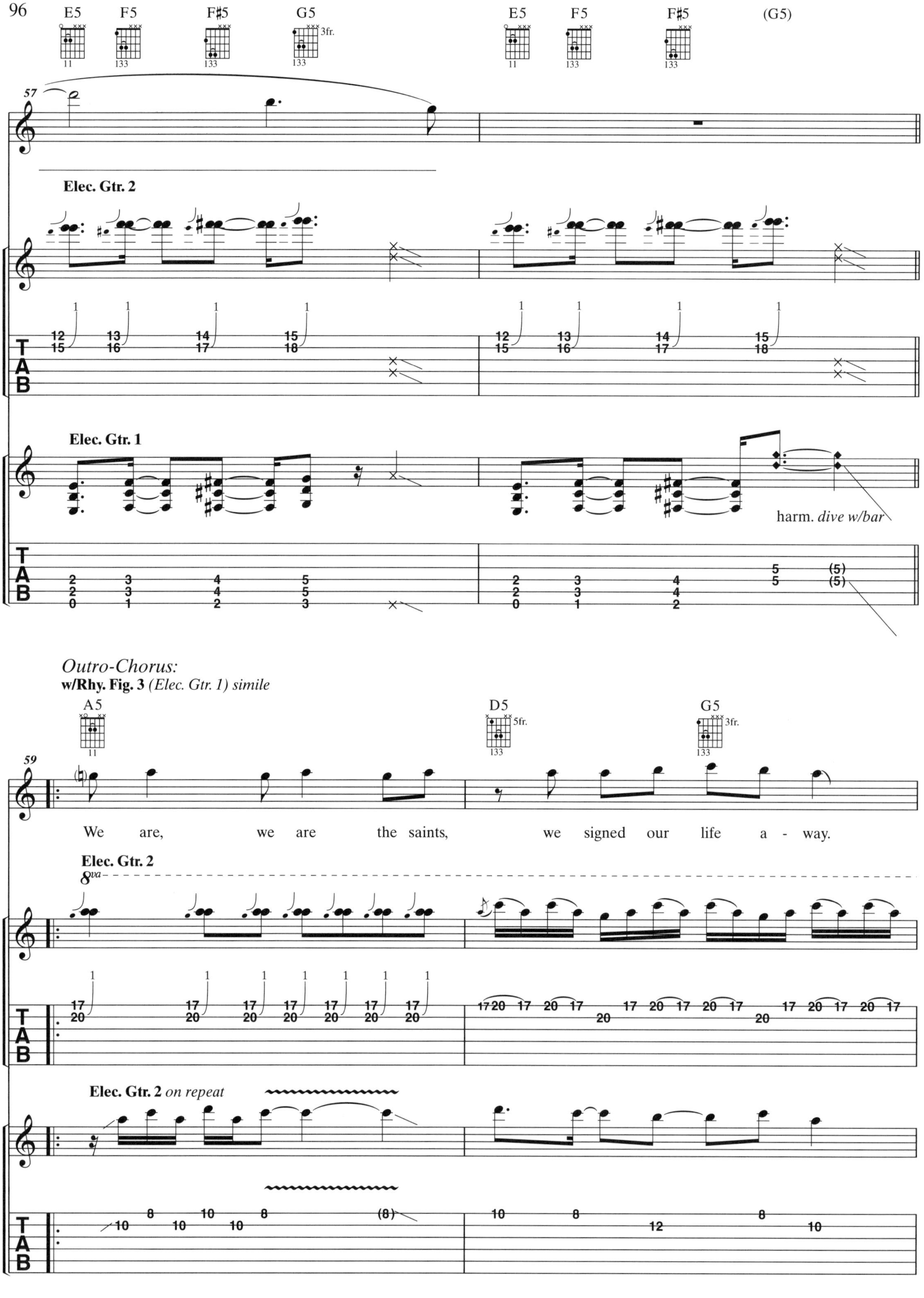
E5 F5 F♯5 G5 E5 F5 F♯5 (G5)
Elec. Gtr. 2
Elec. Gtr. 1
harm. dive w/bar
Outro-Chorus:
w/Rhy. Fig. 3 (Elec. Gtr. 1) simile
A5 D5 G5
We are, we are the saints, we signed our life a - way.
Elec. Gtr. 2
8va
Elec. Gtr. 2 on repeat

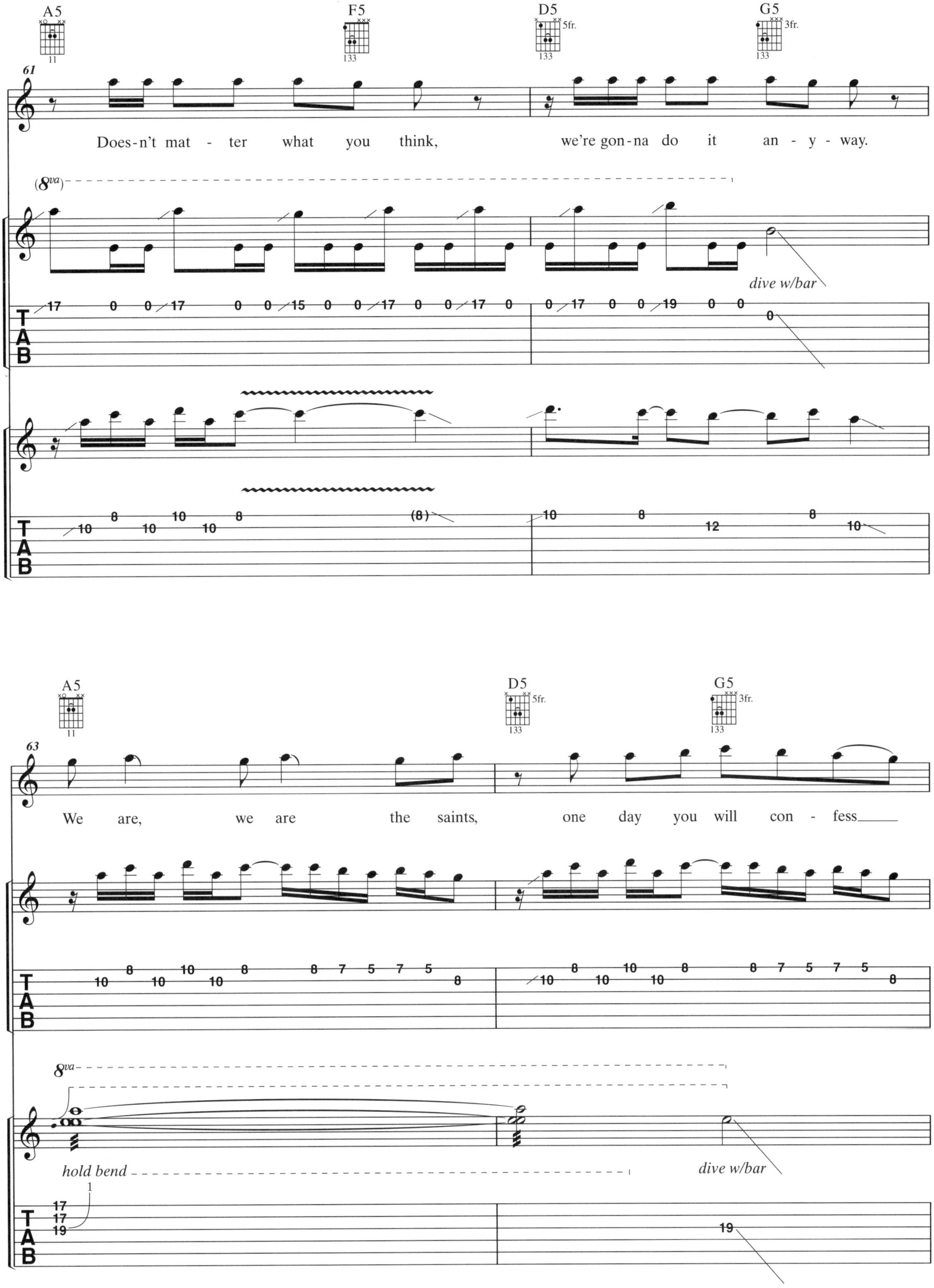
A5
F5
D5
5fr.
G5
3fr.
61
Does-n't mat - ter what you think, we're gon-na do it an - y - way.
(8va)
dive w/bar
A5
D5
5fr.
G5
3fr.
63
We are, we are the saints, one day you will con - fess
8va
hold bend
dive w/bar

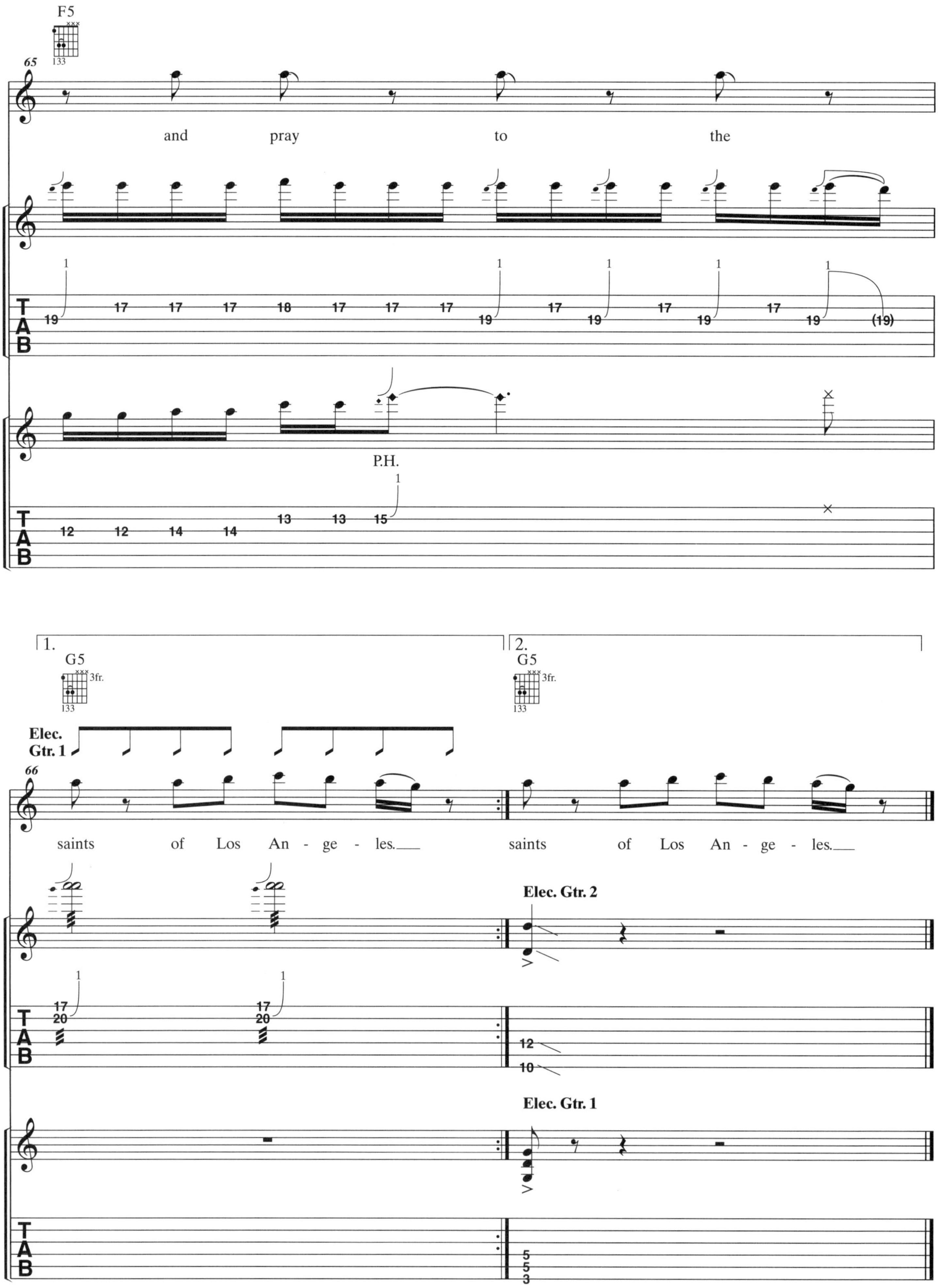
F5
133
65
and pray to the
P.H.
1.
2.
G5
3fr.
133
Elec. Gtr. 1
66
saints of Los An - ge - les.
Elec. Gtr. 2
Elec. Gtr. 1

FOREVER

Words and Musics by
TOBIN ESPERANCE, JACOBY SHADDIX,
JERRY HORTON and DAVE BUCKNER

Drop D tuning:
(low to high) D-A-D-G-B-E

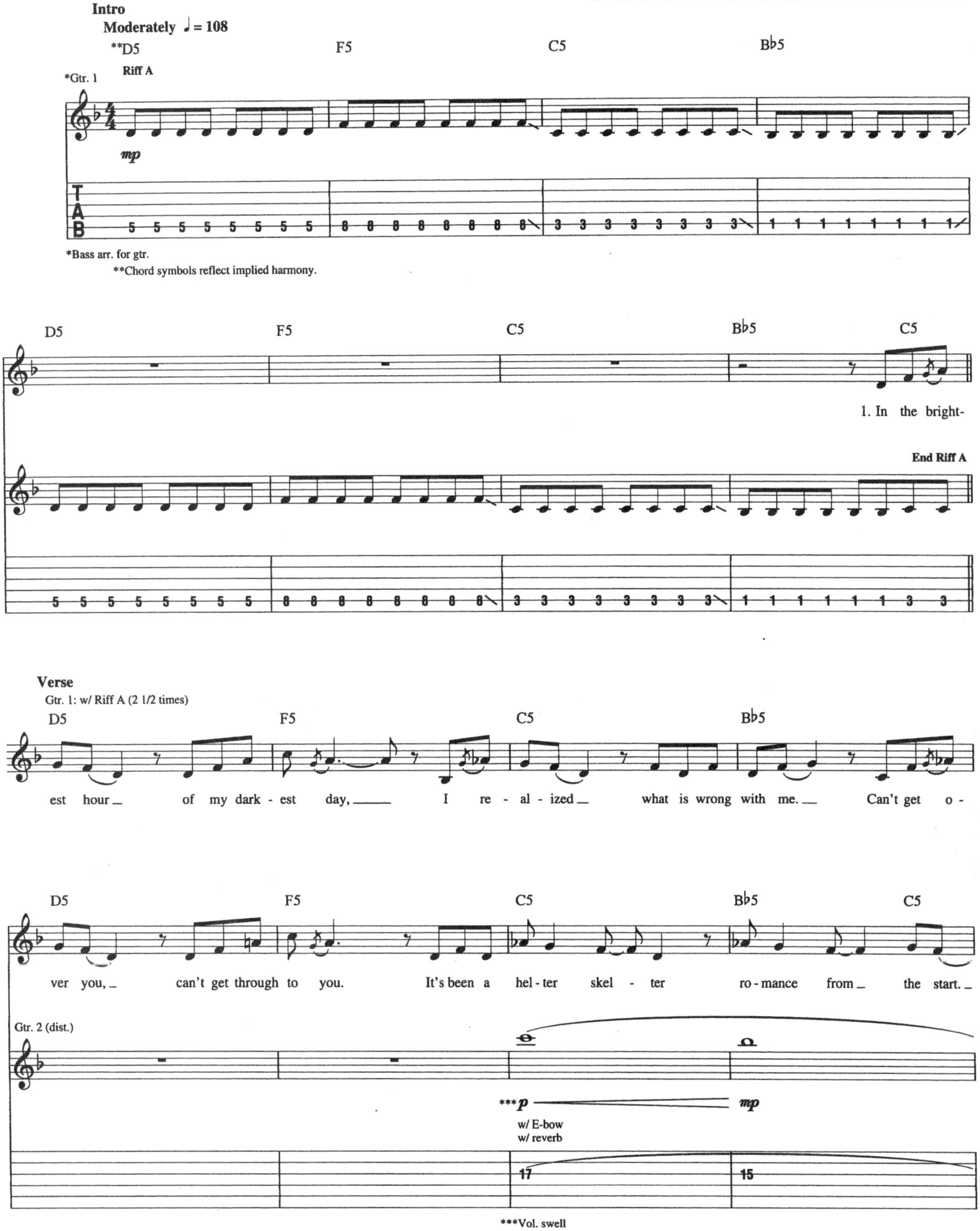

D5 F5 C5 B♭5
Take these mem - o - ries that are haunt - ing me of a pa - per man cut in - to shreds
D5 F5 C5 B♭5 C5
by his own pair of scis - sors. He'll nev - er for - give her, he'll nev - er for - give her.
D5 F5 C5 B♭5
Be - cause
Gtr. 2
Riff B
Gtr. 3 (slight dist.)
End Riff B
mf
*w/ delays
*One set for quarter-note regeneration w/ 1 repeat, one set for eighth-note regeneration w/ 1 repeat.
Gtrs. 4 & 5 (dist.)
f

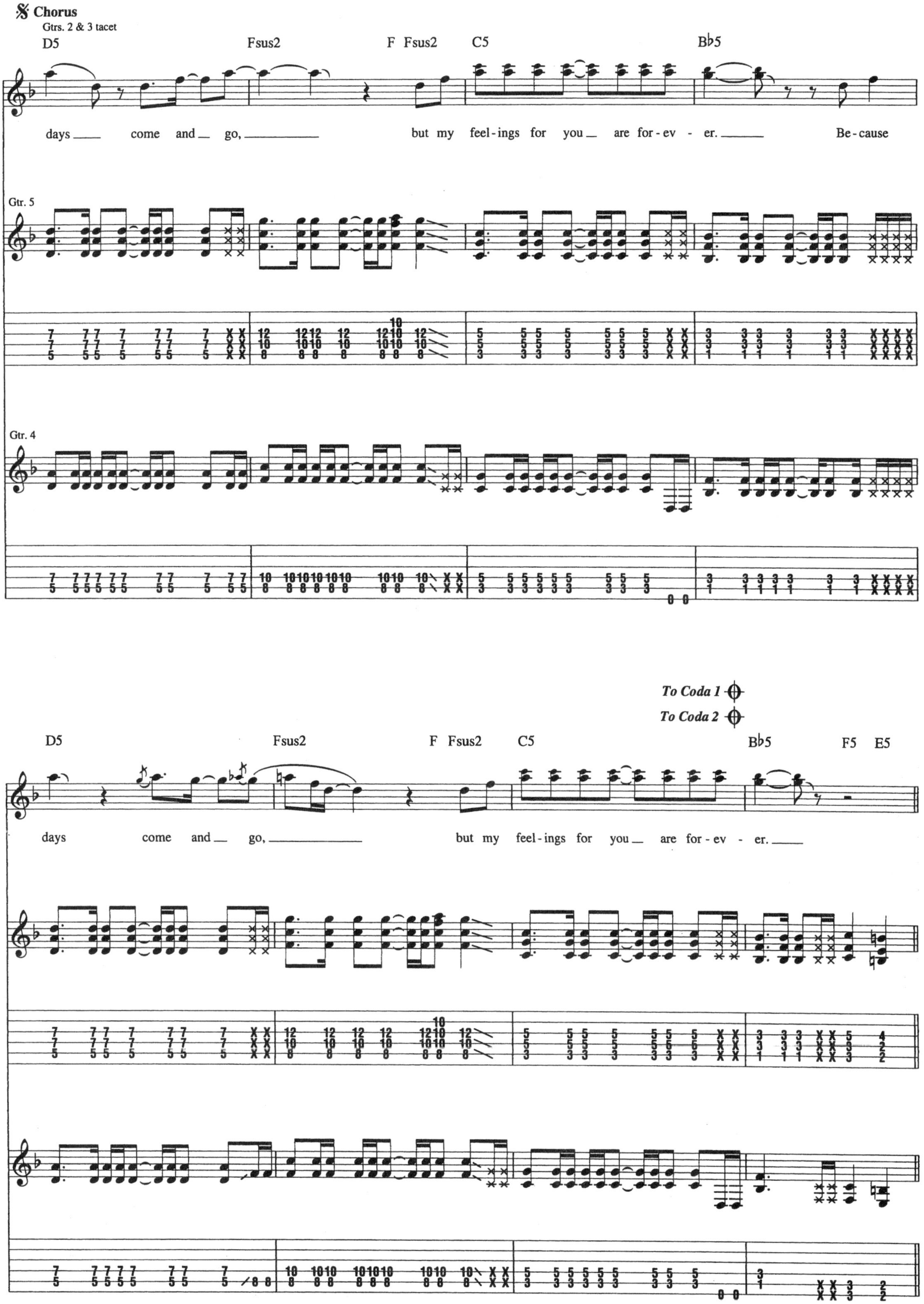
Chorus
Gtrs. 2 & 3 tacet
D5 Fsus2 F Fsus2 C5 B♭5
days come and go, but my feel-ings for you are for-ev - er. Be-cause
Gtr. 5
Gtr. 4
To Coda 1
To Coda 2
D5 Fsus2 F Fsus2 C5 B♭5 F5 E5
days come and go, but my feel-ings for you are for-ev - er.

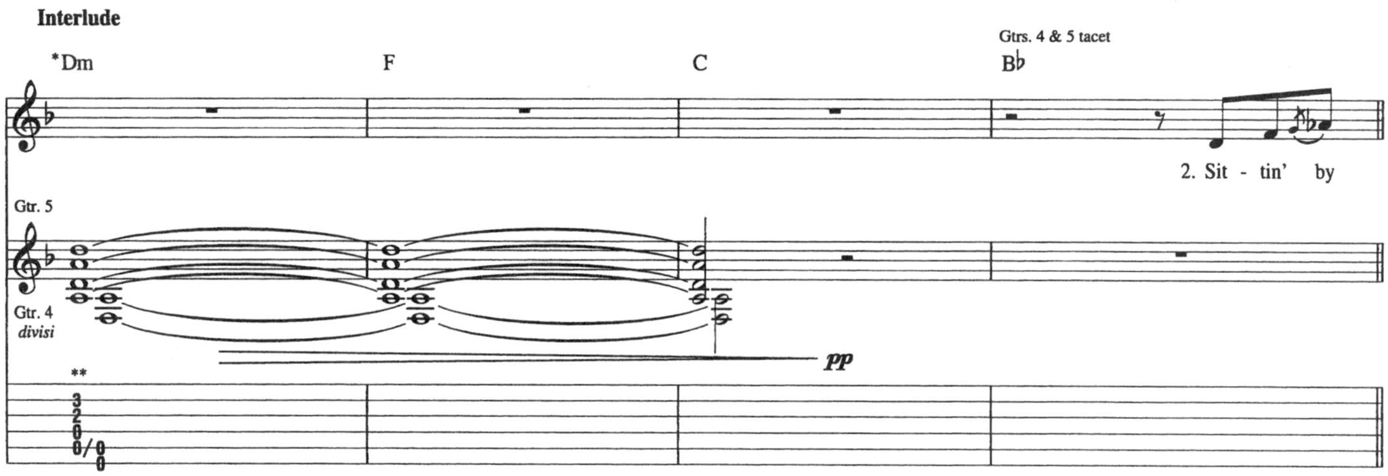

*Chord symbols reflect overall harmony.
**Gtr. 5 to left of slash in tab.

Coda 1
Bridge
B♭5 F5 E5 D5 F5 C/E C5 F5 E5
er. One last kiss be-fore I go. Dry your
Rhy. Fig. 1A
Rhy. Fig. 1
B♭5 F5 C/E G5 F5 G5 A5 F5 C/E
tears, it is time to let you go. One last
End Rhy. Fig. 1A
End Rhy. Fig. 1
Gtrs. 4 & 5: w/ Rhy. Figs. 1 & 1A
D5 F5 C/E C5
*Voc. Fig. 1
kiss be - fore I go.
(One last kiss be - fore I
*Refers to upstemmed voc. only.
F5 E5 B♭5 F5 C/E
End Voc. Fig. 1
go. Dry your tears, it is time
Dry your tears.)

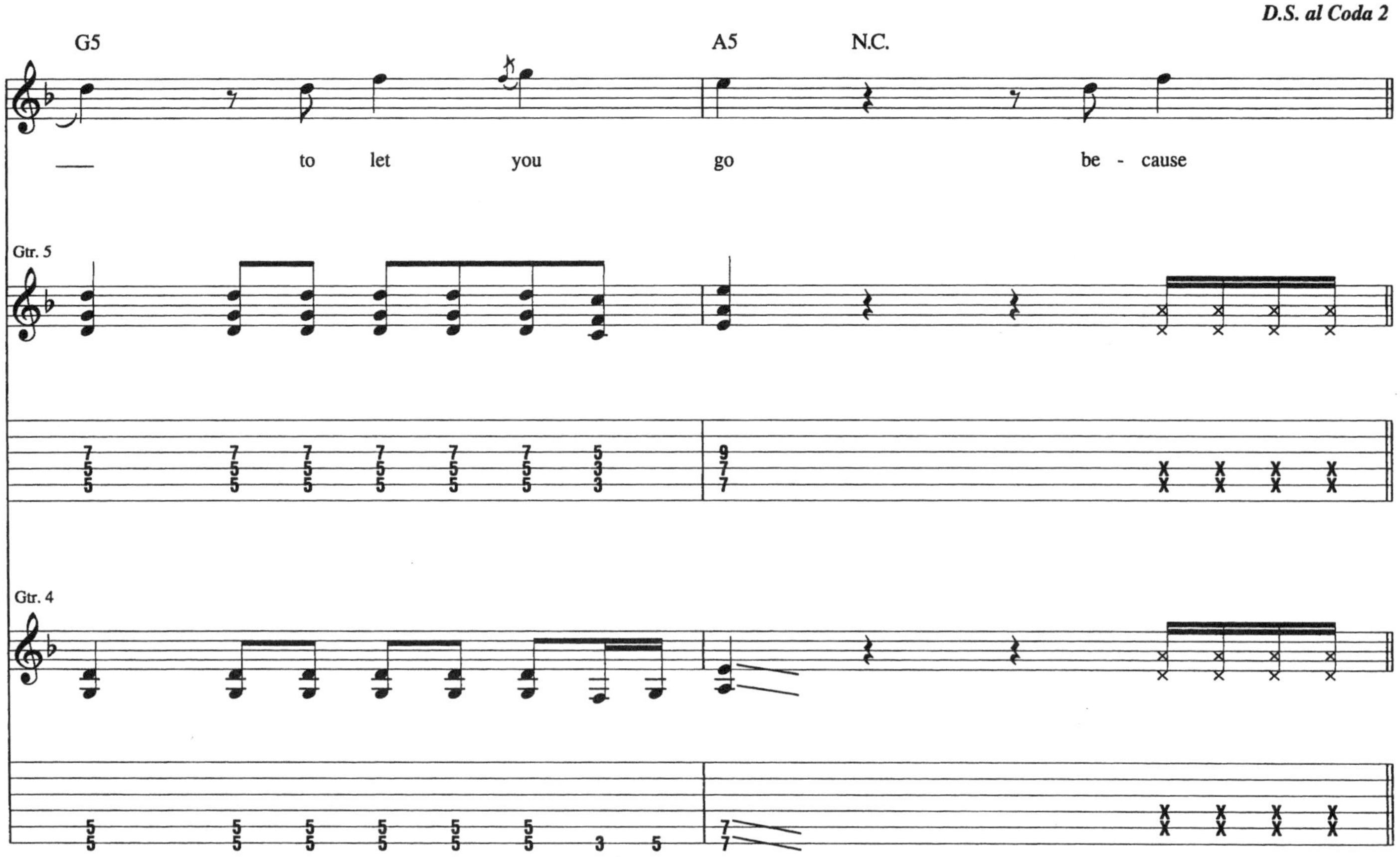
D.S. al Coda 2
G5
A5
N.C.
to let you go be - cause
Gtr. 5
Gtr. 4

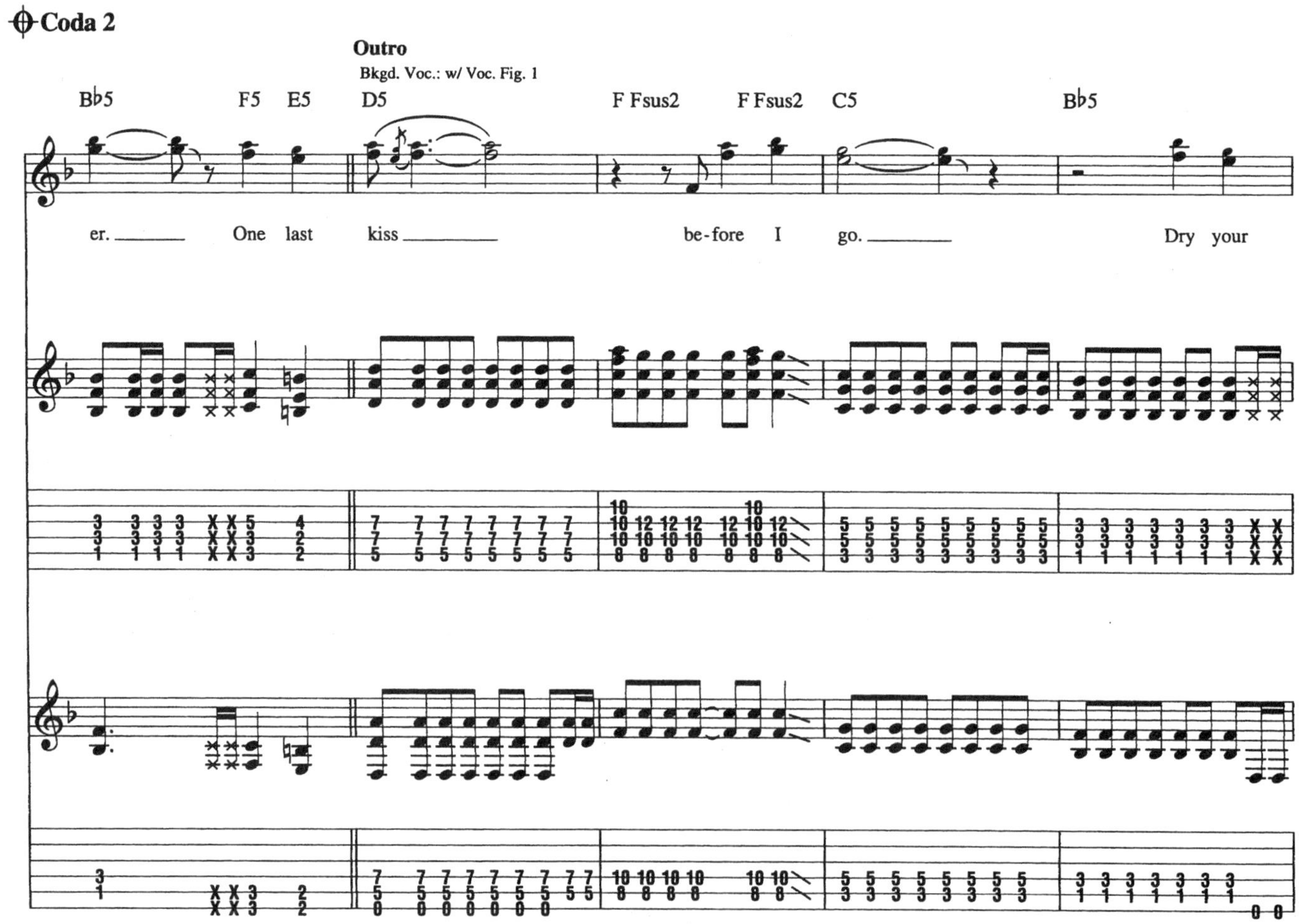
Coda 2
Outro
Bkgd. Voc.: w/ Voc. Fig. 1
B♭5
F5
E5
D5
F Fsus2
F Fsus2
C5
B♭5
er. One last kiss be-fore I go. Dry your

D5 F Fsus2 F Fsus2 C5 B♭5 F5
tears, it is time to let you go. One last
D5 F5 C5 B♭5
kiss be - fore I go. Dry your
Gtr. 5
Gtr. 4 divisi
*Gtr. 5 to left of slash in tab.
D5 F5 C5 B♭5 D5
tears, it is time to let you go. One last kiss.
pp

LAST RESORT

Words and Musics by
PAPA ROACH

Gtr. 1: w/ Riff B (2 times)
E5 D5 C5 B5 D5
Don't give a fuck if I cut my arm bleed - ing. Do you e - ven care if I die bleed - ing?
feed - ing on cha - os and liv - ing in sin. Down - ward spi - ral, where do I be - gin?
E5 D5 C5 B5 D5
Would it be wrong, would it be right if I took my life to - night? Chanc - es are that I might.
It all start - ed when I lost my moth - er. No love for my - self, and no love for an - oth - er. Search - ing
E5 D5 C5 B5 IX D5 XII
Rhy. Fig. 2A
Gtr. 2
End Rhy. Fig. 2A
Mu - ti - la - tion out of sight, and I'm con - tem - plat - ing su - i - cide.
to find a love up - on a high - er lev - el, find - ing noth - ing but ques - tions and dev - ils.
'Cause I'm
Gtr. 1
Rhy. Fig. 2
End Rhy. Fig. 2
P.M.
Chorus
E5 C5 N.C.(D)
los - ing my sight, los - ing my mind. Wish some - bod - y would tell me I'm fine.
Gtrs. 1 & 2
Rhy. Fig. 3
End Rhy. Fig. 3
1.
E5 C5 N.C.(D)
Los - ing my sight, los - ing my mind. Wish some - bod - y would tell me I'm fine.

2.
Gtr. 1: w/ Riff A
Gtr. 2: w/ Rhy. Fig. 1
E5 D5 C5 B5 D5
Gtrs. 1 & 2: w/ Rhy. Fig. 3
E5 C5 N.C.(D)
Los-ing my sight, los-ing my mind. Wish some-bod-y would tell me I'm fine.
Bridge
E5 D5 C5 G5 B5 D5
Noth-ing's al-right, noth-ing is fine.
Gtrs. 1 & 2
E5 D5 C5 D5 G5 B5
To Coda
I'm run-ning and I'm cry-ing.
E5 G5 C5 B5 D5
I'm cry-ing. I'm cry-ing.

E5 G5 C5 B5
I'm cry - ing. I'm cry - ing.
Gtrs. 1 & 2: w/ Rhy. Fig. 1 (4 times)
E5 D5 C5 B5 D5 E5 D5
Whispered: I can't go on liv - ing
C5 B5 D5 E5 D5 C5 B5 D5
this way. Cut my life in - to piec - es, this is my last re - sort.
E5 D5 C5 B5 D5
Suf - fo - ca - tion, no breath - ing. Don't give a fuck if I cut my arm bleed - ing.
Verse
Gtr. 1: w/ Riff A
Gtr. 2: w/ Rhy. Fig. 1
E5 D5 C5 B5 D5
3. Would it be wrong, would it be right if I took my life to-night? Chanc-es are that I might.
Gtrs. 1 & 2: w/ Rhy. Fig. 2
D.S. (take 2nd ending) al Coda
E5 D5 C5 B5 D5
Mu - ti - la - tion out of sight, and I'm con - tem - plat - ing su - i - cide. 'Cause I'm
Coda
E5 C5 N.C.(D) E5 C5
Screamed:
I can't go on liv - ing
Gtrs. 1 & 2

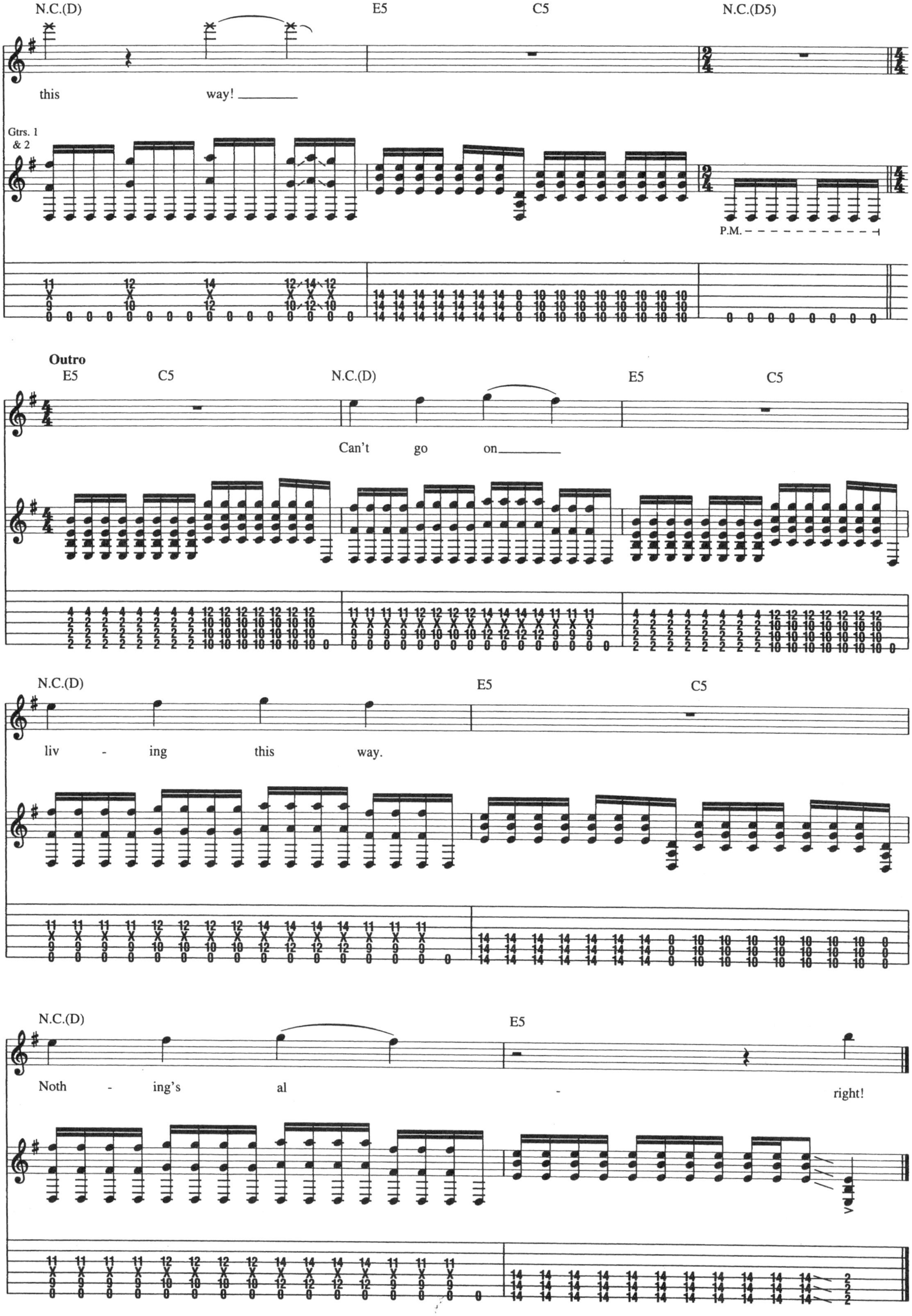
N.C.(D)
E5
C5
N.C.(D5)
this way!
Gtrs. 1 & 2
P.M.
Outro
E5
C5
N.C.(D)
E5
C5
Can't go on
N.C.(D)
E5
C5
liv - ing this way.
N.C.(D)
E5
Noth - ing's al - right!

LIFE IS BEAUTIFUL

Words and Musics by
NIKKI SIXX, JAMES MICHAEL
and DJ ASHBA

All gtrs. in Drop D tuning:
⑥ = D

Moderately ♩ = 90
Intro:

*Stereo delay set for dotted 8th note on left and dotted quarter note on right.

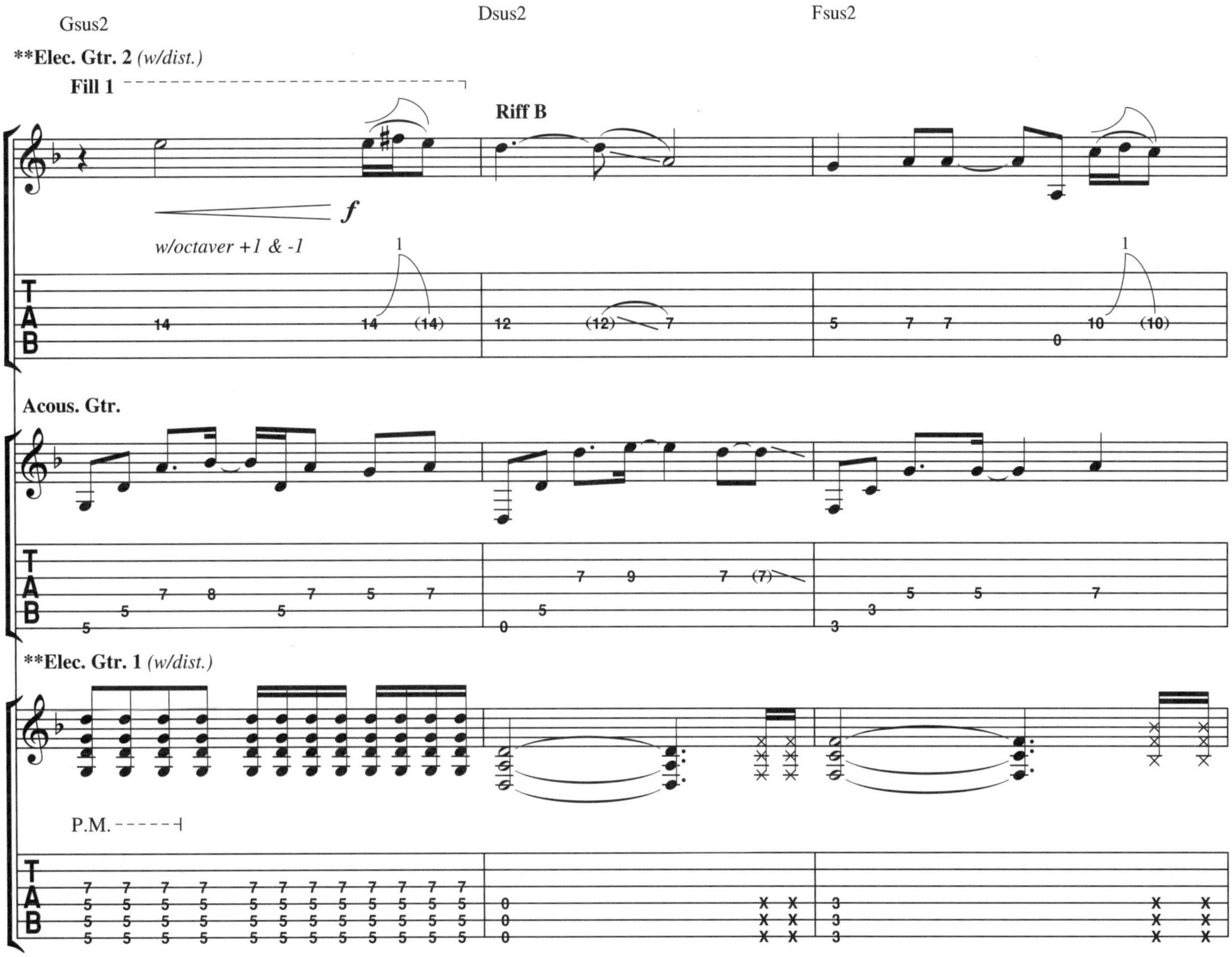

B♭sus2
Gsus2
Elec. Gtr. 2
end Riff B
end Riff A
Elec. Gtr. 1
P.M.
N.C.(D5)
Elec. Gtr. 1
Rhy. Fig. 1
end Rhy. Fig. 1

Verse 1: (0:31)
N.C.
13
You can't quit un - til you try.
You can't live un - til you die.
*Elec. Gtr. 3 (w/dist.)
Riff C
P.M.
*Two gtrs. arr. for one.
**Vcl. dbld. by spoken voice till Chorus.
15
You can't learn to tell the truth un - til you learn to lie.
Elec. Gtr. 3
end Riff C
P.M.
Elec. Gtr. 1
Rhy. Fig 2
w/Riff C (Elec. Gtr. 3) 1st 2 meas.
D5
F5
17
You can't breathe un - til you choke.
You got - ta laugh when you're the joke. There's
Elec. Gtr. 1

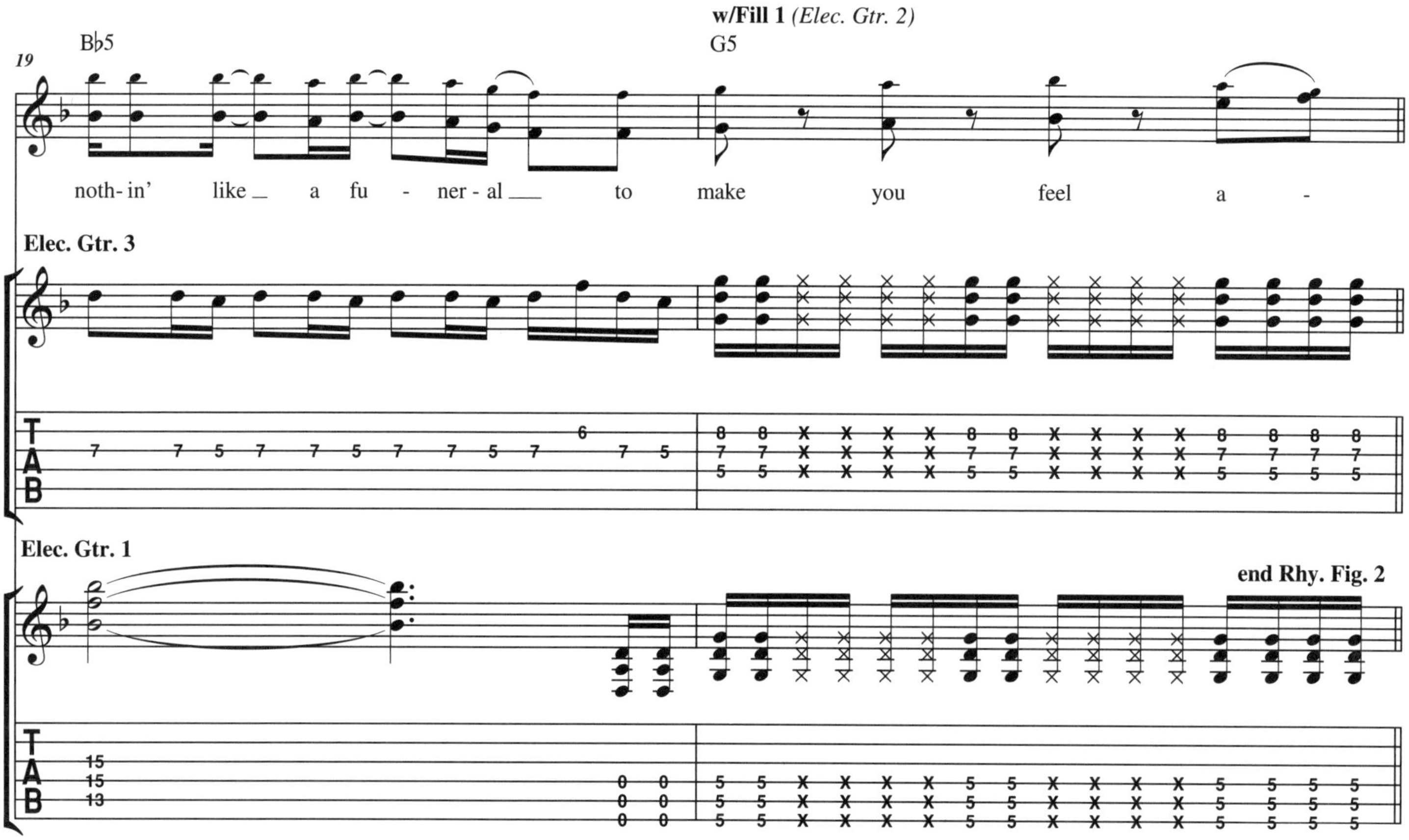
w/Fill 1 (Elec. Gtr. 2)
19
B♭5
G5
noth- in' like a fu - ner - al to make you feel a -
Elec. Gtr. 3
Elec. Gtr. 1
end Rhy. Fig. 2

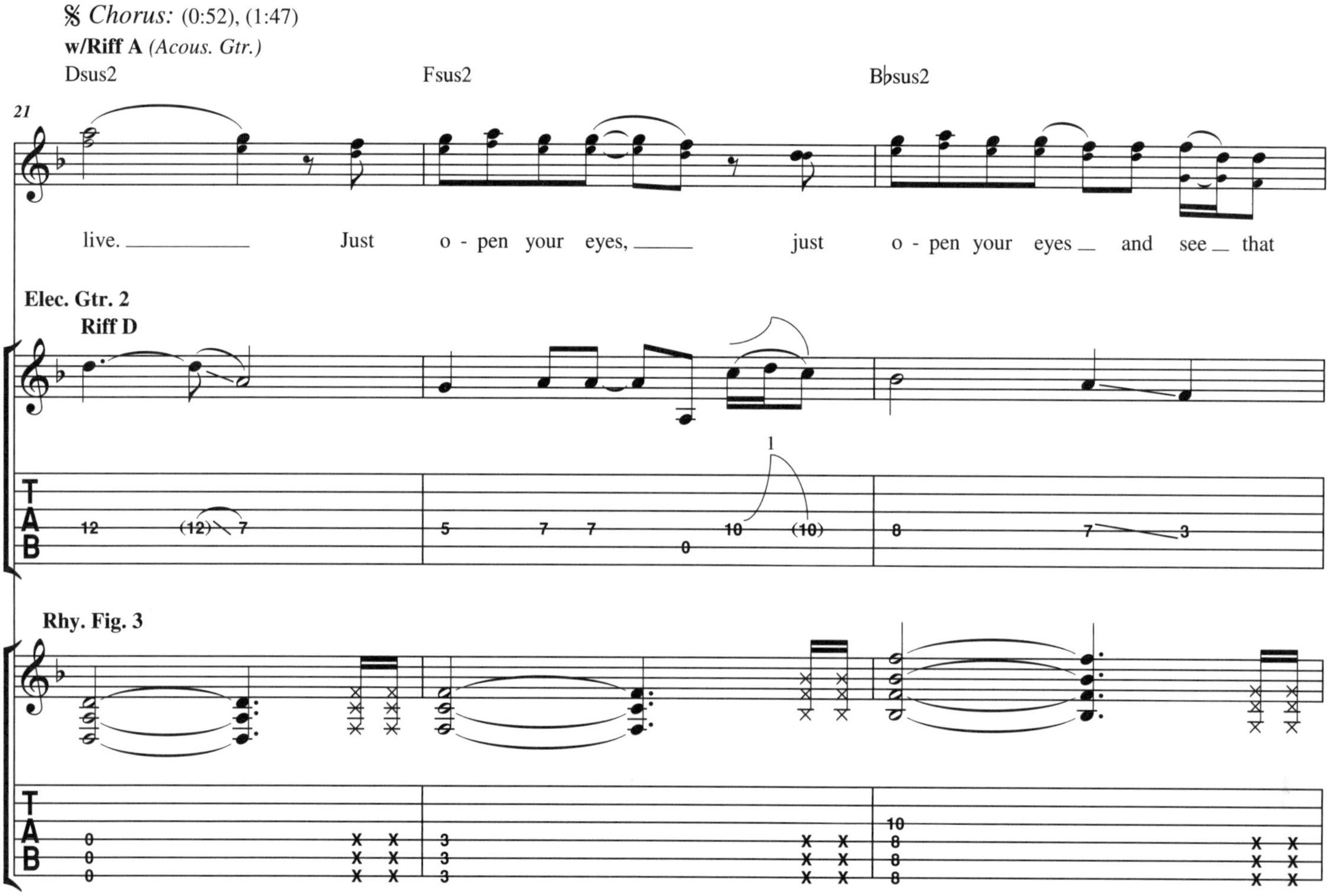
𝄋 Chorus: (0:52), (1:47)
w/Riff A (Acous. Gtr.)
21
Dsus2
Fsus2
B♭sus2
live. Just o - pen your eyes, just o - pen your eyes and see that
Elec. Gtr. 2
Riff D
Rhy. Fig. 3

w/Riff B (Elec. Gtr. 2)
Gsus2
Dsus2
Fsus2
24
life is beau - ti - ful. Will you swear on your life that
end Riff D
harm.
Bbsus2
Gsus2
27
no one will cry at my fu - ner -
Elec. Gtr. 2
end Rhy. Fig. 3
P.M.
Interlude: (1:15)
w/Rhy. Fig. 1 (Elec. Gtr. 1)
N.C.(D5)
29
al?
Verse 2: (1:26)
w/Riff B (Elec. Gtr. 3)
N.C.
33
I know some things that you don't. I've done things that you won't. There's

w/Rhy. Fig. 2 (Elec. Gtr. 1)
35
noth - in' like a trail of blood to find your way back home.
Elec. Gtr. 4 (w/dist. & wah as filter)
mf
D5
37
F5
I was wait - in' for my hearse. What came next was so much worse.
w/Fill 1 (Elec. Gtr. 2)
D.S. 𝄋 al Coda
B♭5
39
G5
It took a fu - ner - al to make me feel a -
Coda
Guitar Solo: (2:10)
N.C.
41
al?
Elec. Gtr. 5 (w/dist.)
Riff E
end Riff E
mf

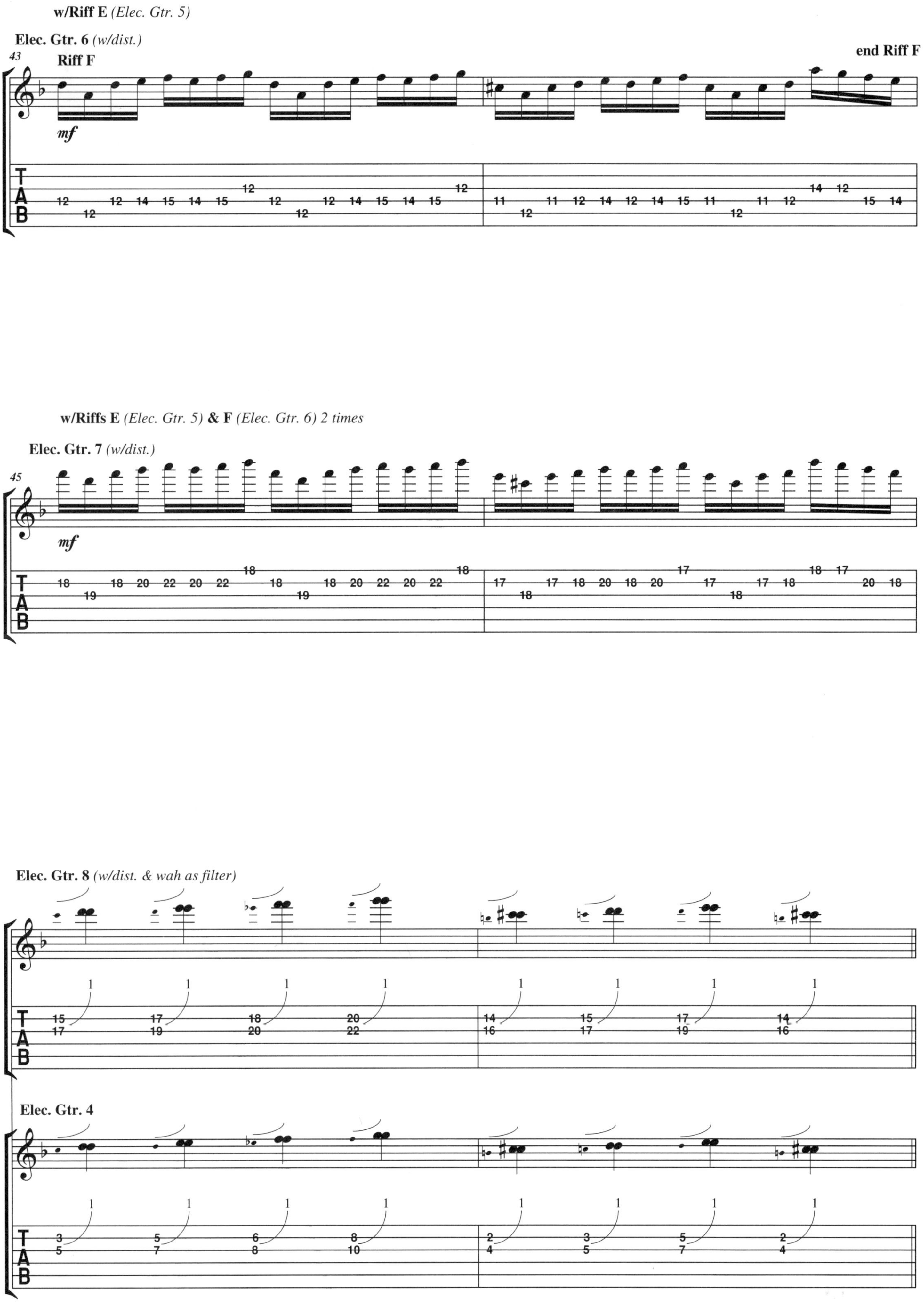
w/Riff E (Elec. Gtr. 5)
Elec. Gtr. 6 (w/dist.)
43
Riff F
end Riff F
mf
w/Riffs E (Elec. Gtr. 5) & F (Elec. Gtr. 6) 2 times
Elec. Gtr. 7 (w/dist.)
45
mf
Elec. Gtr. 8 (w/dist. & wah as filter)
Elec. Gtr. 4

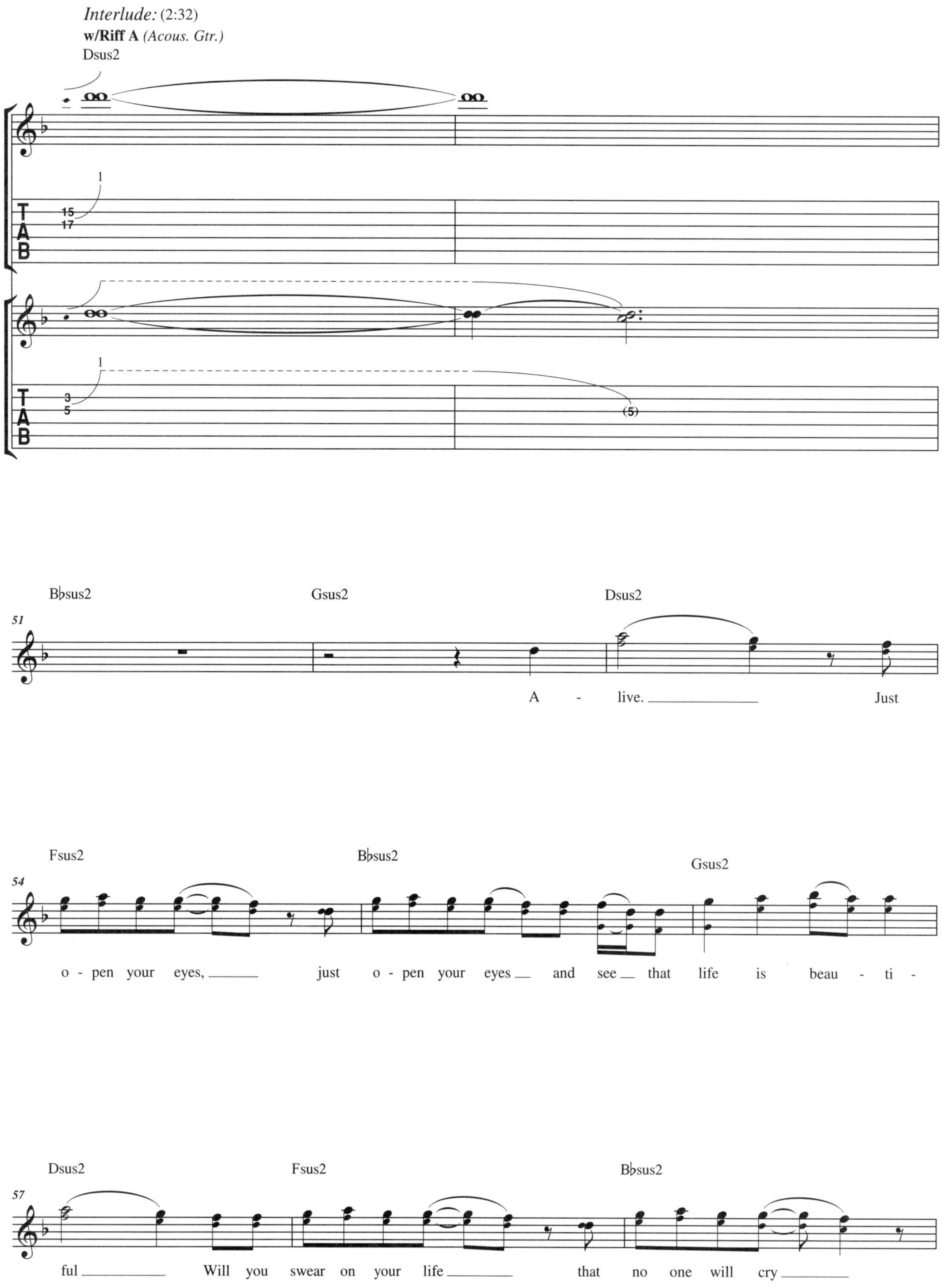
Interlude: (2:32)
w/Riff A (Acous. Gtr.)
Dsus2
1
15
17
1
3
5
(5)
51
B♭sus2
Gsus2
Dsus2
A - live. Just
54
Fsus2
B♭sus2
Gsus2
o - pen your eyes, just o - pen your eyes and see that life is beau - ti -
57
Dsus2
Fsus2
B♭sus2
ful Will you swear on your life that no one will cry

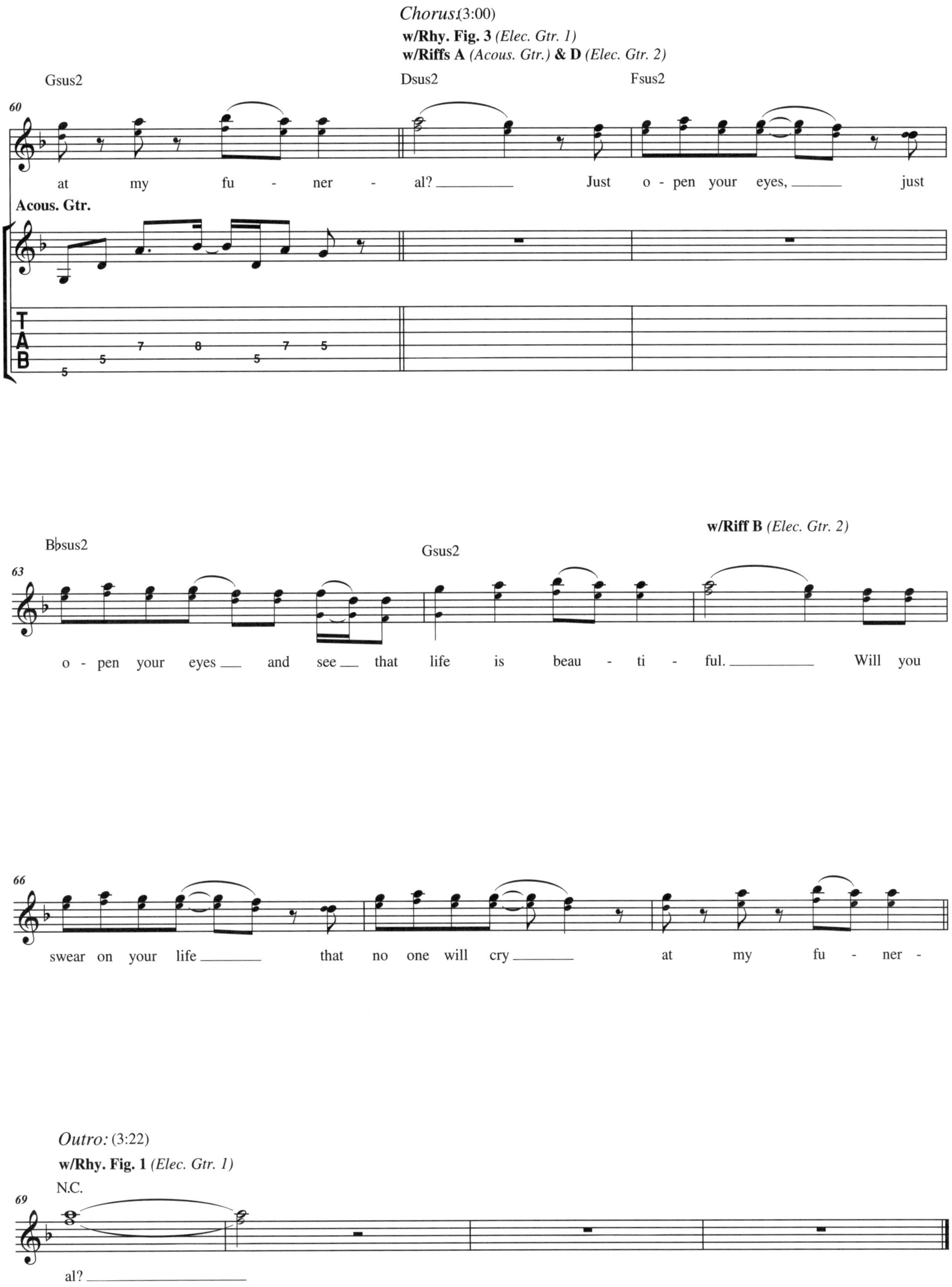
Chorus: (3:00)
w/Rhy. Fig. 3 (Elec. Gtr. 1)
w/Riffs A (Acous. Gtr.) & D (Elec. Gtr. 2)
Gsus2
Dsus2
Fsus2
60
at my fu - ner - al? Just o - pen your eyes, just
Acous. Gtr.
T
A
B
Bbsus2
Gsus2
w/Riff B (Elec. Gtr. 2)
63
o - pen your eyes and see that life is beau - ti - ful. Will you
66
swear on your life that no one will cry at my fu - ner -
Outro: (3:22)
w/Rhy. Fig. 1 (Elec. Gtr. 1)
N.C.
69
al?

PRAY FOR ME

Words and Musics by
NIKKI SIXX, JAMES MICHAEL
and DJ ASHBA

All gtrs in Drop D tuning:
⑥ = D

Moderately ♩ = 132

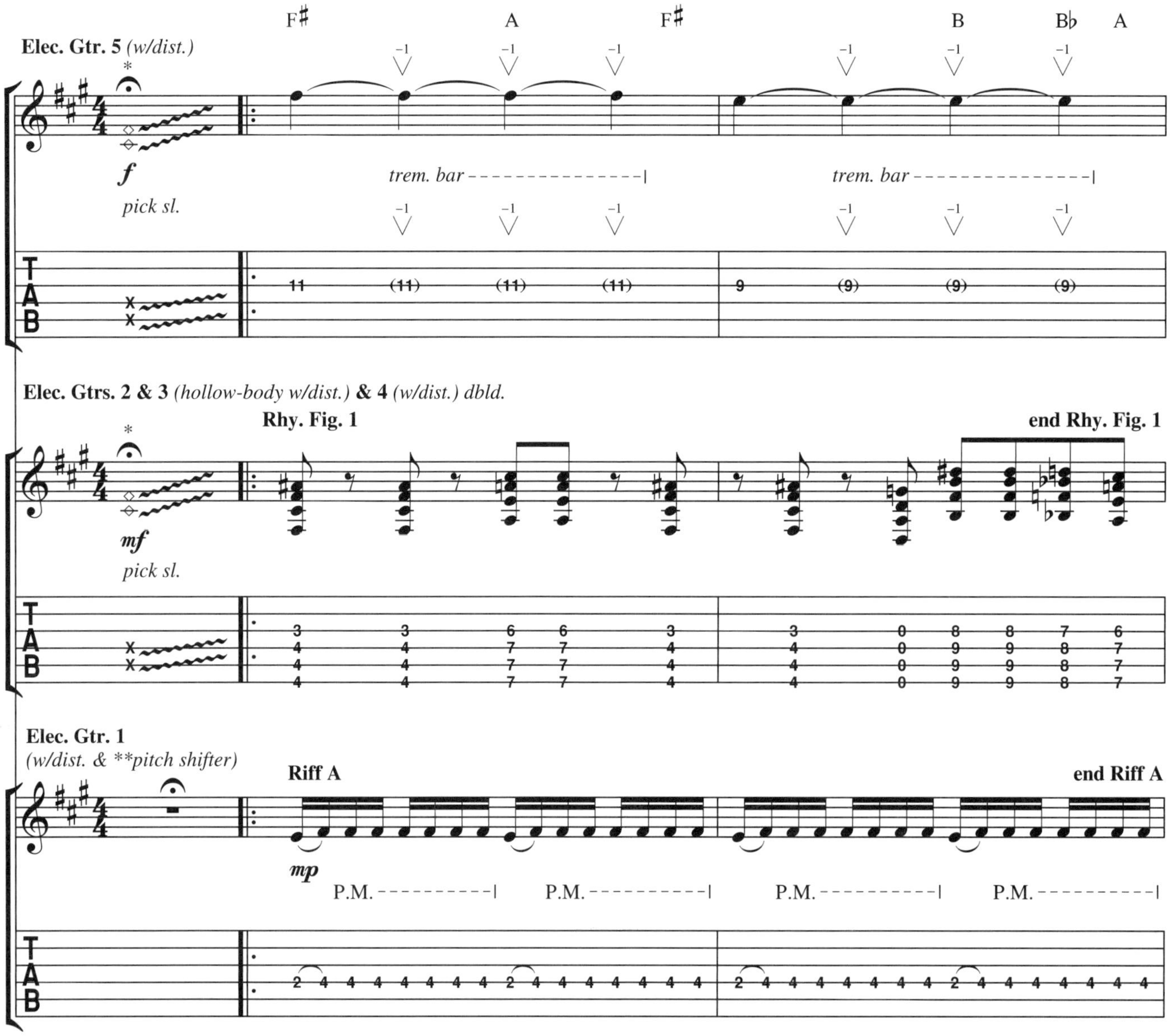

*Drag pick along strings with pressure to produce ascending scratch sound.
**Set for one octave down.

1.
2.
w/Riff A (Elec. Gtr. 1)
F♯ A F♯ B B♭ B
Elec. Gtr. 5
trem. bar
Elec. Gtrs. 2 & 3
F♯ A F♯ B B♭ A D5 A C♯5 G♯5 A5G♯5 E5
She lights a
Elec. Gtr. 2
Rhy. Fig. 2
end Rhy. Fig. 2
Verse 1: (0:24)
w/Rhy. Fig. 2 (Elec. Gtr. 2)
F♯ A F♯ B B♭ A
can - dle, but she does - n't know why. She wants to
Elec. Gtr. 1
Riff B
P.M.

13
D5 A C#5 G#5 A5 G#5 A5
save me, but I'm bare - ley a - live. My soul is
end Riff B
P.M.
P.M.
1/2
w/Riff B (Elec. Gtr. 1) 3 times
w/Rhy. Fig. 2 (Elec. Gtrs. 2 & 3)
15
F# A F# B B♭ A D5 A C#5 G#5 A5 G#5 E5
thirst - y. I just wan-na get high and make her go a - way.
w/Rhy. Fig. 2 (Elec. Gtrs. 2-4) 2 times
19
F# A F# B B♭ A
And now I'm hit - tin' the wall and she begs me to quit,
Elec. Gtr. 5
Riff C
mp
21
D5 A C#5 G#5 A5 G#5 E5
and she drags me to church but I'm scared to com - mit.
end Riff C

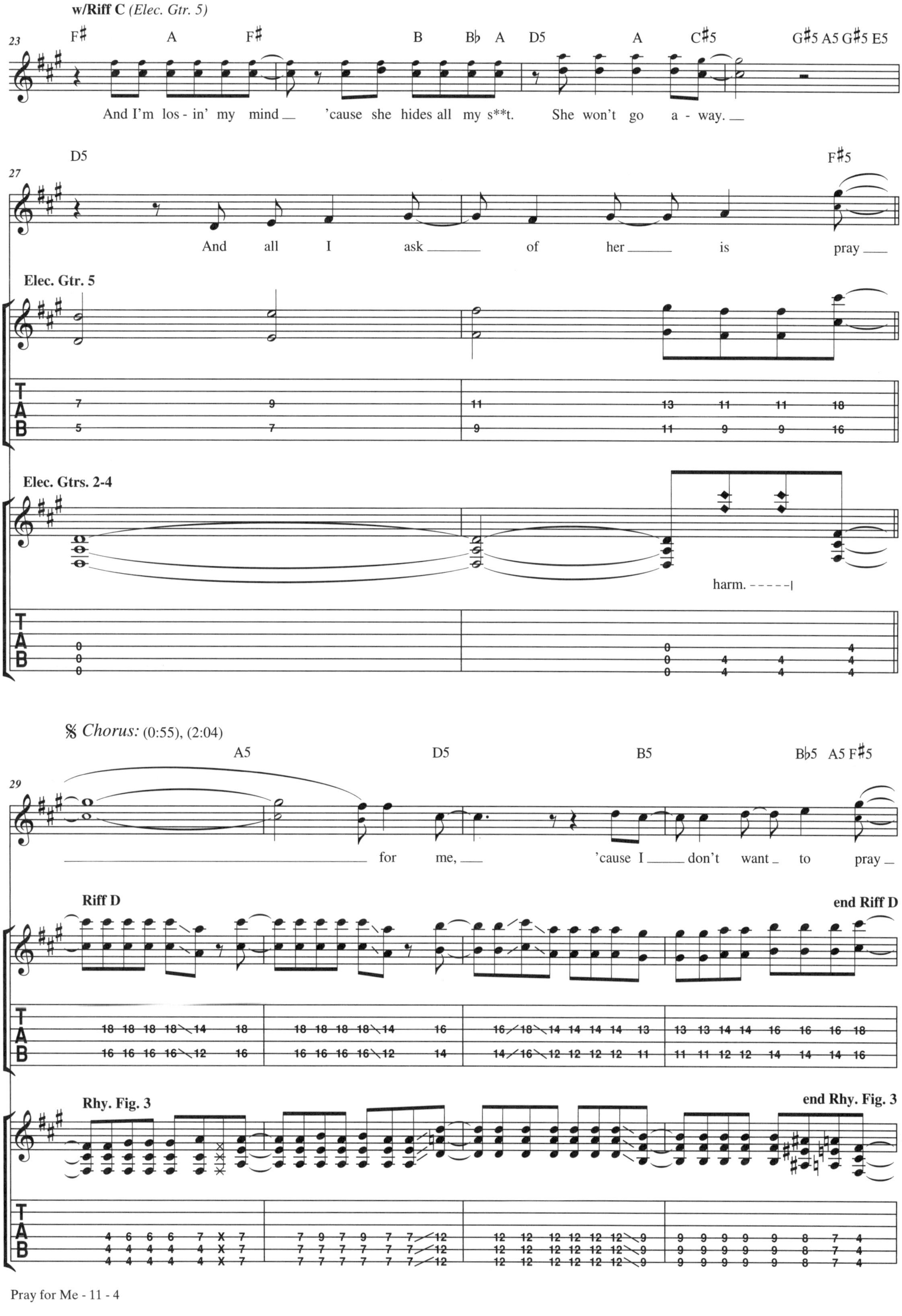

w/Riff C (Elec. Gtr. 5)
F♯ A F♯ B B♭ A D5 A C♯5 G♯5 A5 G♯5 E5
And I'm los - in' my mind 'cause she hides all my s**t. She won't go a - way.
D5 F♯5
And all I ask of her is pray
Elec. Gtr. 5
Elec. Gtrs. 2-4
harm.
𝄋 Chorus: (0:55), (2:04)
A5 D5 B5 B♭5 A5 F♯5
for me, 'cause I don't want to pray
Riff D
end Riff D
Rhy. Fig. 3
end Rhy. Fig. 3

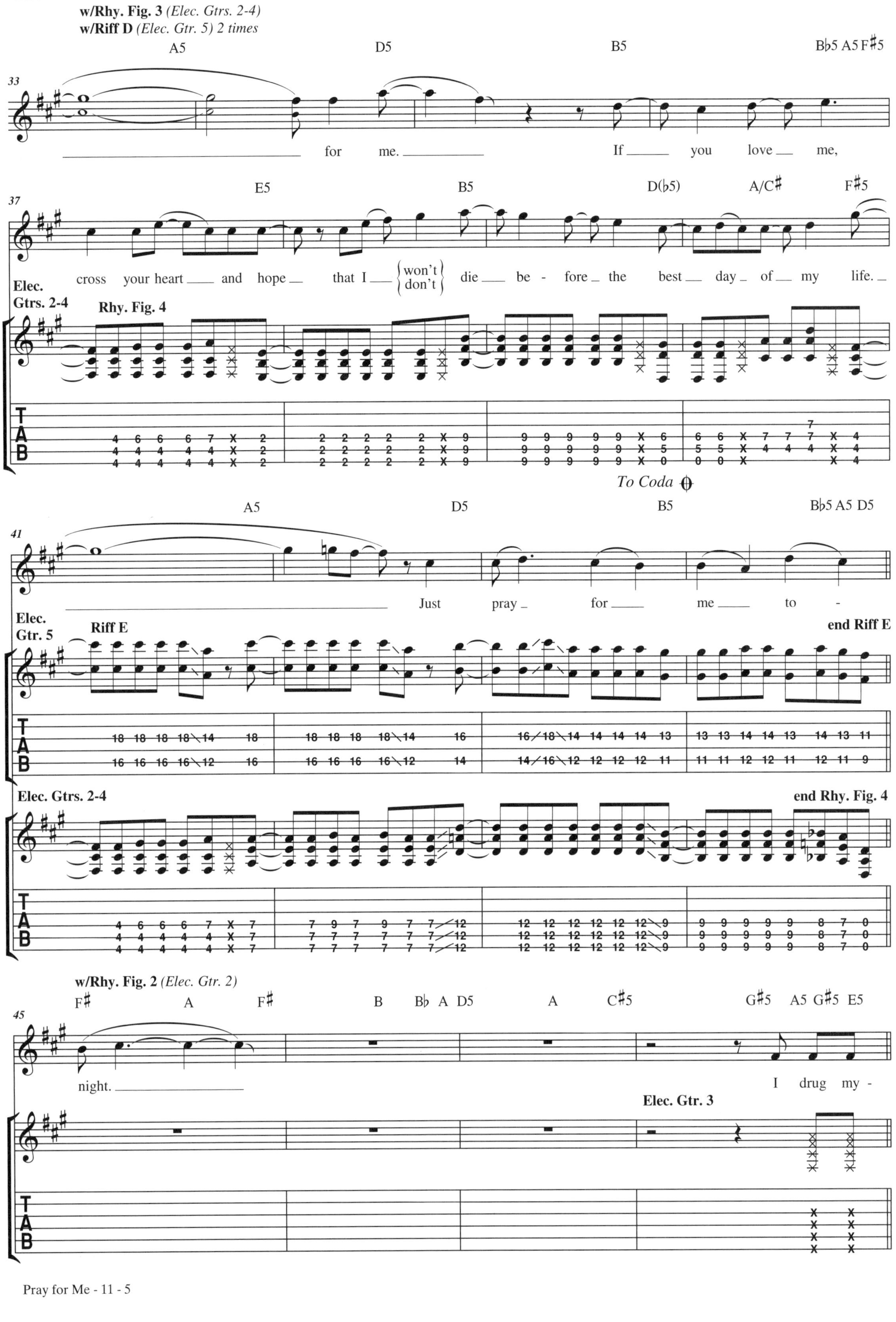
w/Rhy. Fig. 3 (Elec. Gtrs. 2-4)
w/Riff D (Elec. Gtr. 5) 2 times
A5 D5 B5 B♭5 A5 F♯5
for me. If you love me,
E5 B5 D(♭5) A/C♯ F♯5
cross your heart and hope that I won't / don't die be - fore the best day of my life.
Elec. Gtrs. 2-4
Rhy. Fig. 4
To Coda
A5 D5 B5 B♭5 A5 D5
Just pray for me to -
Elec. Gtr. 5
Riff E
end Riff E
Elec. Gtrs. 2-4
end Rhy. Fig. 4
w/Rhy. Fig. 2 (Elec. Gtr. 2)
F♯ A F♯ B B♭ A D5 A C♯5 G♯5 A5 G♯5 E5
night. I drug my -
Elec. Gtr. 3

Verse 2: (1:32)
w/Riff B (Elec. Gtr. 1) & Riff C (Elec. Gtr. 5) both 4 times
w/Rhy. Fig. 2 (Elec. Gtrs. 2 & 3) 2 times
F♯ A F♯ B B♭ A D5 A C♯5 G♯5 A5 G♯5 E5
self out of the bed that she made and I es - cape her in a black mot - or - cade. She's push - in'
F♯ A F♯ B B♭ A D5 A C♯5 G♯5 A5 G♯5 E5
bi - bles and a clean bill of health. I can't make her go a - way.
w/Rhy. Fig. 2 (Elec. Gtrs. 2-4) 2 times
F♯ A F♯ B B♭ A D5 A C♯5 G♯5 A5 G♯5 E5
And now I'm hit - tin' the wall and she begs me to quit, and she drags me to church but I'm scared to com - mit.
F♯ A F♯ B B♭ A D5 A C♯5 G♯5 A5 G♯5 E5
And I'm los - in' my mind 'cause she hides all my s**t. She won't go a - way.
D.S. 𝄋 al Coda
D5 E5 F♯5
And all I ask of her is pray
Elec. Gtr. 5
Elec. Gtrs. 2-4

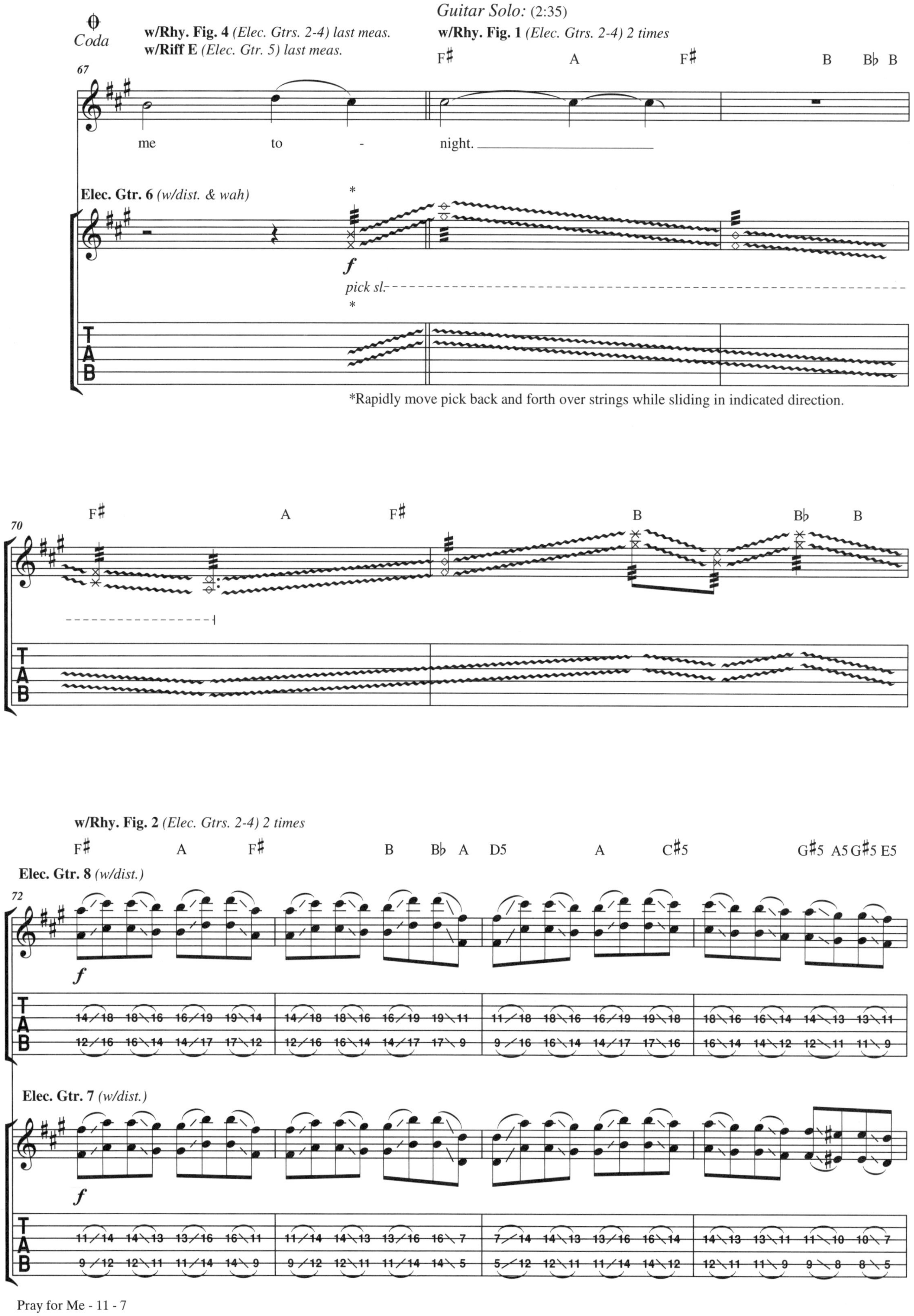
Coda
w/Rhy. Fig. 4 (Elec. Gtrs. 2-4) last meas.
w/Riff E (Elec. Gtr. 5) last meas.
Guitar Solo: (2:35)
w/Rhy. Fig. 1 (Elec. Gtrs. 2-4) 2 times
F♯ A F♯ B B♭ B
me to - night.
Elec. Gtr. 6 (w/dist. & wah)
pick sl.
*Rapidly move pick back and forth over strings while sliding in indicated direction.
F♯ A F♯ B B♭ B
w/Rhy. Fig. 2 (Elec. Gtrs. 2-4) 2 times
F♯ A F♯ B B♭ A D5 A C♯5 G♯5 A5 G♯5 E5
Elec. Gtr. 8 (w/dist.)
Elec. Gtr. 7 (w/dist.)

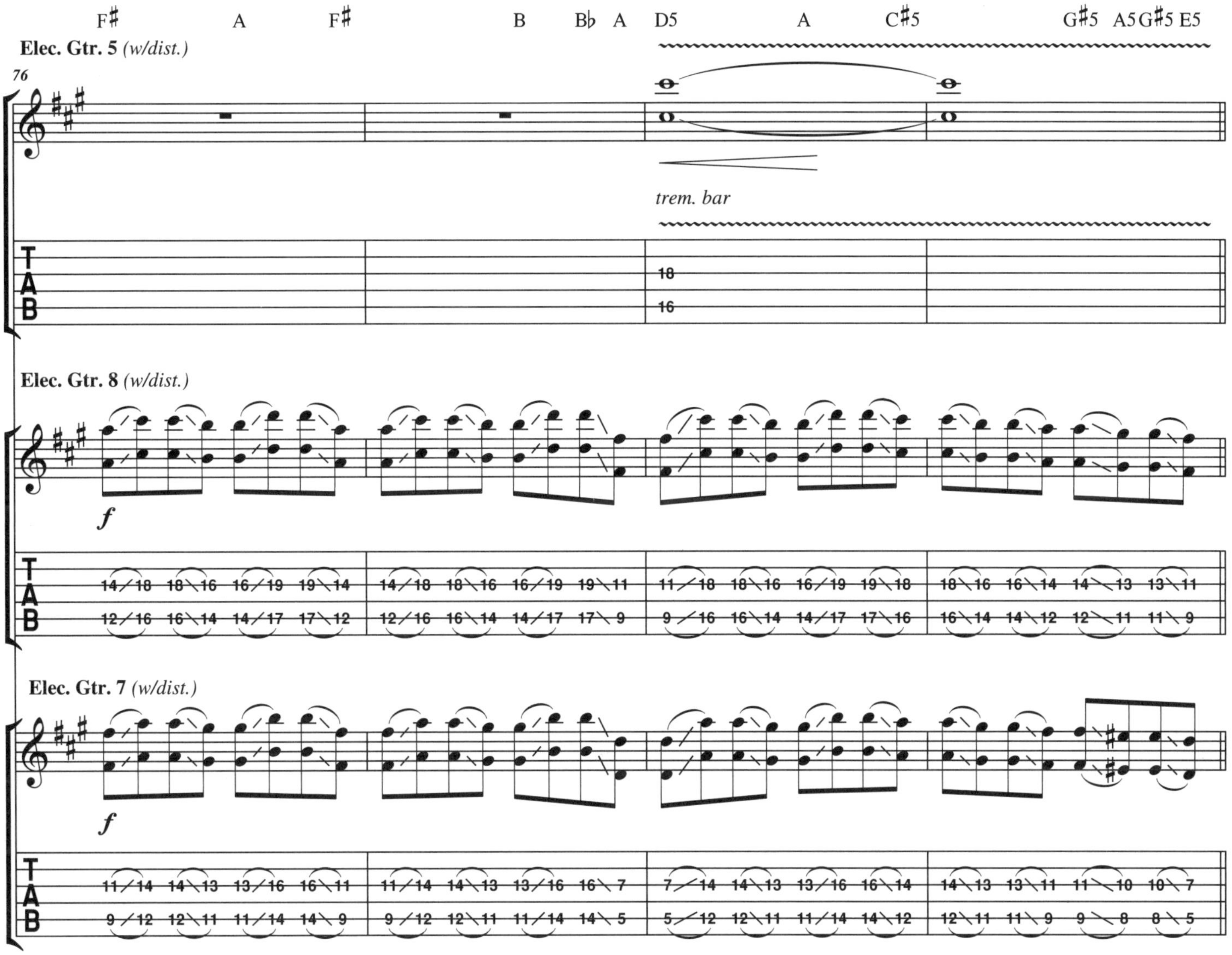

Interlude: (2:58)

w/misc. fdbk. & tremolo effects *(Elec. Gtr. 5)*

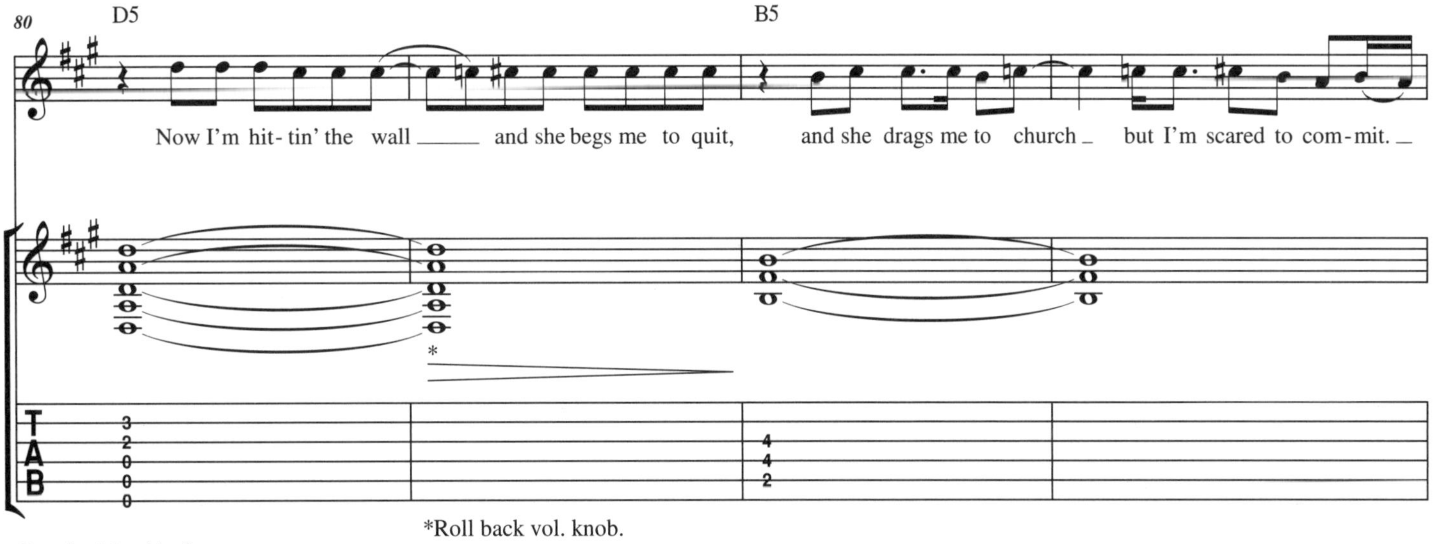

*Roll back vol. knob.

D5 C♯5 N.C. F♯5
And I'm los - in' my mind 'cause she hides all my s**t. And all I ask of her is pray
pick sl.
*Vol. knob full.
Chorus: (3:09)
w/Rhy. Fig. 3 (Elec. Gtrs. 2-4) 2 times
w/Riff D (Elec. Gtr. 5) 3 times
A5 D5 B5 B♭5 A5 F♯5
for me, 'cause I don't want to pray
A5 D5 B5 B♭5 A5 F♯5
for me. If you love me,
w/Rhy. Fig. 4 (Elec. Gtrs. 2-4)
E5 B5 D(♭5) A/C♯ F♯5
cross your heart and hope that I don't die be - fore the best day of my life.
w/Riff E (Elec. Gtrs. 2-4)
A5 D5 B5 B♭5 A5 D5
Pray
Vcl. Fig. 1
Pray for me to - night.
Elec. Gtr. 6
mp

Outro/Guitar Solo: (3:40)

w/Rhy. Fig. 3 *(Elec. Gtrs. 2-4) 2 times* **w/Vcl. Fig. 1** *4 times*

w/Riff D *(Elec. Gtr. 5) 3 times*

w/Rhy. Fig. 4 (Elec. Gtrs. 2-4)
E5
B5
D(♭5)
A/C♯
F♯5
112
for me.
Pray
116
A5
D5
B5
B♭5
for me.
Pray for me to...
Elec. Gtr. 6
8va
Elec. Gtr. 5
Elec. Gtrs. 2-4

BAD GIRLFRIEND

Lyrics by TYLER CONNOLLY and CHRISTINE CONNOLLY
Music by TYLER CONNOLLY, DAVID BRENNER
and DEAN BACK

*All Gtrs. tune down 1 whole step:

⑥ = D ③ = F
⑤ = G ② = A
④ = C ① = D

Moderately ♩ = 135
Intro:
D5

*Recording sounds a whole step lower than written.

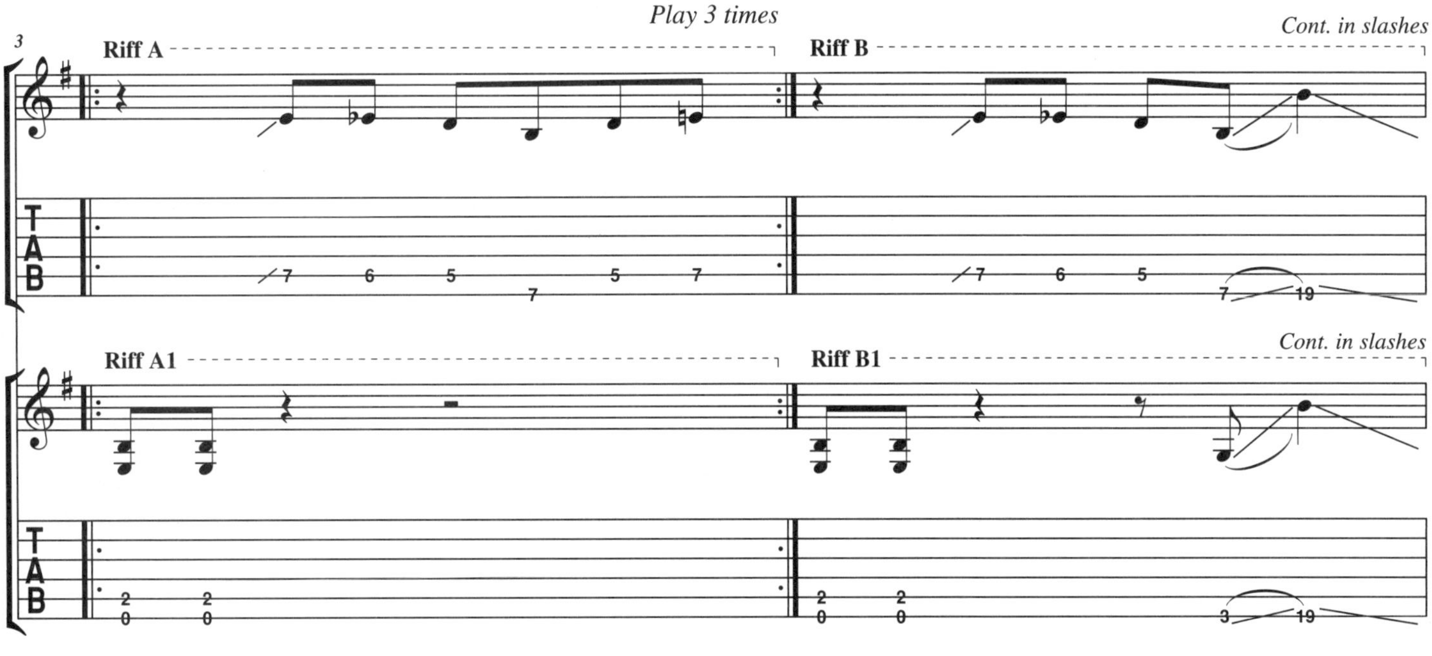

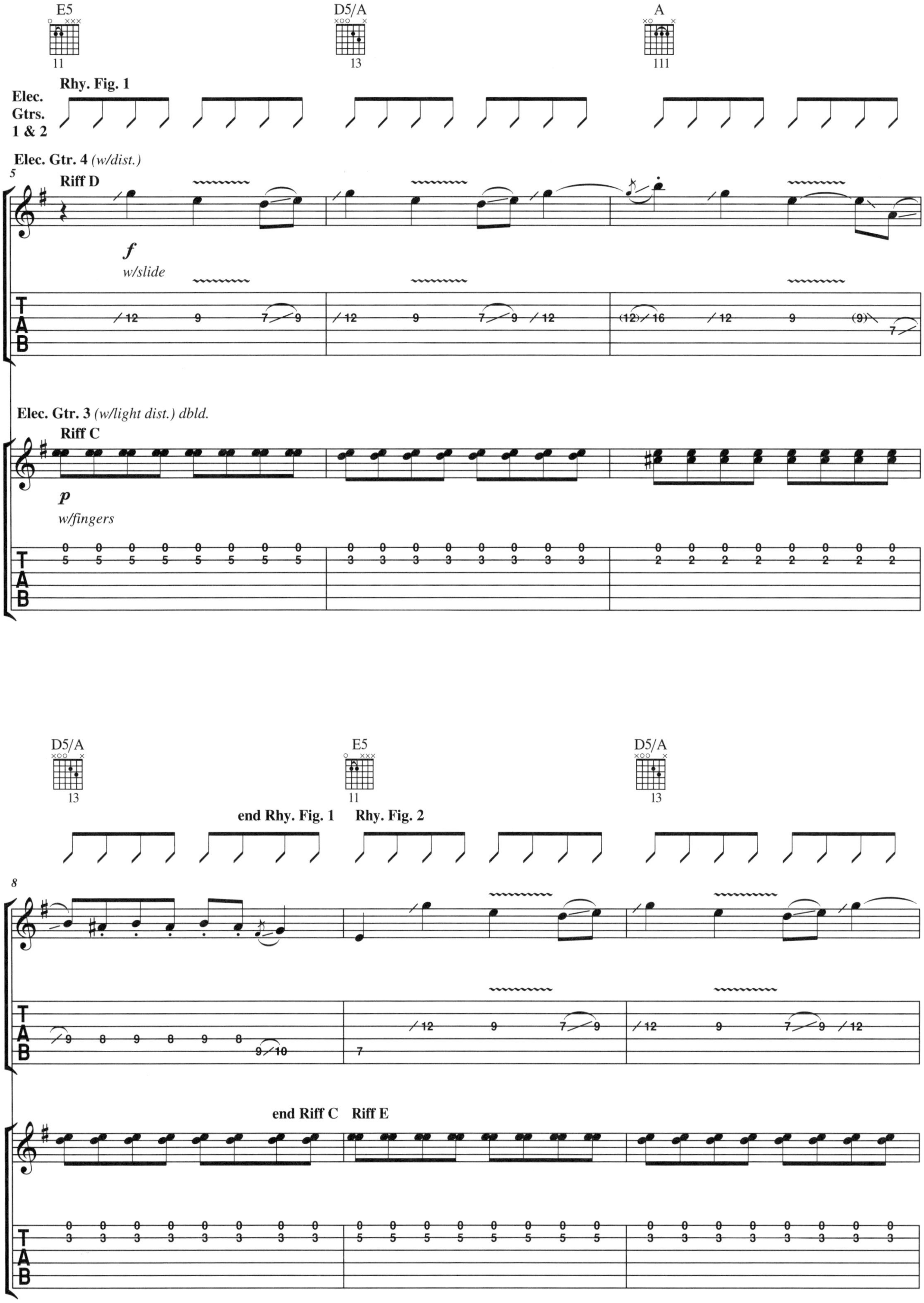
E5
D5/A
A
Rhy. Fig. 1
Elec. Gtrs. 1 & 2
Elec. Gtr. 4 (w/dist.)
Riff D
f
w/slide
Elec. Gtr. 3 (w/light dist.) dbld.
Riff C
p
w/fingers
D5/A
E5
D5/A
end Rhy. Fig. 1
Rhy. Fig. 2
end Riff C
Riff E

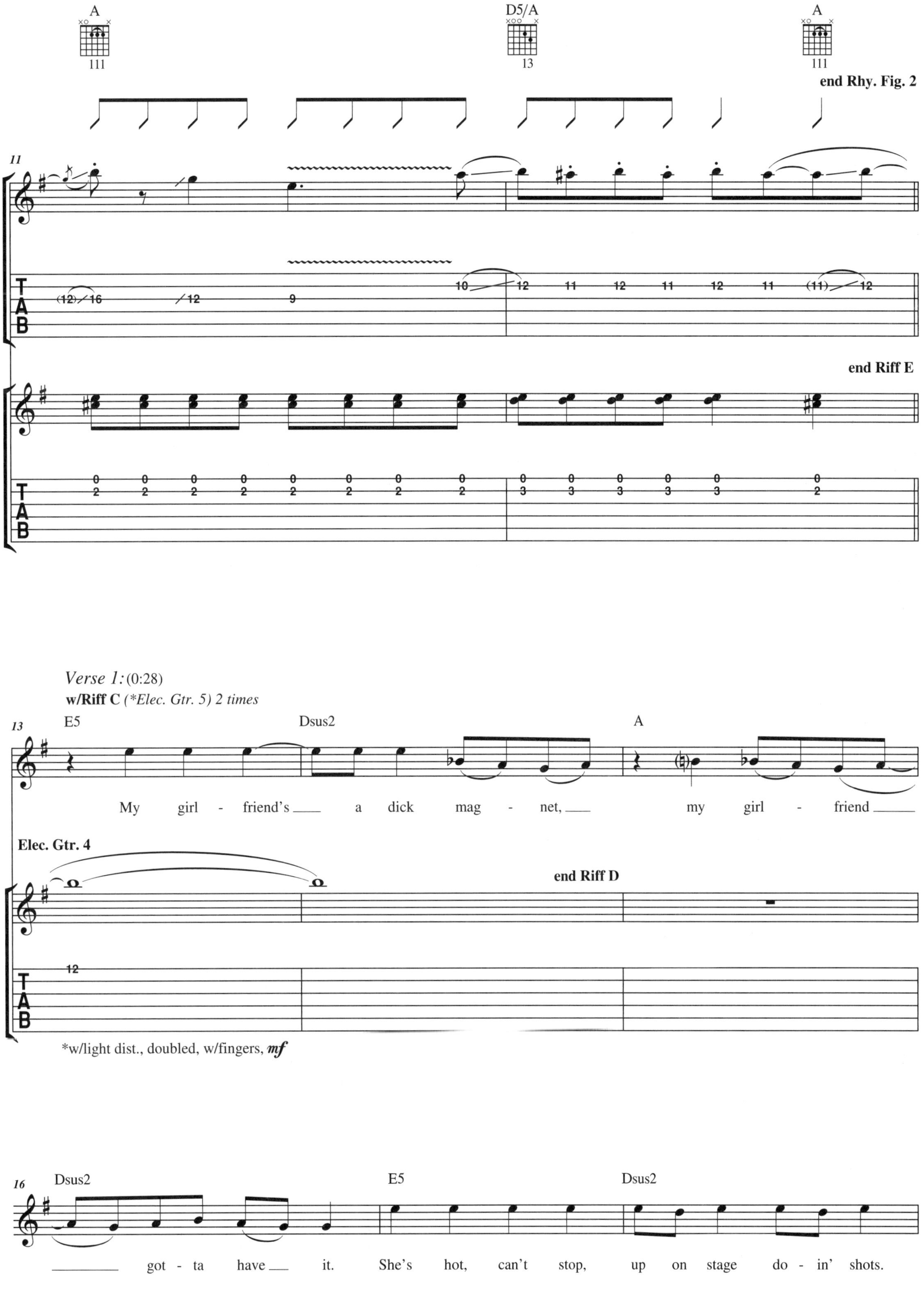
A
D5/A
A
end Rhy. Fig. 2
11
end Riff E
Verse 1: (0:28)
w/Riff C (*Elec. Gtr. 5) 2 times
13
E5
Dsus2
A
My girl - friend's a dick mag - net, my girl - friend
Elec. Gtr. 4
end Riff D
*w/light dist., doubled, w/fingers, mf
16
Dsus2
E5
Dsus2
got - ta have it. She's hot, can't stop, up on stage do - in' shots.

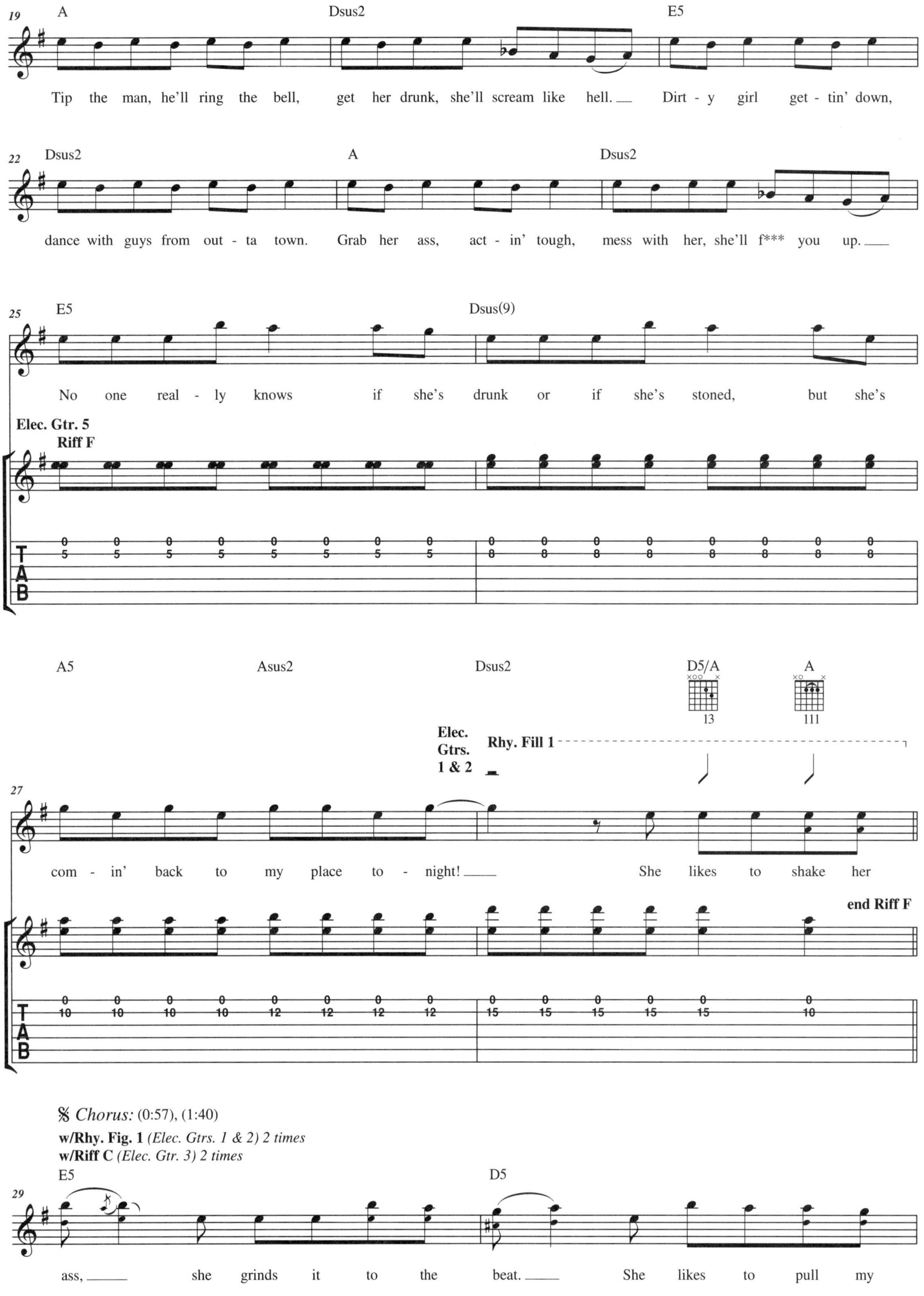

19
A
Dsus2
E5
Tip the man, he'll ring the bell, get her drunk, she'll scream like hell. Dirt - y girl get - tin' down,
22
Dsus2
A
Dsus2
dance with guys from out - ta town. Grab her ass, act - in' tough, mess with her, she'll f*** you up.
25
E5
Dsus(9)
No one real - ly knows if she's drunk or if she's stoned, but she's
Elec. Gtr. 5
Riff F
A5
Asus2
Dsus2
D5/A
A
Elec. Gtrs. 1 & 2
Rhy. Fill 1
27
com - in' back to my place to - night! She likes to shake her
end Riff F
Chorus: (0:57), (1:40)
w/Rhy. Fig. 1 (Elec. Gtrs. 1 & 2) 2 times
w/Riff C (Elec. Gtr. 3) 2 times
E5
D5
29
ass, she grinds it to the beat. She likes to pull my

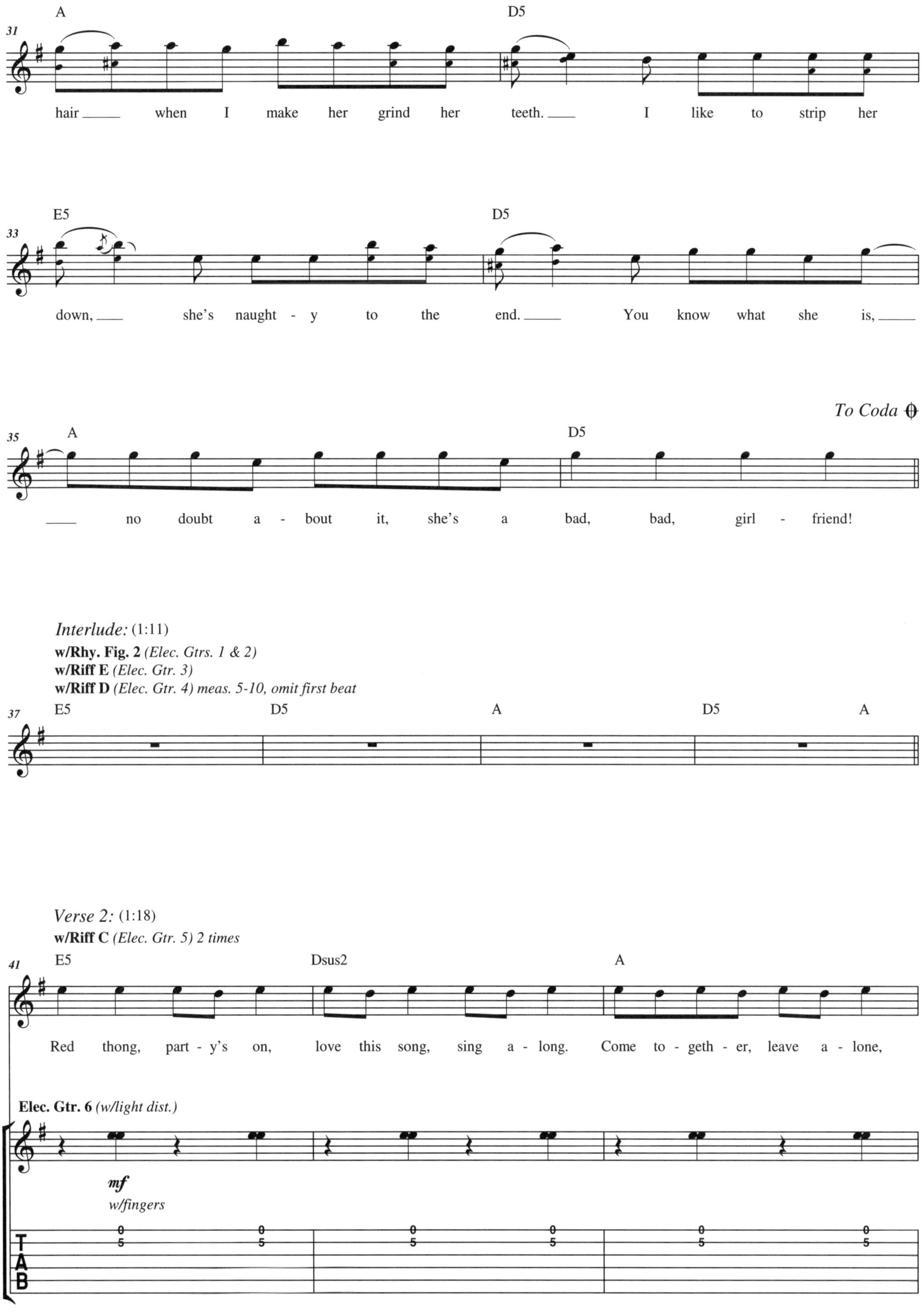
A
D5
31
hair when I make her grind her teeth. I like to strip her
E5
D5
33
down, she's naught - y to the end. You know what she is,
To Coda
A
D5
35
no doubt a - bout it, she's a bad, bad, girl - friend!
Interlude: (1:11)
w/Rhy. Fig. 2 (Elec. Gtrs. 1 & 2)
w/Riff E (Elec. Gtr. 3)
w/Riff D (Elec. Gtr. 4) meas. 5-10, omit first beat
37
E5
D5
A
D5
A
Verse 2: (1:18)
w/Riff C (Elec. Gtr. 5) 2 times
41
E5
Dsus2
A
Red thong, part - y's on, love this song, sing a - long. Come to - geth - er, leave a - lone,
Elec. Gtr. 6 (w/light dist.)
mf
w/fingers
T
A
B

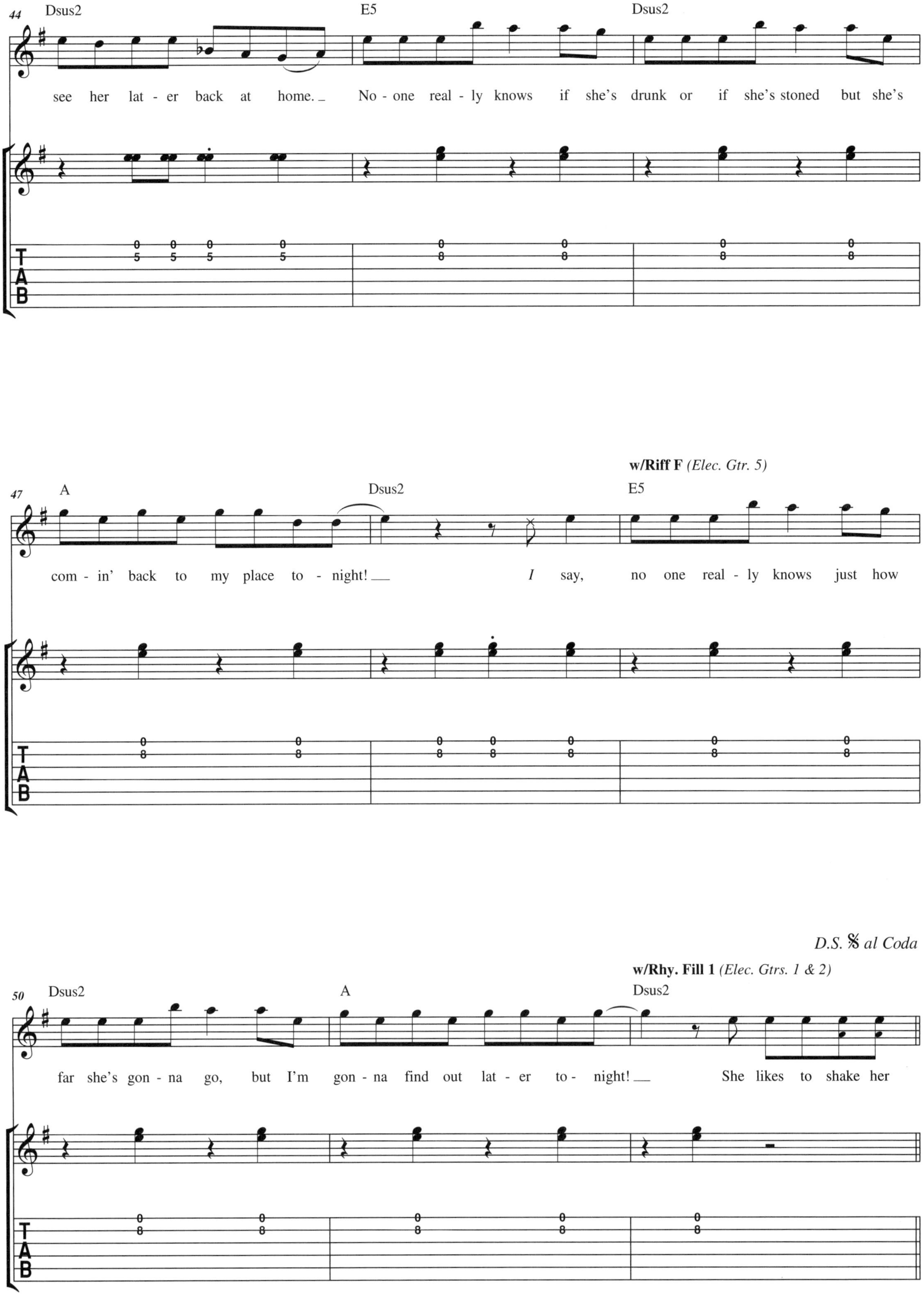
44
Dsus2
E5
Dsus2
see her lat - er back at home. _ No - one real - ly knows if she's drunk or if she's stoned but she's
47
A
Dsus2
w/Riff F (Elec. Gtr. 5)
E5
com - in' back to my place to - night! _ I say, no one real - ly knows just how
D.S. 𝄋 al Coda
50
Dsus2
A
w/Rhy. Fill 1 (Elec. Gtrs. 1 & 2)
Dsus2
far she's gon - na go, but I'm gon - na find out lat - er to - night! _ She likes to shake her
TAB

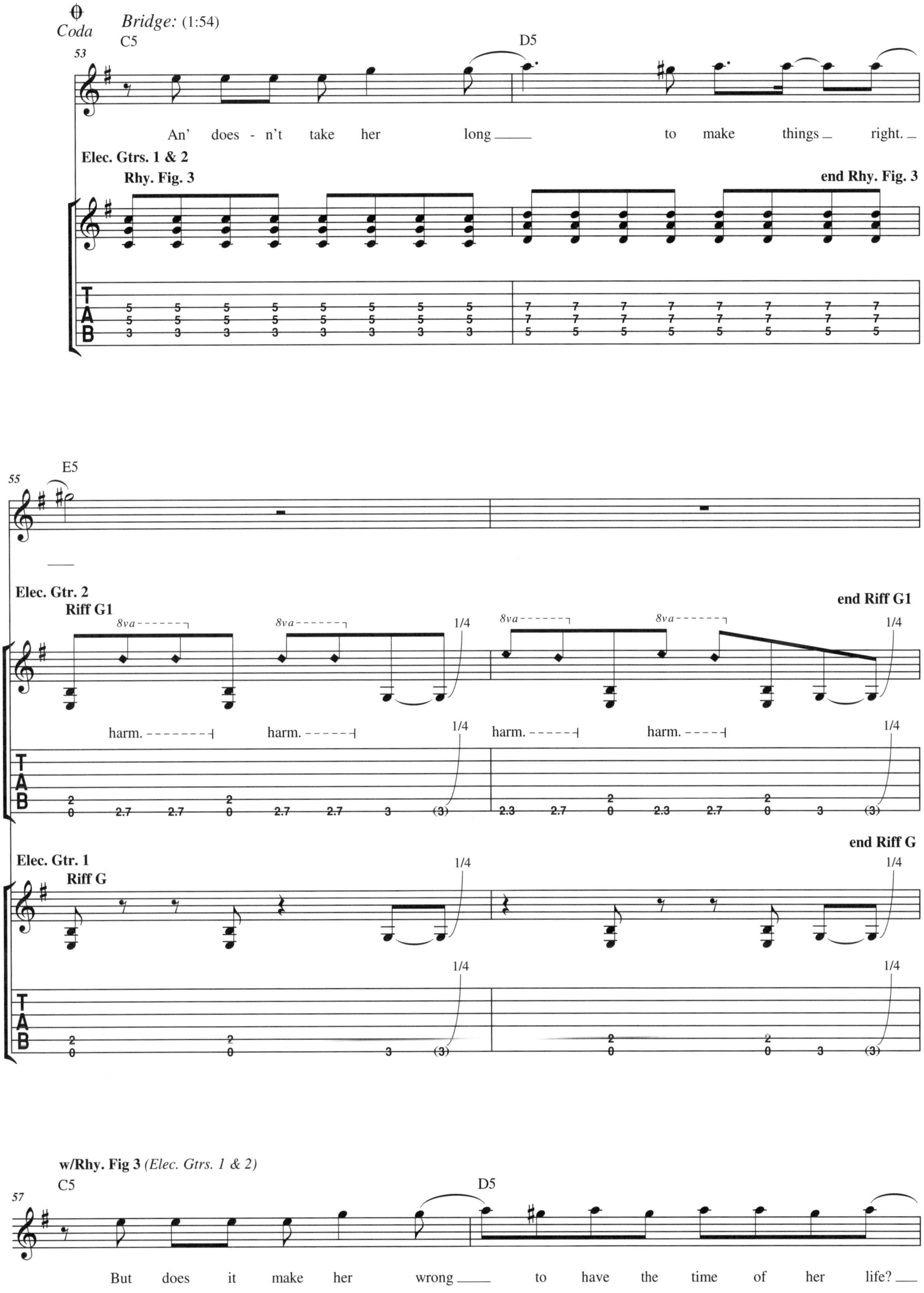
Coda
Bridge: (1:54)
C5
D5
53
An' does - n't take her long to make things right.
Elec. Gtrs. 1 & 2
Rhy. Fig. 3
end Rhy. Fig. 3
E5
55
Elec. Gtr. 2
Riff G1
end Riff G1
8va
harm.
1/4
Elec. Gtr. 1
Riff G
end Riff G
w/Rhy. Fig 3 (Elec. Gtrs. 1 & 2)
C5
D5
57
But does it make her wrong to have the time of her life?

w/Riffs G (Elec. Gtr. 1) & G1 (Elec. Gtr. 2) 2 times
E5
The time of her life.
w/Riffs A (Elec. Gtr. 1) & A1 (Elec. Gtr. 2) 3 times
w/Riffs B (Elec. Gtr. 1) & B1 (Elec. Gtr. 2)
My girl - friend's a dick mag - net, My girl - friend, got - ta have it.
Guitar Solo: (2:19)
w/Rhy. Fig. 1 (Elec. Gtrs. 1 & 2)
w/Riff C (Elec. Gtr. 3)
E5
D5
A
Elec. Gtr. 6 (w/dist.)
8va
w/Rhy. Fig. 2 (Elec. Gtrs. 1 & 2)
w/Riff E (Elec. Gtr. 3)
D5
E5
D5
A
D5
A
She's a
8va

Verse 3: (2:33)
w/Rhy. Fig. 1 (Elec. Gtrs. 1 & 2)
w/Riff C (Elec. Gtr. 3)
75
E5
D5
A
gold dig - ger, now I fig - ured out it's o - ver, pull the trig - ger. Fu - ture's fin - ished, there it went,
(8va)
17
w/Rhy. Fig. 2 (Elec. Gtrs. 1 & 2)
w/Riff E (Elec. Gtr. 3)
78
D5
E5
D5
sav - ings gone, the mon - ey's spent. Look a - round and all I see, no good, bad and ug - ly.
(8va)
81
A
D5
A
N.C.
Man, she's hot and fixed to be the fu - ture ex - Miss Con - nol - ly! She likes to shake her
(8va)
Chorus: (2:49)
w/Rhy. Fig. 1 (Elec. Gtr. 1)
w/Riff C (Elec. Gtr. 3)
84
E5
D5
A
ass, she grinds it to the beat. She likes to pull my hair when I make her grind her

w/Rhy. Fig. 2 (Elec. Gtrs. 1 & 2)
w/Riff E (Elec. Gtr. 3)
87
D5
E5
D5
teeth. _ I like to strip her down, _ she's naught - y to the end. _ You know what she is _
Outro: (3:03)
w/Rhy. Fig. 1 (Elec. Gtrs. 1 & 2)
w/Riff C (Elec. Gtr. 3)
w/Riff D (Elec. Gtr. 4) first 8 meas.
90
A
D5
A
E5
_ no doubt a - bout it, she's a bad, bad, girl - friend!
w/Rhy. Fig. 2 (Elec. Gtrs. 1 & 2)
w/Riff E (Elec. Gtr. 3)
93
D5
A
D5
E5
She's a bad, bad, girl - friend! _
97
D5
A
D5
A
She's a bad, bad, girl - friend!
E5
100
Elec. Gtr. 2
Elec. Gtr. 1

HATE MY LIFE

Lyrics by TYLER CONNOLLY and CHRISTINE CONNOLLY
Music by TYLER CONNOLLY, DAVID BRENNER
and DEAN BACK

*All Gtrs. tune down 1/2 step:

⑥ = E♭ ③ = G♭
⑤ = A♭ ② = B♭
④ = D♭ ① = E♭

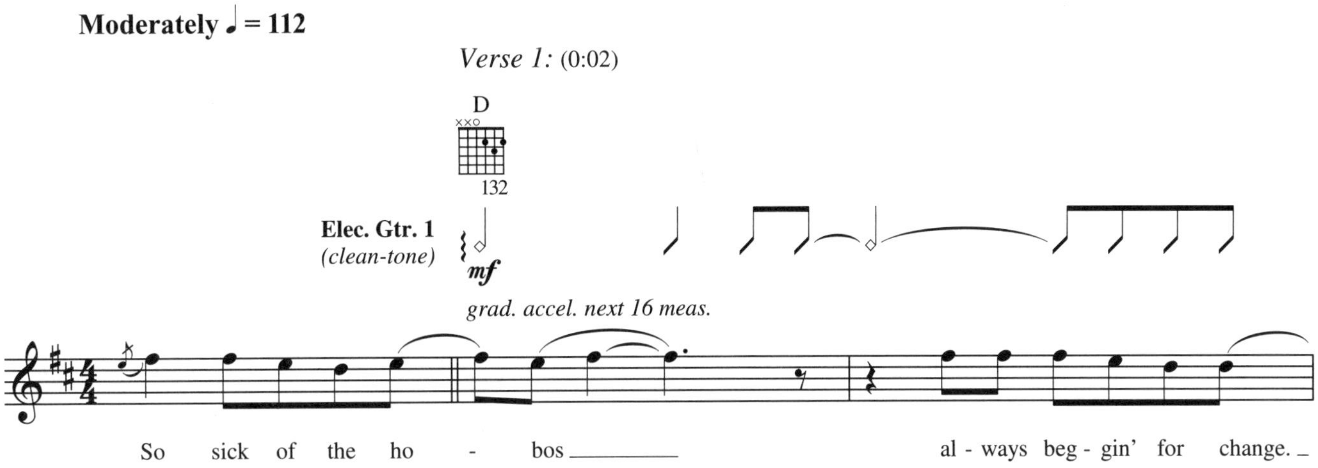
Moderately ♩ = 112
Verse 1: (0:02)
D
132
Elec. Gtr. 1
(clean-tone)
mf
grad. accel. next 16 meas.
So sick of the ho - bos
al - ways beg - gin' for change.

*Recording sounds a half step lower than written.

A
234
G5
2 34
3
I don't like how I got - ta work and

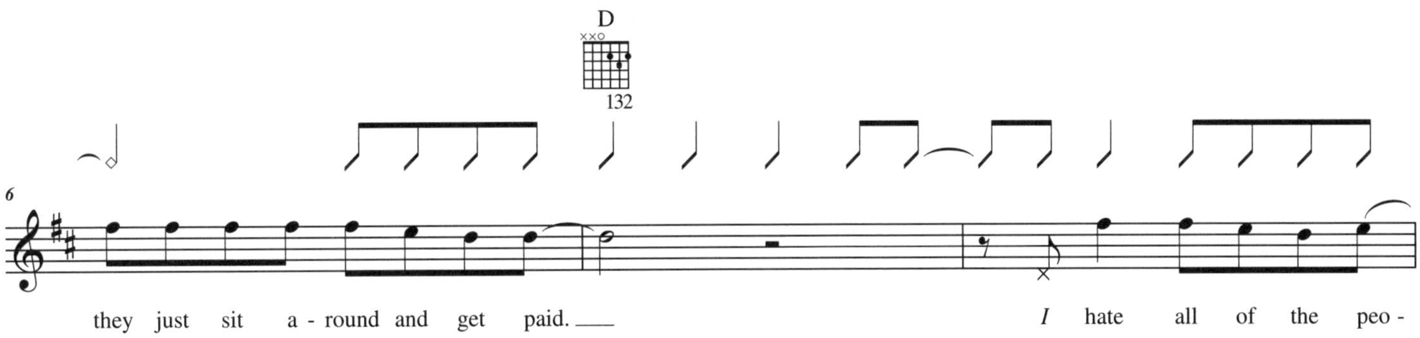
D
132
6
they just sit a - round and get paid.
I hate all of the peo -

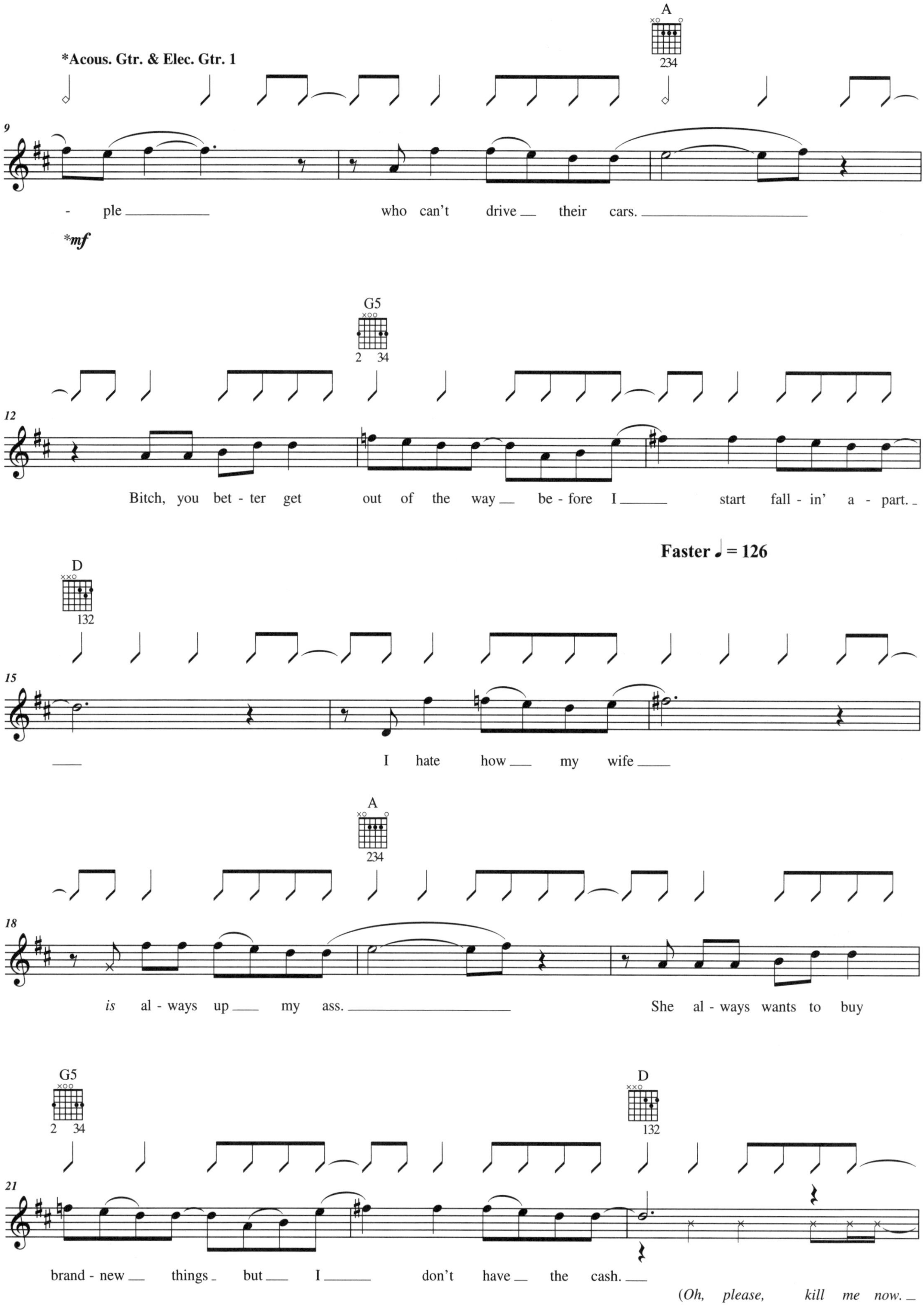
A
234
*Acous. Gtr. & Elec. Gtr. 1
9
- ple who can't drive their cars.
*mf
G5
2 34
12
Bitch, you bet - ter get out of the way be - fore I start fall - in' a - part.
D
132
Faster ♩ = 126
15
I hate how my wife
A
234
18
is al - ways up my ass. She al - ways wants to buy
G5
2 34
D
132
21
brand - new things but I don't have the cash.
(Oh, please, kill me now.

Chorus: (0:49)
A
Elec. Gtrs. 1 & *2, Acous. Gtr.
Rhy. Fig. 1
Oh, I hate my job, all of my rich friends, I hate ev - 'ry - one
)
* w/light. dist., mf
G5
D
A
G5
to the bit - ter end. Noth - in' turns out right, there's no end in sight.
D
end Rhy. Fig. 1
I hate my life. How come I nev - er get laid?
Verse 2: (1:04)
D
A
Elec. Gtrs. 1 & 2, Acous. Gtr.
Rhy. Fig. 2
Nice guys al - ways lose.
Elec. Gtr. 3 (w/dist.)
Rhy. Fig. 2A
mf
P.M.
TAB

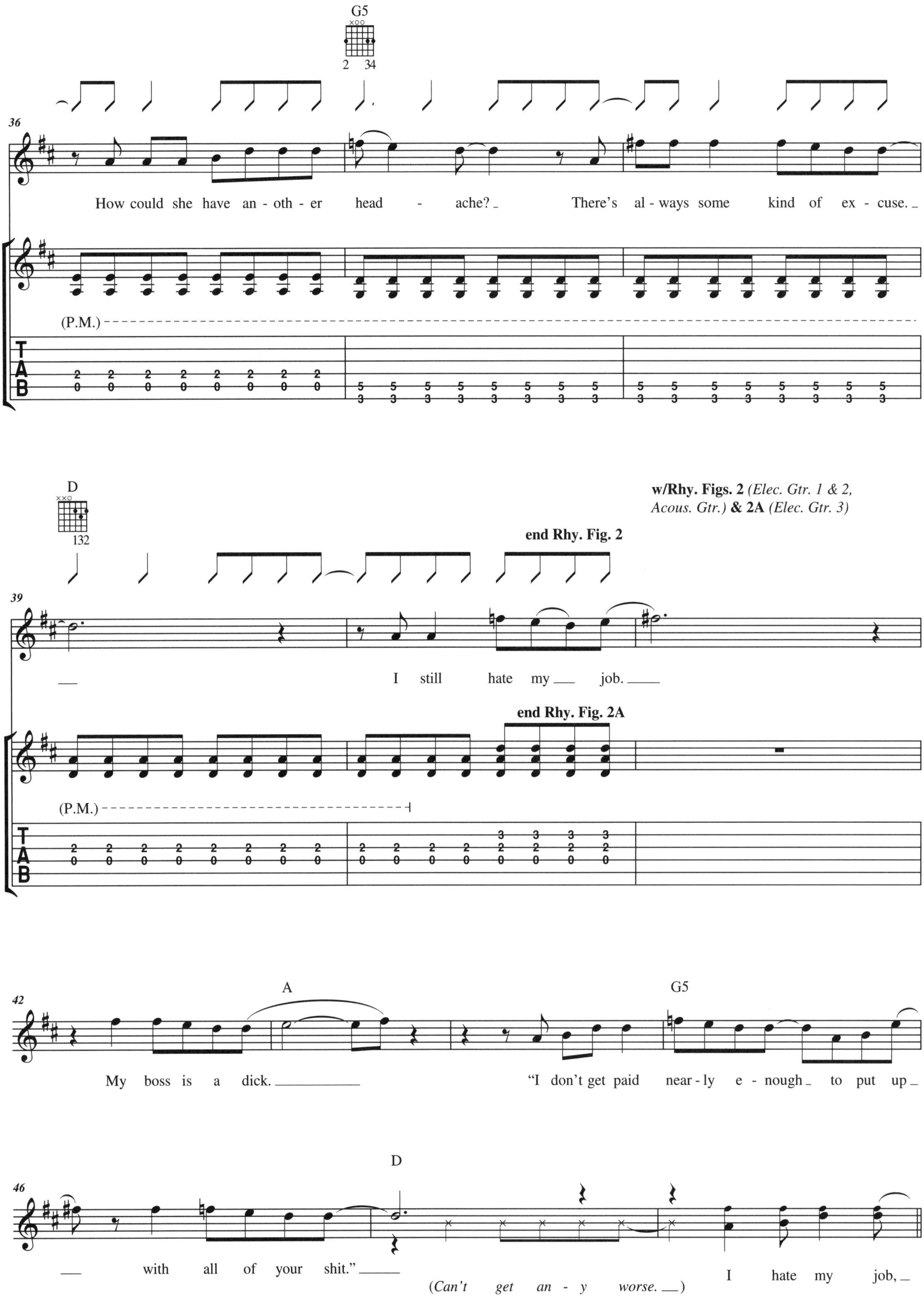
G5
How could she have an - oth - er head - ache? There's al - ways some kind of ex - cuse.
(P.M.)
D
w/Rhy. Figs. 2 (Elec. Gtr. 1 & 2, Acous. Gtr.) & 2A (Elec. Gtr. 3)
end Rhy. Fig. 2
I still hate my job.
end Rhy. Fig. 2A
(P.M.)
A
G5
My boss is a dick. "I don't get paid near - ly e - nough to put up with all of your shit."
D
(Can't get an - y worse.) I hate my job,

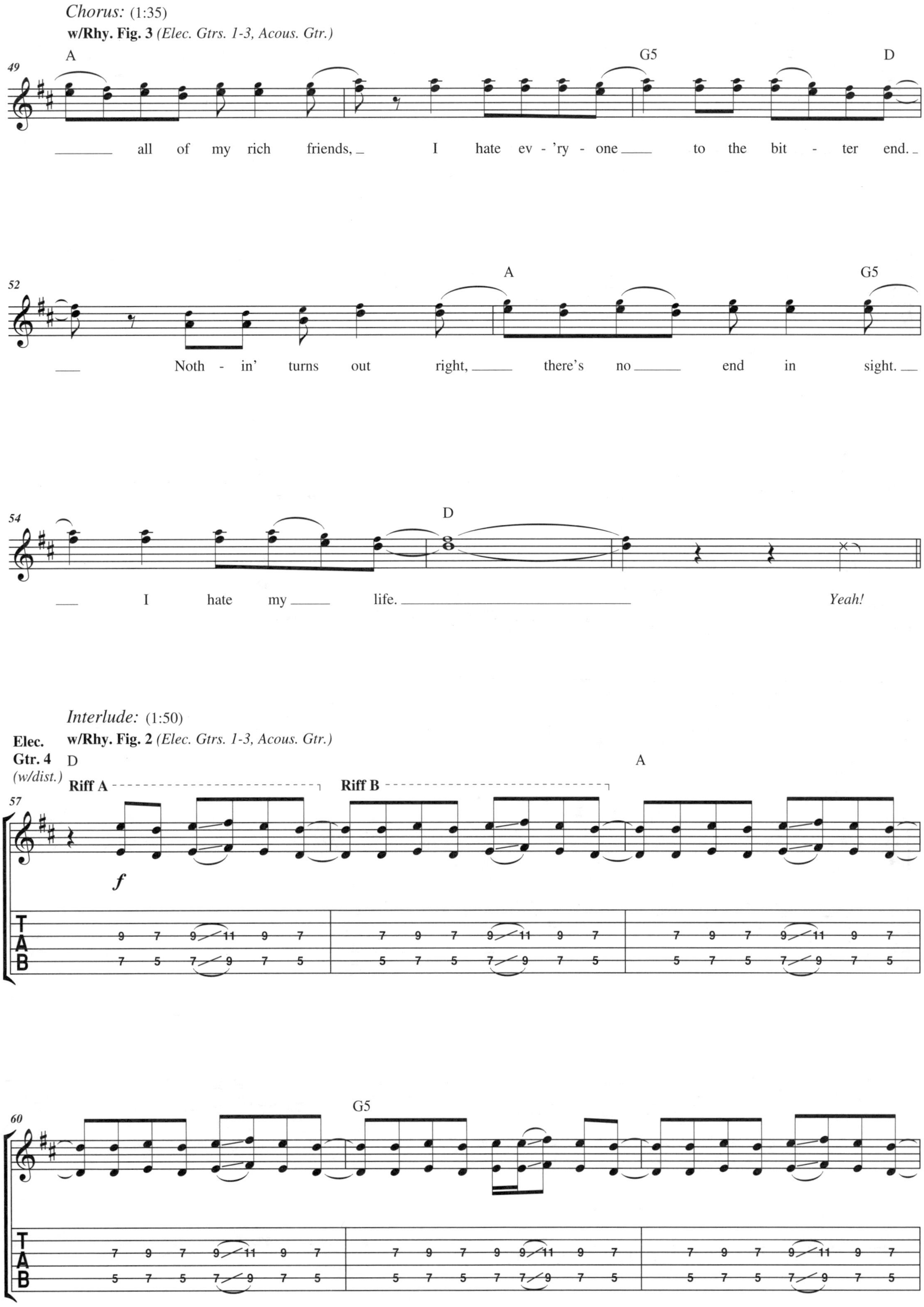
Chorus: (1:35)
w/Rhy. Fig. 3 (Elec. Gtrs. 1-3, Acous. Gtr.)
A
G5
D
all of my rich friends, I hate ev - 'ry - one to the bit - ter end.
A
G5
Noth - in' turns out right, there's no end in sight.
D
I hate my life.
Yeah!
Interlude: (1:50)
Elec. Gtr. 4 (w/dist.)
w/Rhy. Fig. 2 (Elec. Gtrs. 1-3, Acous. Gtr.)
D
A
Riff A
Riff B
f
G5
TAB

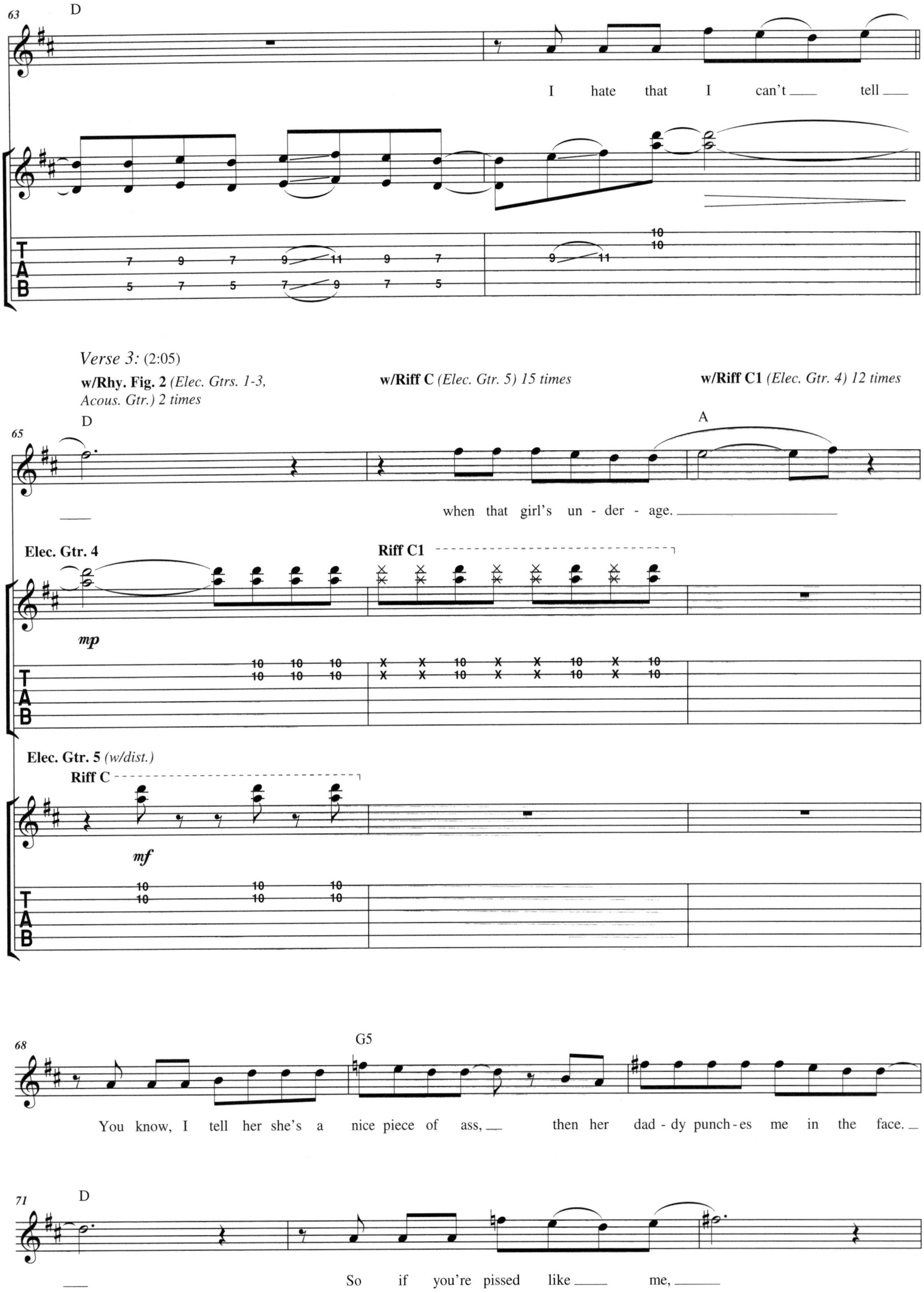
63
D
I hate that I can't tell
T
A
B
Verse 3: (2:05)
w/Rhy. Fig. 2 (Elec. Gtrs. 1-3, Acous. Gtr.) 2 times
w/Riff C (Elec. Gtr. 5) 15 times
w/Riff C1 (Elec. Gtr. 4) 12 times
65
D
A
when that girl's un - der - age.
Elec. Gtr. 4
Riff C1
mp
Elec. Gtr. 5 (w/dist.)
Riff C
mf
68
G5
You know, I tell her she's a nice piece of ass, then her dad - dy punch - es me in the face.
71
D
So if you're pissed like me,

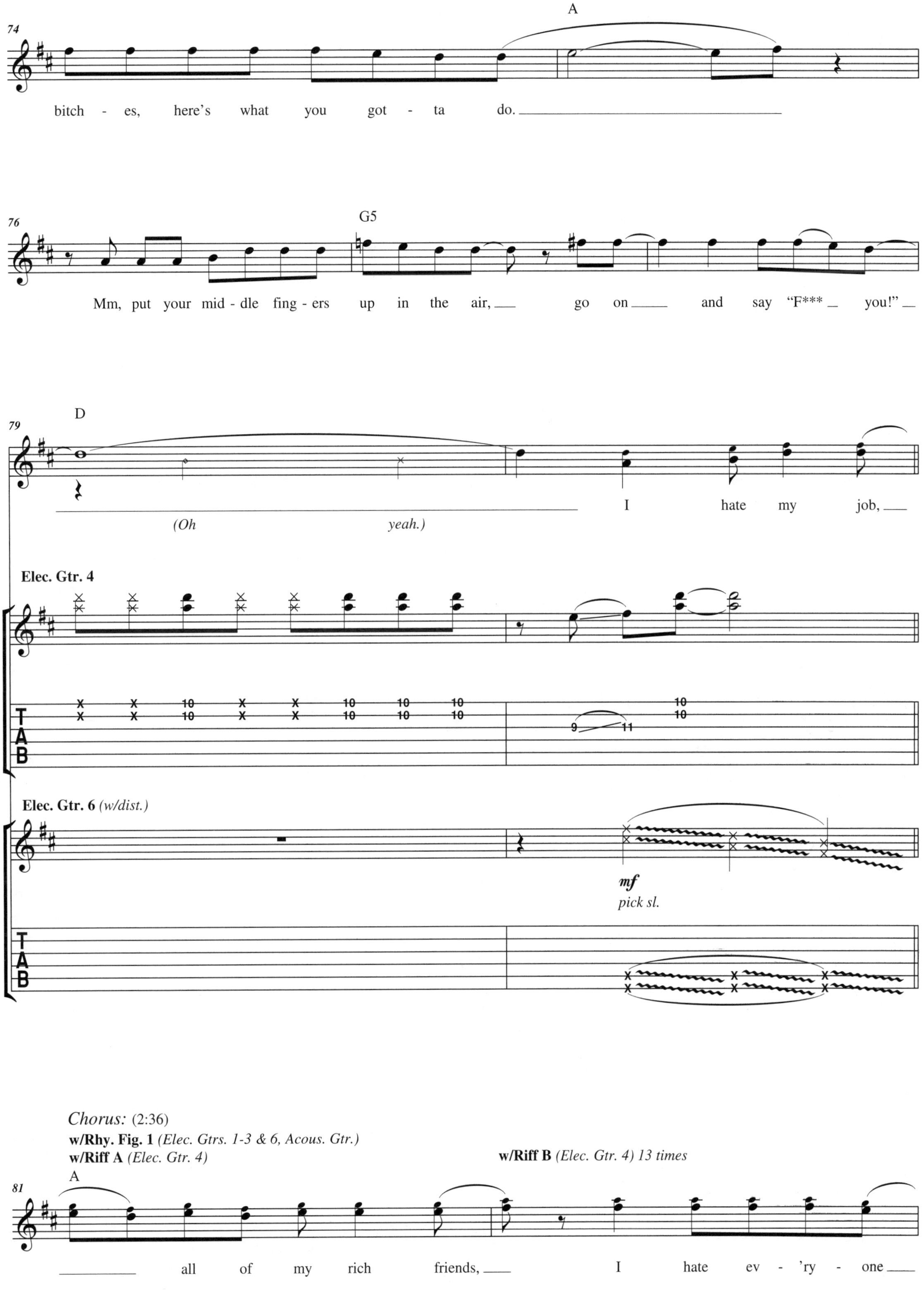
74
A
bitch - es, here's what you got - ta do.
76
G5
Mm, put your mid - dle fing - ers up in the air, go on and say "F*** you!"
79
D
(Oh yeah.)
I hate my job,
Elec. Gtr. 4
Elec. Gtr. 6 (w/dist.)
mf
pick sl.
Chorus: (2:36)
w/Rhy. Fig. 1 (Elec. Gtrs. 1-3 & 6, Acous. Gtr.)
w/Riff A (Elec. Gtr. 4)
w/Riff B (Elec. Gtr. 4) 13 times
81
A
all of my rich friends, I hate ev - 'ry - one

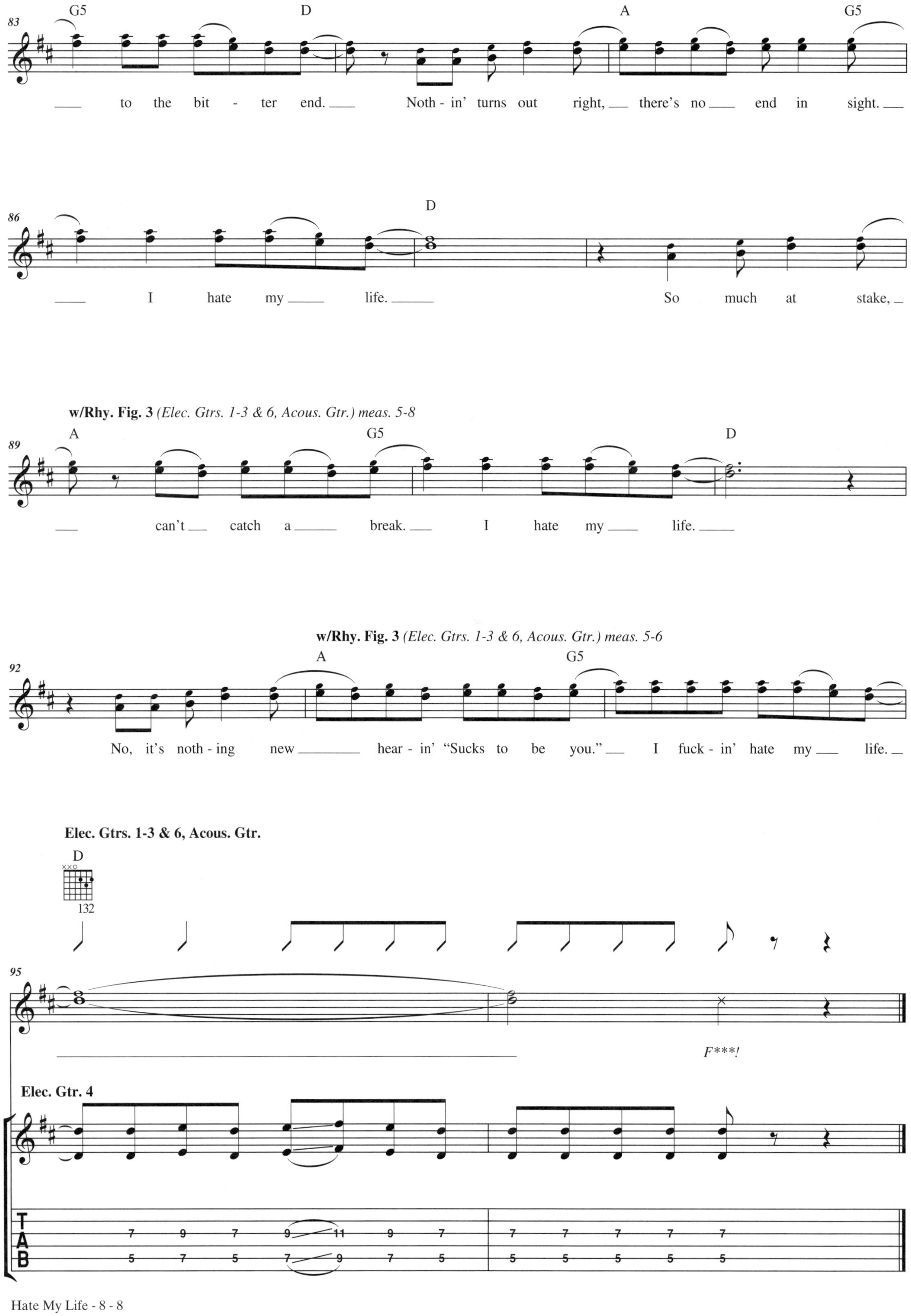
83
G5 D A G5
to the bit - ter end. Noth - in' turns out right, there's no end in sight.
86
D
I hate my life. So much at stake,
w/Rhy. Fig. 3 (Elec. Gtrs. 1-3 & 6, Acous. Gtr.) meas. 5-8
89
A G5 D
can't catch a break. I hate my life.
w/Rhy. Fig. 3 (Elec. Gtrs. 1-3 & 6, Acous. Gtr.) meas. 5-6
92
A G5
No, it's noth - ing new hear - in' "Sucks to be you." I fuck - in' hate my life.
Elec. Gtrs. 1-3 & 6, Acous. Gtr.
D
132
95
F***!
Elec. Gtr. 4
T
A
B

HEADSTRONG

Words and Music by
CHRISTOPHER BROWN, PETER CHARELL
and SIMON ORMANDY

Moderate rock ♩ = 92
Intro:

*Tune 7th string to B.

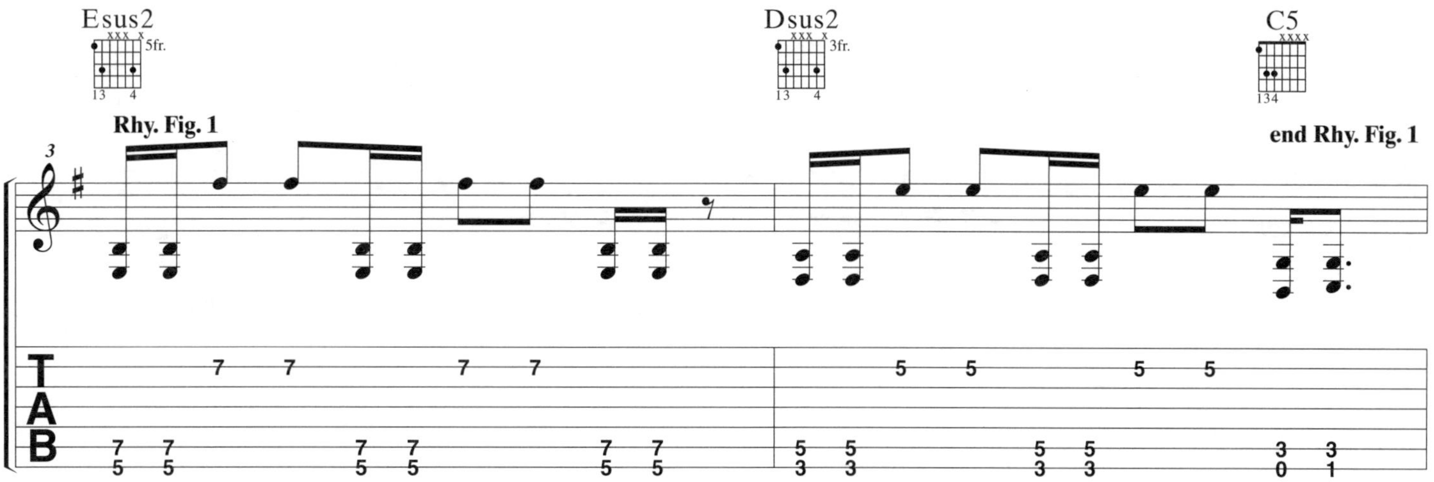

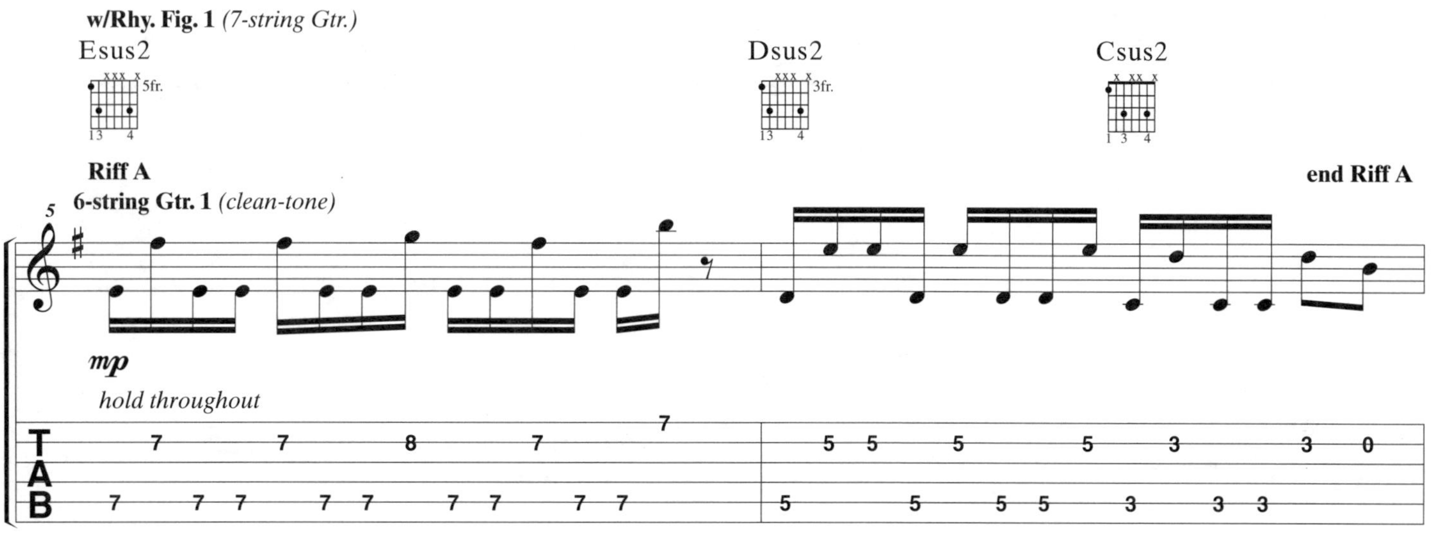

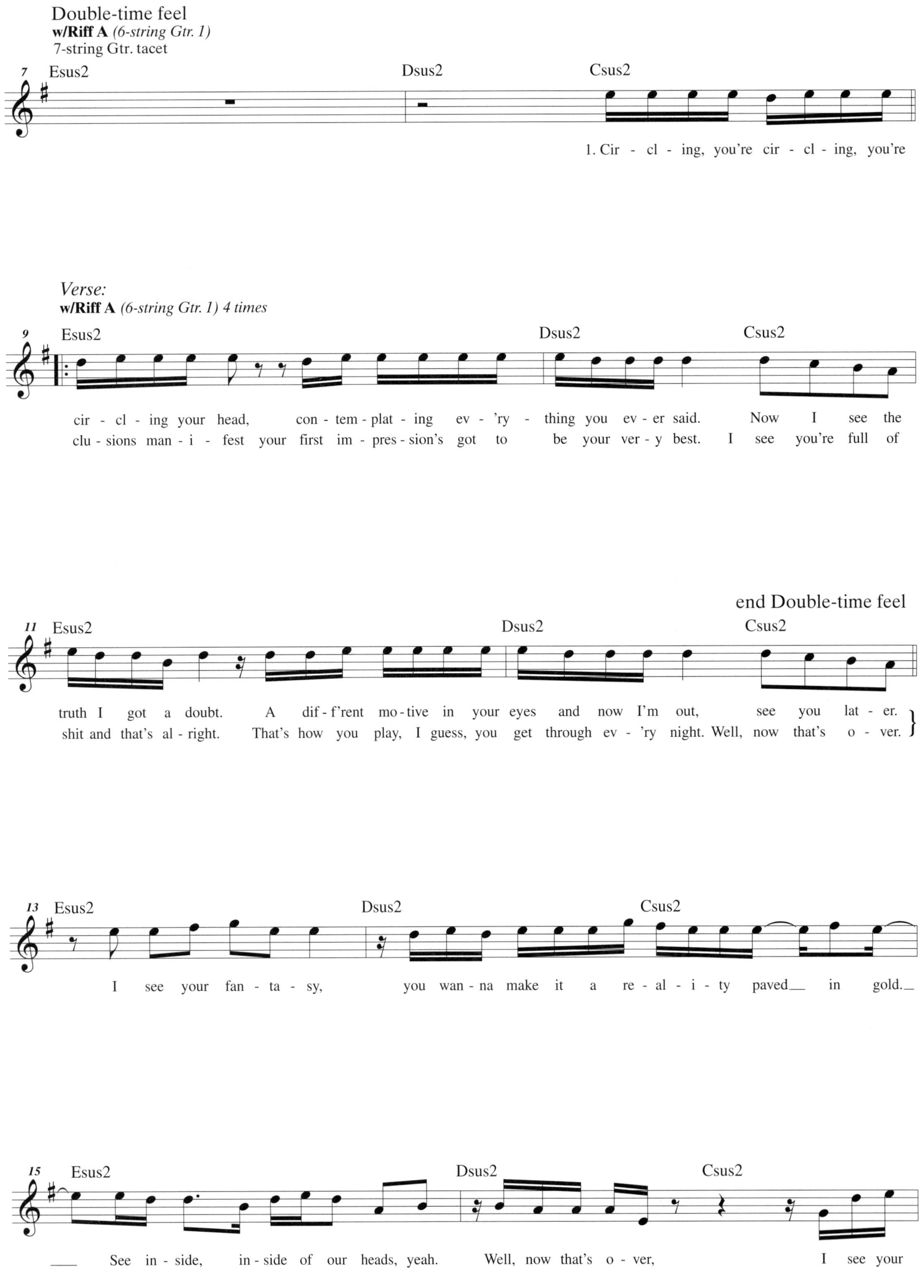
Double-time feel
w/Riff A (6-string Gtr. 1)
7-string Gtr. tacet
7
Esus2
Dsus2
Csus2
1. Cir - cl - ing, you're cir - cl - ing, you're
Verse:
w/Riff A (6-string Gtr. 1) 4 times
9
Esus2
Dsus2
Csus2
cir - cl - ing your head, con - tem - plat - ing ev - 'ry - thing you ev - er said. Now I see the
clu - sions man - i - fest your first im - pres - sion's got to be your ver - y best. I see you're full of
end Double-time feel
11
Esus2
Dsus2
Csus2
truth I got a doubt. A dif - f'rent mo - tive in your eyes and now I'm out, see you lat - er.
shit and that's al - right. That's how you play, I guess, you get through ev - 'ry night. Well, now that's o - ver.
13
Esus2
Dsus2
Csus2
I see your fan - ta - sy, you wan - na make it a re - al - i - ty paved in gold.
15
Esus2
Dsus2
Csus2
See in - side, in - side of our heads, yeah. Well, now that's o - ver, I see your

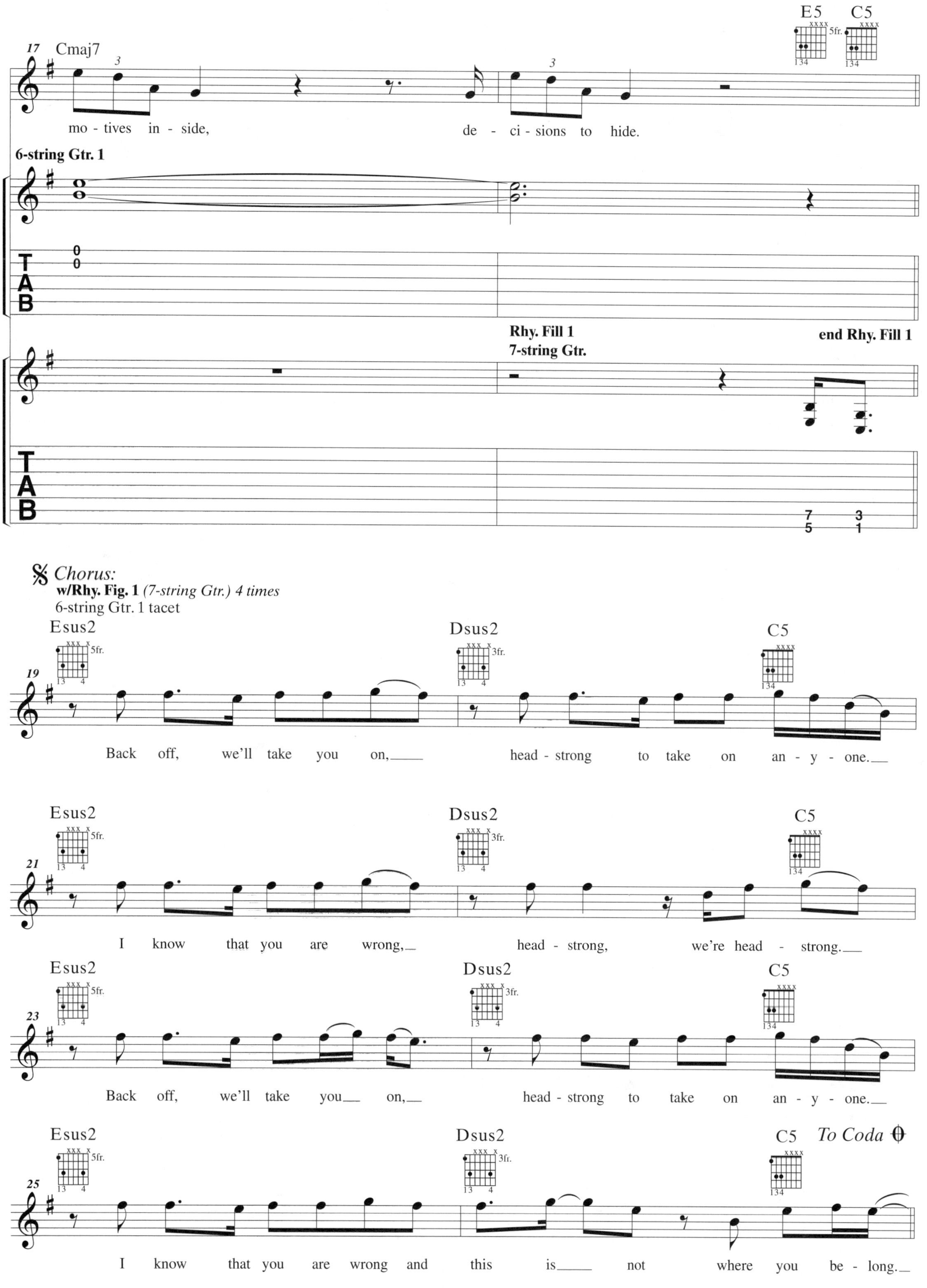
Cmaj7
E5
C5
5fr.
mo - tives in - side,
de - ci - sions to hide.
6-string Gtr. 1
Rhy. Fill 1
7-string Gtr.
end Rhy. Fill 1
Chorus:
w/Rhy. Fig. 1 (7-string Gtr.) 4 times
6-string Gtr. 1 tacet
Esus2
Dsus2
C5
Back off, we'll take you on,
head - strong to take on an - y - one.
I know that you are wrong,
head - strong, we're head - strong.
Back off, we'll take you on,
head - strong to take on an - y - one.
To Coda
I know that you are wrong and this is not where you be - long.

Bridge:

2nd time. w/misc. background vocals

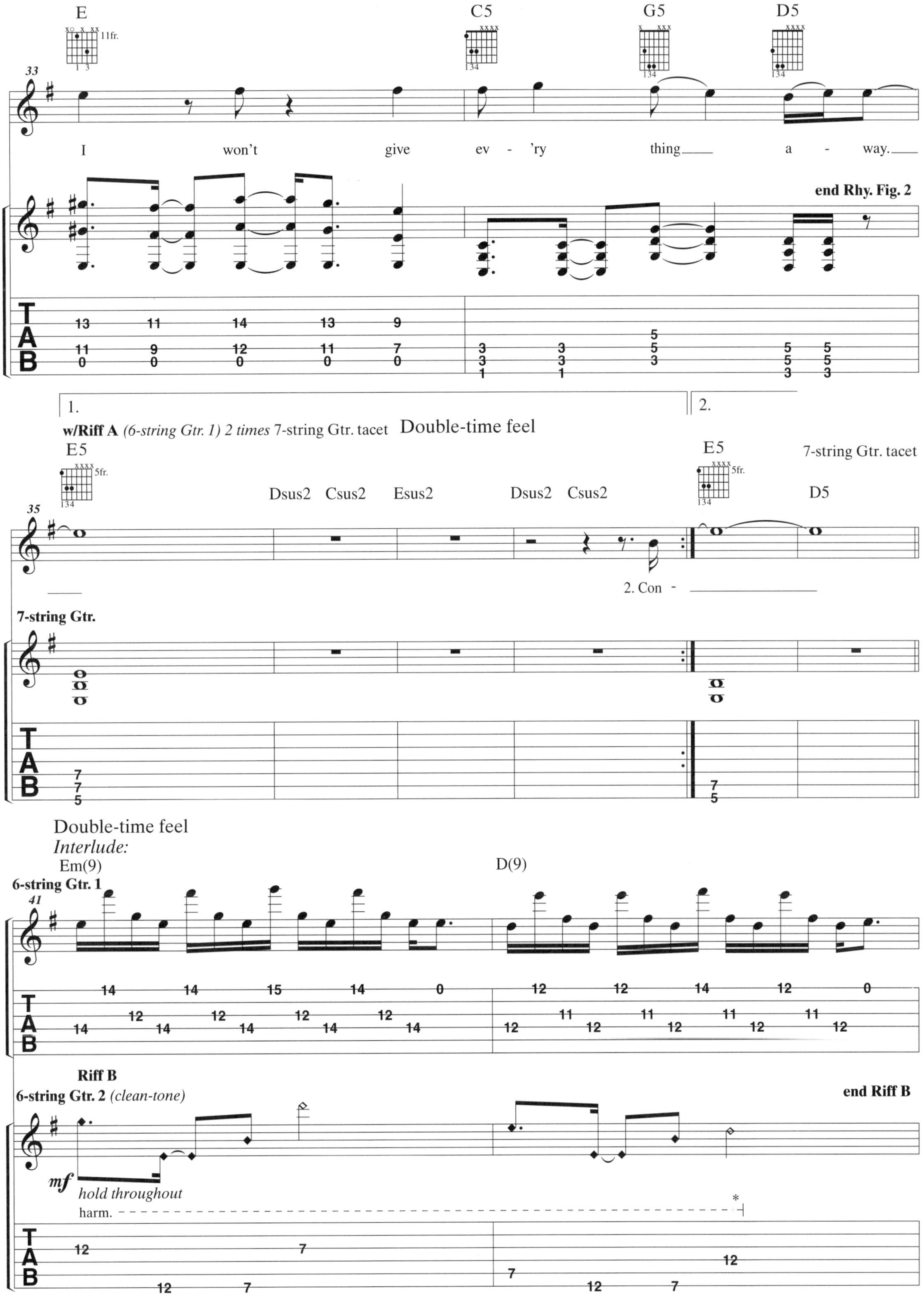

*On repeats play 12th fret harm. on 5th string.

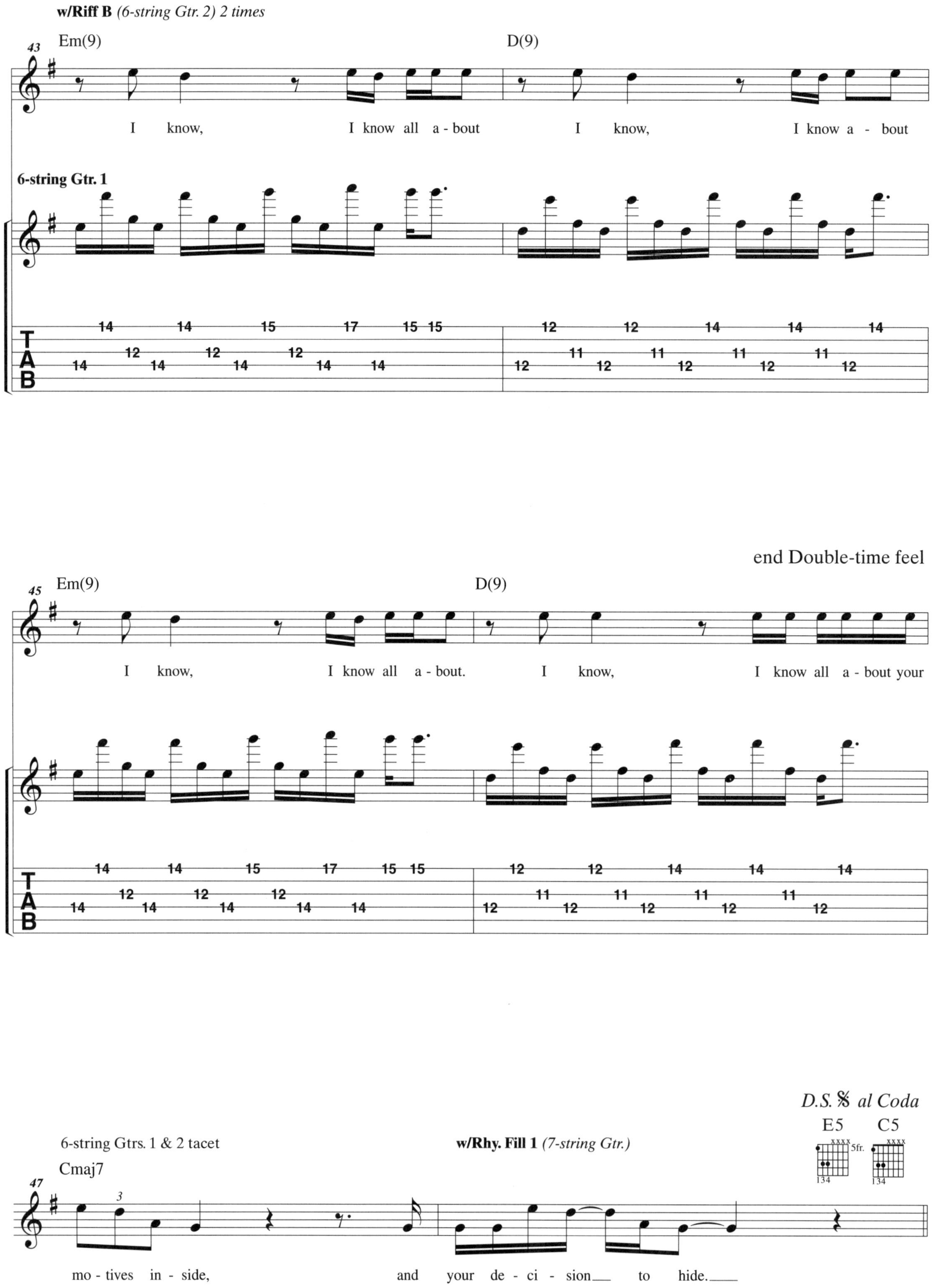
w/Riff B (6-string Gtr. 2) 2 times
43
Em(9)
D(9)
I know, I know all a - bout I know, I know a - bout
6-string Gtr. 1
T
A
B
14 14 15 17 15 15 12 12 14 14 14
12 12 12 11 11 11 11
14 14 14 14 14 12 12 12 12 12
end Double-time feel
45
Em(9)
D(9)
I know, I know all a - bout. I know, I know all a - bout your
T
A
B
14 14 15 17 15 15 12 12 14 14 14
12 12 12 11 11 11 11
14 14 14 14 14 12 12 12 12 12
D.S. 𝄋 al Coda
E5
C5
5fr.
134
134
6-string Gtrs. 1 & 2 tacet
w/Rhy. Fill 1 (7-string Gtr.)
47
Cmaj7
3
mo - tives in - side, and your de - ci - sion__ to hide.__

Bridge:
w/Rhy. Fig. 2 (7-string Gtr.) 1 1/2 times
w/misc. background vocals
Coda
E5
C5
D5
where you be - long.
E5
C5
G5
D5
1.
E5
I can't give
C5
D5
E5
C5
G5
D5
ev - 'ry - thing a - way.
This is not where you be - long.
2.
w/Rhy. Fig. 1 (7-string Gtr.)
& Riff A (6-string Gtr. 1) both 1 1/2 times
Dsus2
C5
Repeat and fade
6-string Gtr. 1
Cmaj7
7-string Gtr.

STAND UP

All gtrs. are 7-string gtrs. tuned:
⑦ = A ③ = G
⑥ = D ② = B
⑤ = A ① = E
④ = D

Words by CHRIS BROWN
Music by TRAPT

Moderately ♩ = 80
Intro:

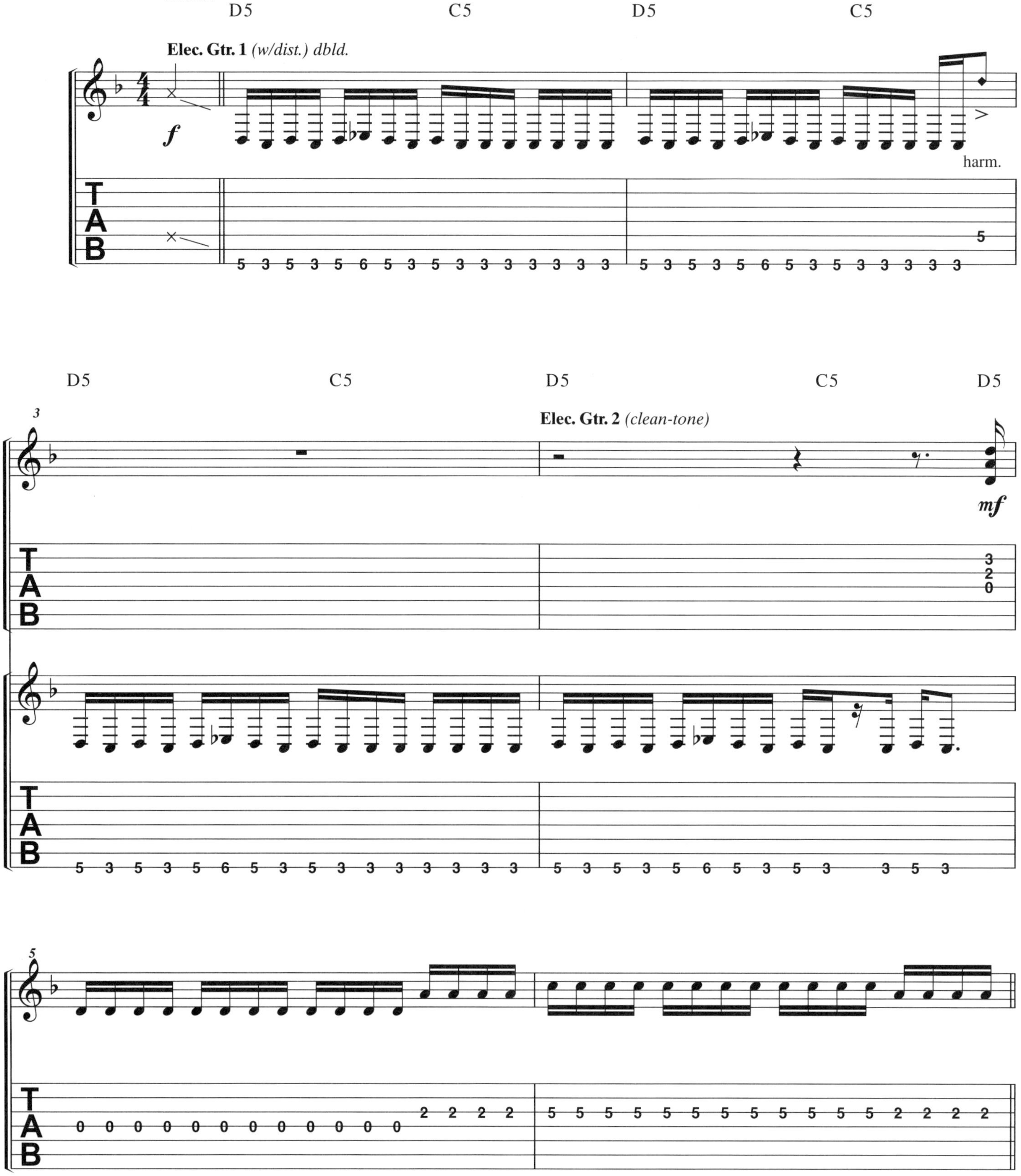

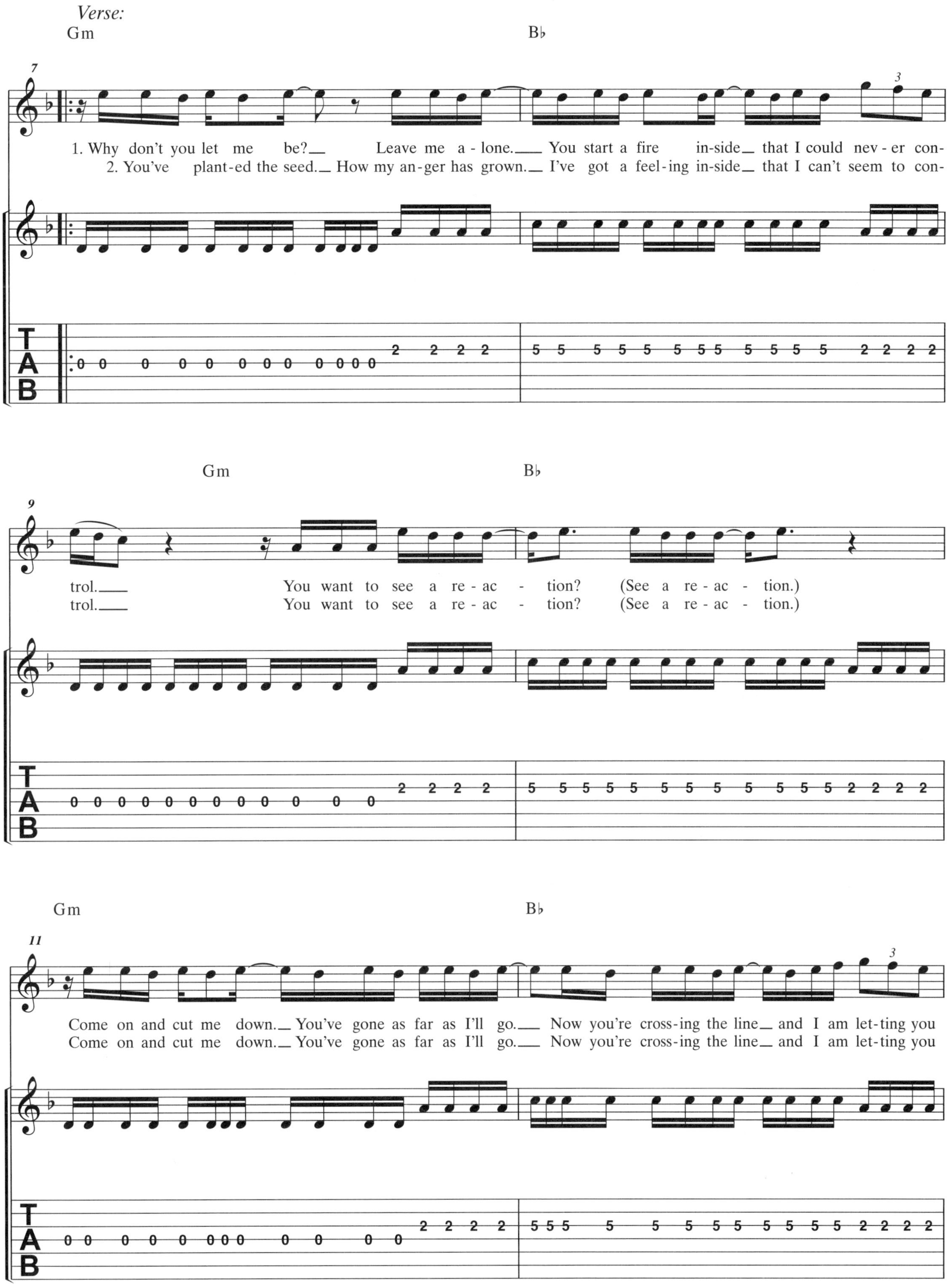
Verse:
Gm
Bb
7
1. Why don't you let me be? Leave me a-lone. You start a fire in-side that I could nev-er con-
2. You've plant-ed the seed. How my an-ger has grown. I've got a feel-ing in-side that I can't seem to con-
Gm
Bb
9
trol. You want to see a re-ac-tion? (See a re-ac-tion.)
trol. You want to see a re-ac-tion? (See a re-ac-tion.)
Gm
Bb
11
Come on and cut me down. You've gone as far as I'll go. Now you're cross-ing the line and I am let-ting you
Come on and cut me down. You've gone as far as I'll go. Now you're cross-ing the line and I am let-ting you

Gm
Bb
13
know. Well, here's your re - ac - tion.
know. So here's your re - ac - tion.
T
A
B
0 0 0 0 0 0 0 0 0 0 0 0 2 2 2 2
5 5 5 5 5 5 5 5 5 5 5 5 5 5 5 5

𝄋 *Pre-chorus:*

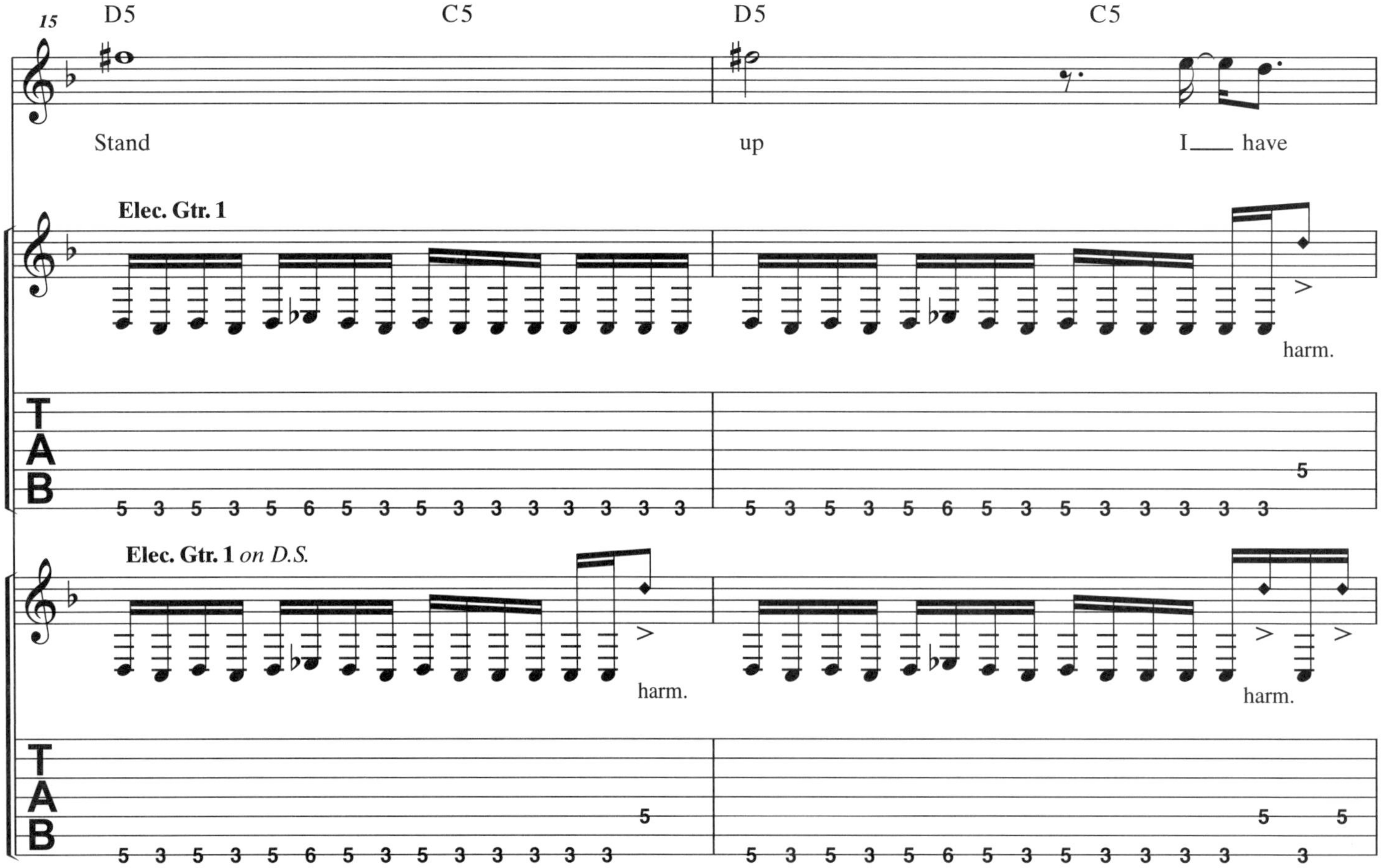
15
D5
C5
D5
C5
Stand up I have
Elec. Gtr. 1
harm.
5 3 5 3 5 6 5 3 5 3 3 3 3 3 3 3
5 3 5 3 5 6 5 3 5 3 3 3 3 3 5 3
Elec. Gtr. 1 on D.S.
harm.
harm.
5 3 5 3 5 6 5 3 5 3 3 3 3 3 5
5 3 5 3 5 6 5 3 5 3 3 3 3 5 3 5

17
D5
C5
D5
C5
had e - nough.
harm.
Moderately fast ♩ = 160
Chorus:
D5
B♭sus2
F5
C5
12fr.
8fr.
3fr.
3fr.
333
1113
111
1314
19
Walk a - way be - fore I fin - ish what
Elec. Gtr. 1
hold
22
D5
B♭sus2
12fr.
8fr.
333
1113
you start - ed. Face to face I will
hold

C5
3fr.
1314
Gsus2
5fr.
1113
D5
12fr.
333
B♭sus2
8fr.
1113
25
put you in___ your place. End this___ game___
hold
F5
3fr.
111
C5
3fr.
1314
28
___ be - fore I fin - ish___ what___ you___ start - ed.
To Coda
D5
12fr.
333
B♭sus2
8fr.
1113
C5
3fr.
1314
B♭5
1314
31
Face to___ face,___ ev - 'ry - thing___ will change.
hold

1. Moderately ♩ = 80
35
D5
Elec. Gtr. 2
2. Moderately ♩ = 80
37
D5
Af-ter
Elec. Gtr. 3 (w/dist.)
mf w/effects
39
Bridge:
in - sult, af-ter in - sult, af-ter in - sult, af-ter in - sult, af-ter in - sult, af-ter in -
41
D.S. 𝄋 al Coda
sult, af-ter in - sult, af-ter in - sult, af-ter in - sult, af-ter in - sult.
trem. pick
TAB

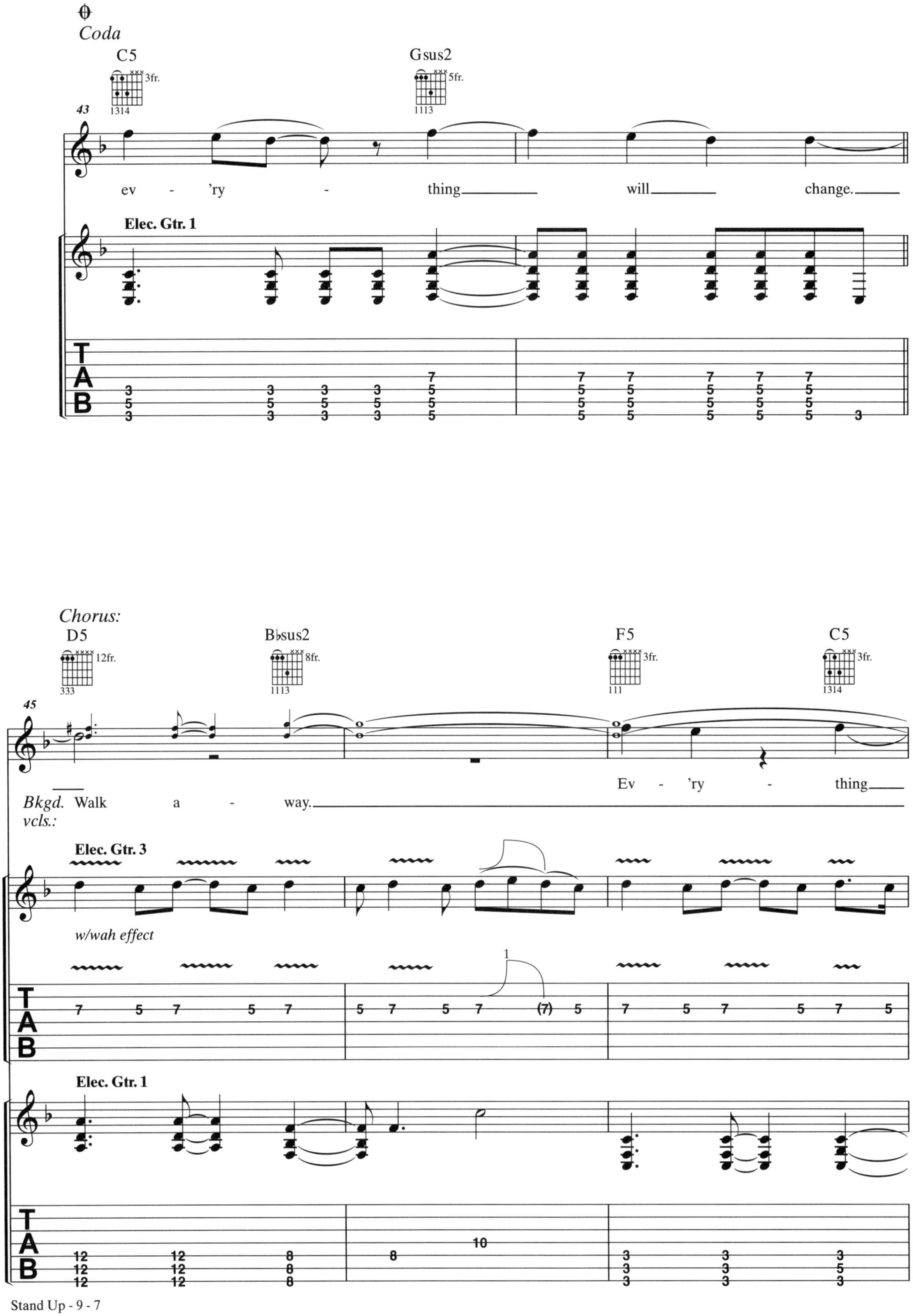
Coda
C5
3fr.
1314
Gsus2
5fr.
1113
43
ev - 'ry - thing will change.
Elec. Gtr. 1
Chorus:
D5
12fr.
333
B♭sus2
8fr.
1113
F5
3fr.
111
C5
3fr.
1314
45
Bkgd. vcls.: Walk a - way.
Ev - 'ry - thing
Elec. Gtr. 3
w/wah effect
Elec. Gtr. 1

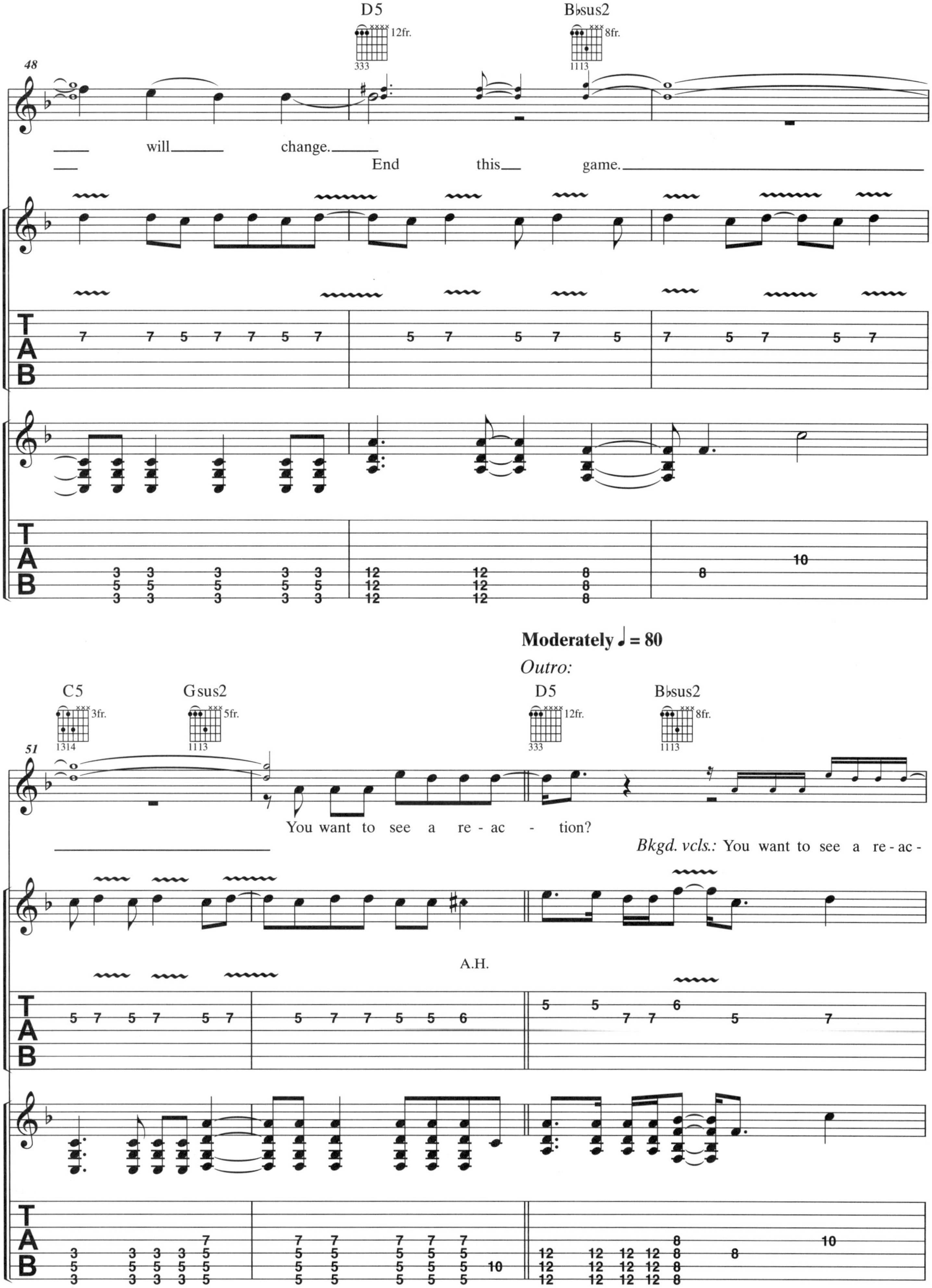

48
D5
12fr.
333
B♭sus2
8fr.
1113
will change.
End this game.
C5
3fr.
1314
Gsus2
5fr.
1113
51
Moderately ♩ = 80
Outro:
D5
12fr.
333
B♭sus2
8fr.
1113
You want to see a re - ac - tion?
Bkgd. vcls.: You want to see a re - ac -
A.H.

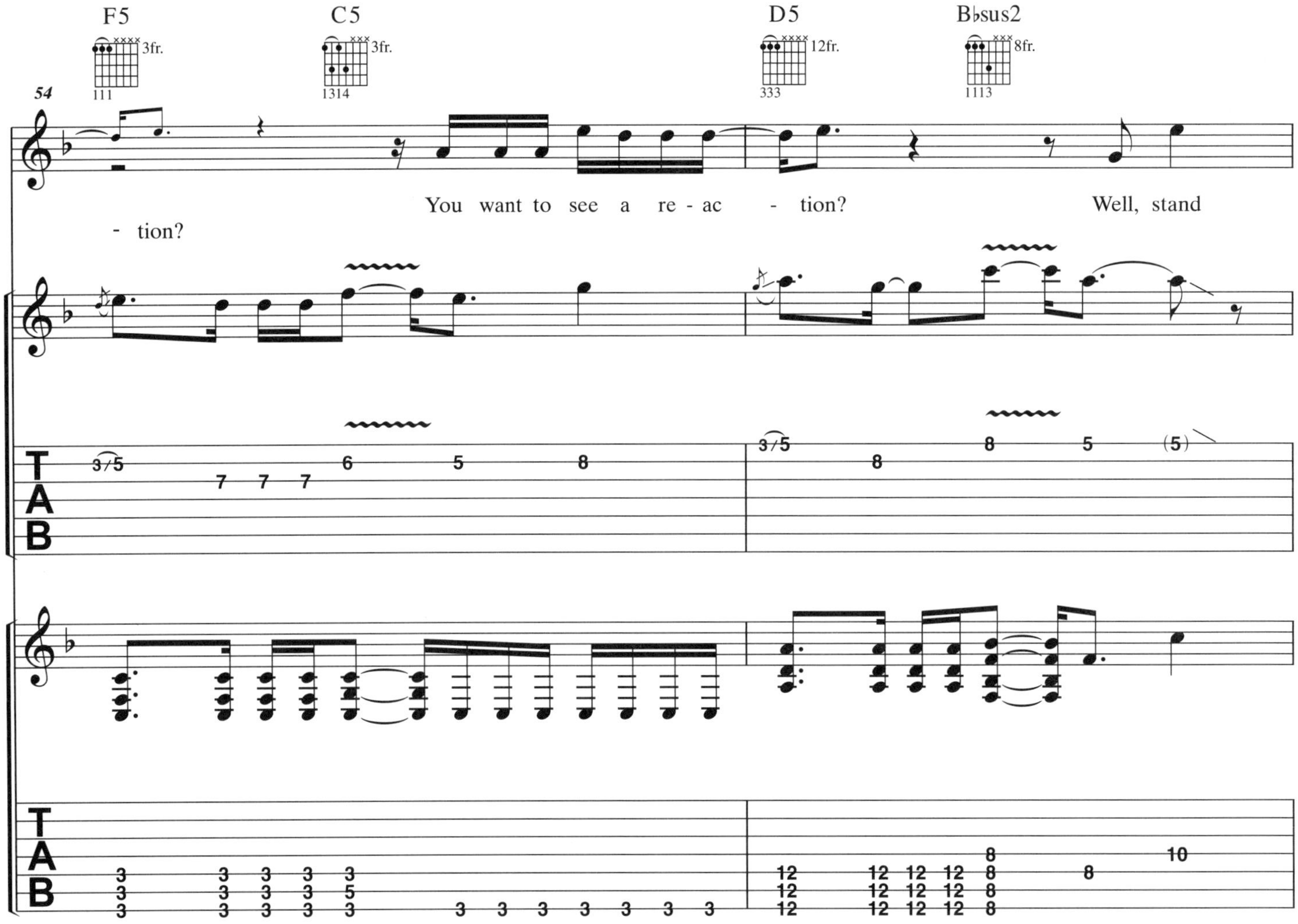
F5
C5
D5
B♭sus2
3fr.
3fr.
12fr.
8fr.
111
1314
333
1113
54
You want to see a re - ac - tion? Well, stand
- tion?

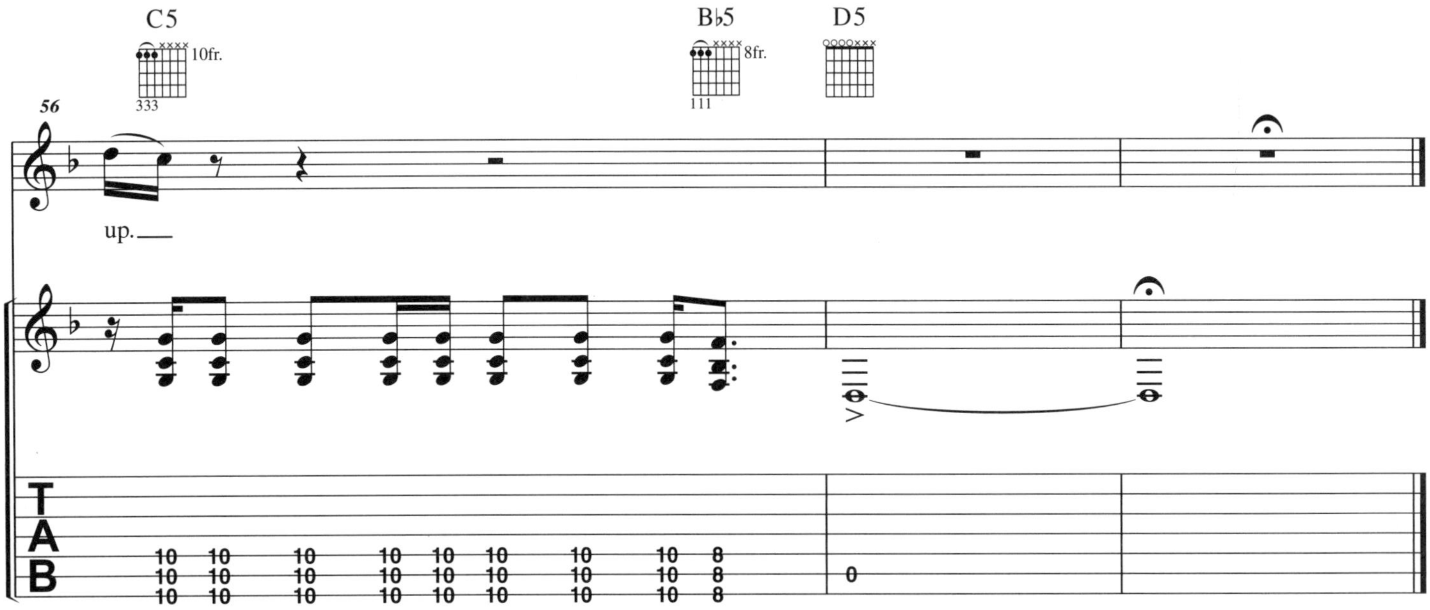
C5
B♭5
D5
10fr.
8fr.
333
111
56
up.

GUITAR TAB GLOSSARY

TABLATURE EXPLANATION

TAB illustrates the six strings of the guitar.
Notes and chords are indicated by the placement of fret numbers on each string.

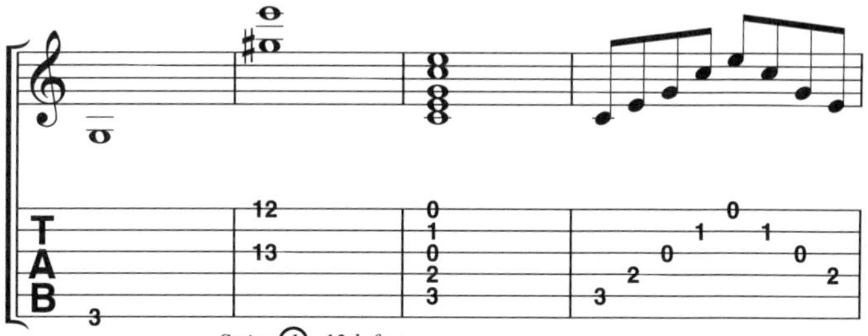

String ⑥, 3rd fret — *String ①, 12th fret / String ③, 13th fret* — *A "C" chord* — *C chord arpeggiated*

BENDING NOTES

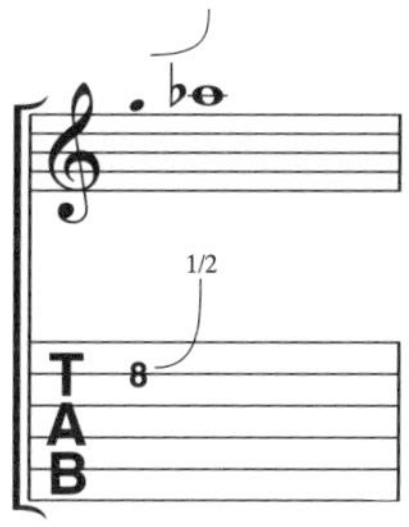

Half Step:
Play the note and bend string one half step (one fret).

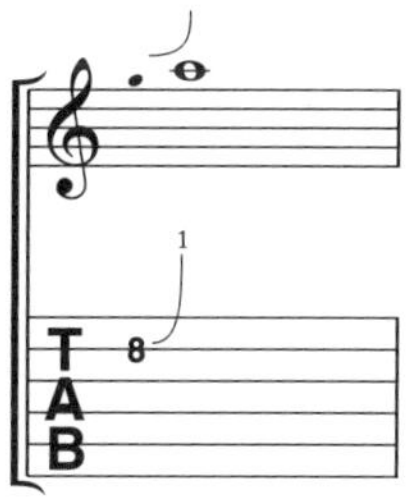

Whole Step:
Play the note and bend string one whole step (two frets).

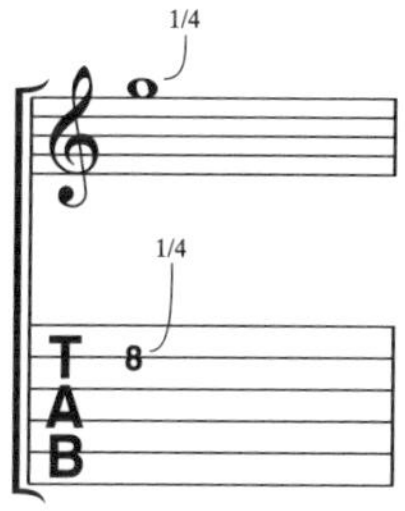

Slight Bend/ Quarter-Tone Bend:
Play the note and bend string sharp.

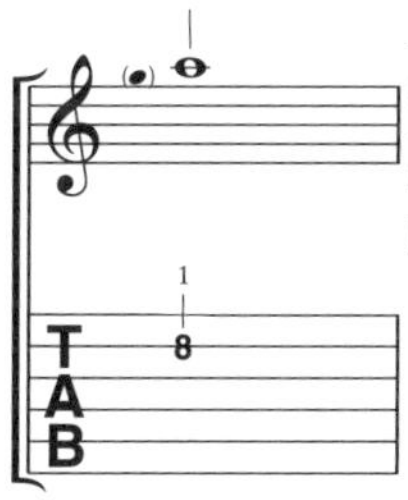

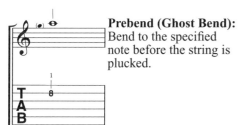

Prebend (Ghost Bend):
Bend to the specified note before the string is plucked.

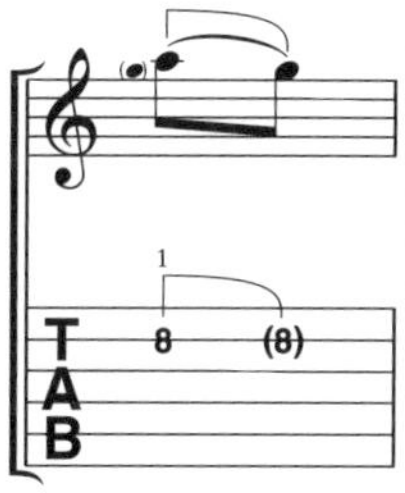

Prebend and Release:
Play the already-bent string, then immediately drop it down to the fretted note.

Unison Bend:
Play both notes and immediately bend the lower note to the same pitch as the higher note.

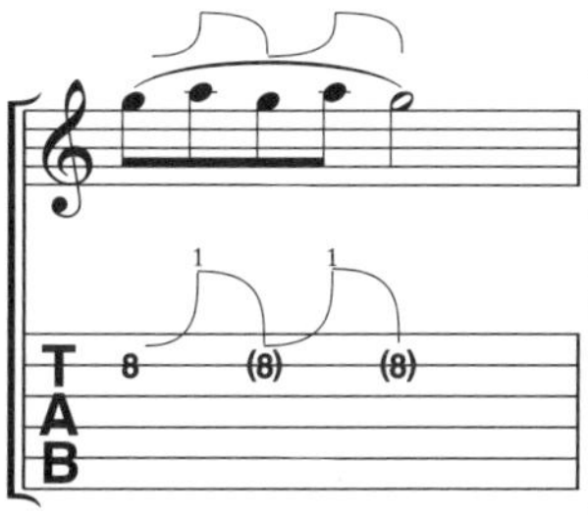

Bend and Release:
Play the note and bend to the next pitch, then release to the original note. Only the first note is attacked.

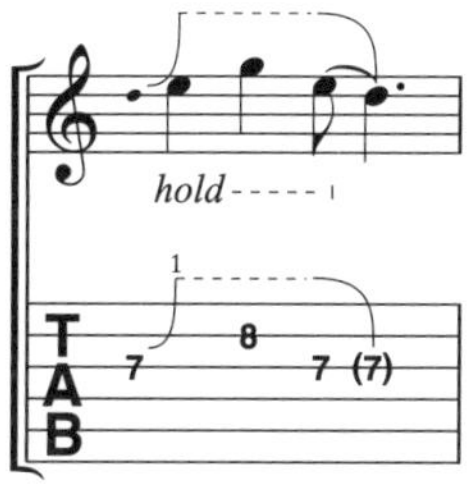

Bends Involving More Than One String:
Play the note and bend the string while playing an additional note on another string. Upon release, relieve the pressure from the additional note allowing the original note to sound alone.

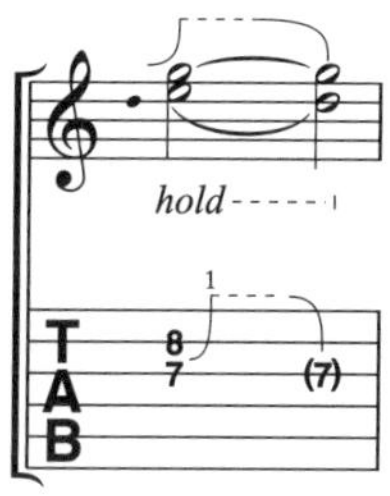

Bends Involving Stationary Notes:
Play both notes and immediately bend the lower note up to pitch. Release bend as indicated.

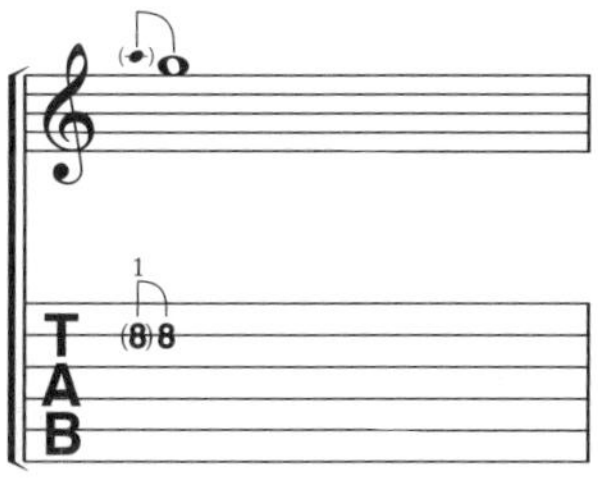

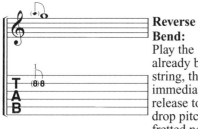

Reverse Bend:
Play the already bent string, then immediately release to drop pitch to fretted note.

Unison Bend:
Play both notes and immediately bend the lower note to the same pitch as the higher note.

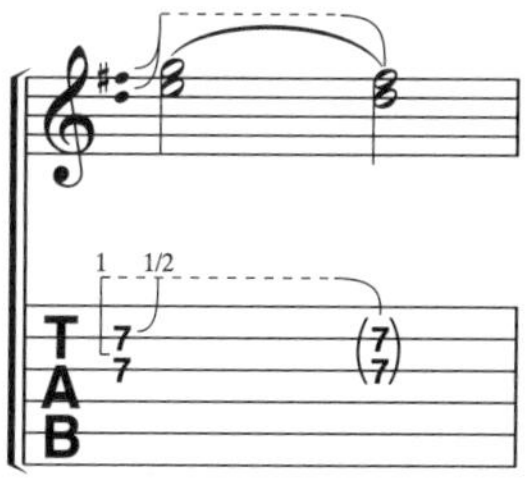

Double Note Bend:
Play both notes and immediately bend both strings simultaneously up the indicated intervals.

Hammer On (Ascending Slur): Play the lower note, then "hammer" your finger to the higher note. Only the first note is plucked.

Pull Off (Descending Slur): Play the higher note with your first finger already in position on the lower note. Pull your finger off the first note with a strong downward motion that plucks the string—sounding the lower note.

Legato Slide: Play the first note and, keeping pressure applied on the string, slide up to the second note. The diagonal line shows that it is a slide and not a hammer-on or a pull-off.

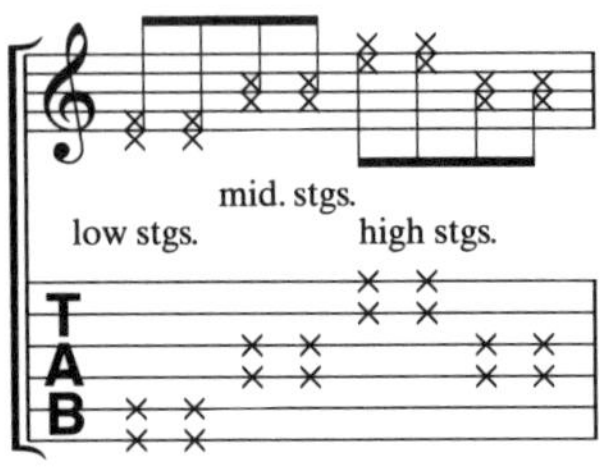

Muted Strings: A percussive sound is produced by striking the strings while laying the fret hand across them.

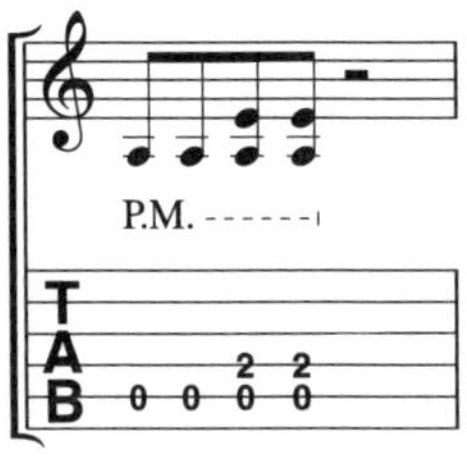

Palm Mute: The notes are muted (muffled) by placing the palm of the pick hand lightly on the strings, just in front of the bridge.

Left Hand Hammer: Using only the left hand, hammer on the first note played on each string.

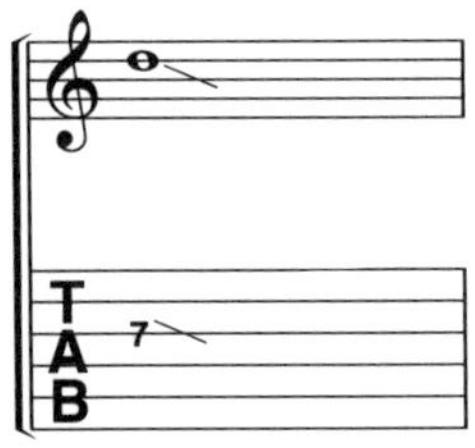

Glissando: Play note and slide in specified direction.

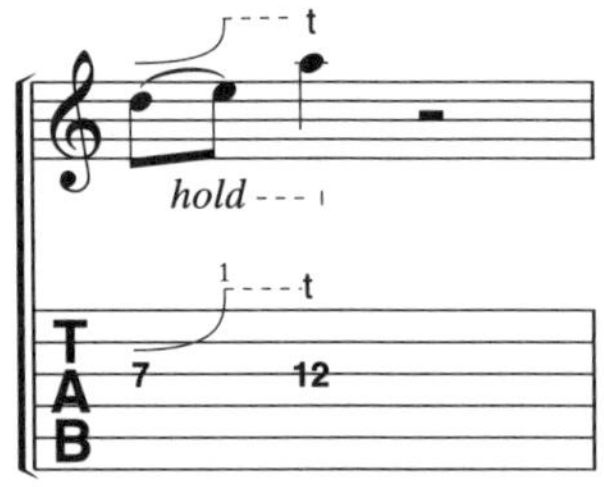

Bend and Tap Technique: Play note and bend to specified interval. While holding bend, tap onto fret indicated with a "t."

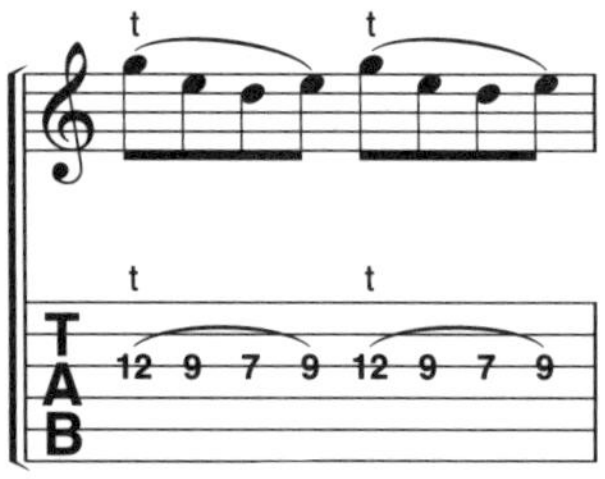

Fretboard Tapping: Tap onto the note indicated by the "t" with a finger of the pick hand, then pull off to the following note held by the fret hand.

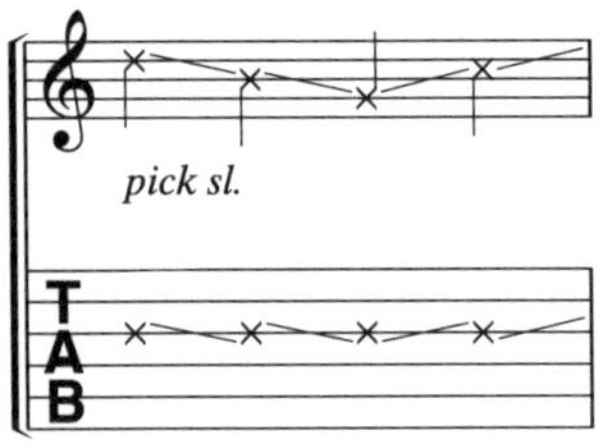

Pick Slide: Slide the edge of the pick in specified direction across the length of the strings.

Tremolo Picking: The note or notes are picked as fast as possible.

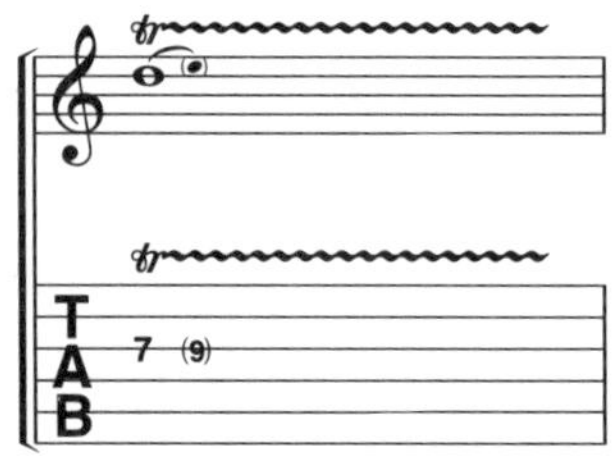

Trill: Hammer on and pull off consecutively and as fast as possible between the original note and the grace note.

Vibrato: The pitch of a note is varied by a rapid shaking of the fret-hand finger, wrist, and forearm.

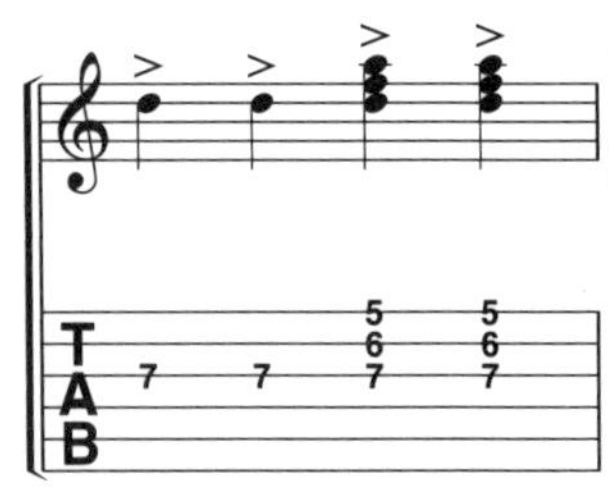

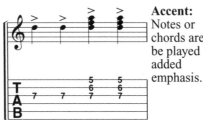

Accent: Notes or chords are to be played with added emphasis.

Staccato (Detached Notes): Notes or chords are to be played about half their noted value and with separation.

HARMONICS

Natural Harmonic: A finger of the fret hand lightly touches the string at the note indicated in the TAB and is plucked by the pick producing a bell-like sound called a harmonic.

Artificial Harmonic: Fret the note at the first TAB number, lightly touch the string at the note indicated in parens (usually 12 frets higher than the fretted note), then pluck the string with an available finger or your pick.

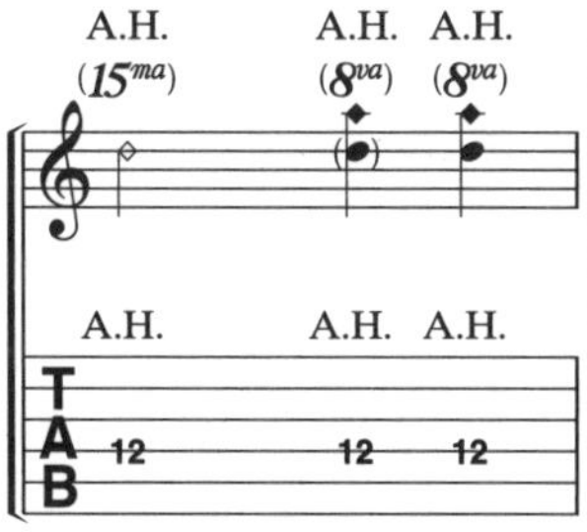

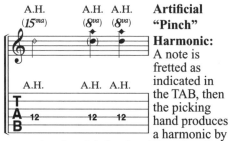

Artificial "Pinch" Harmonic: A note is fretted as indicated in the TAB, then the picking hand produces a harmonic by squeezing the pick firmly while using the tip of the index finger in the pick attack. If parenthesis are found around the fretted note, it does not sound. No parenthesis means both the fretted note and the A.H. are heard simultaneously.

RHYTHM SLASHES

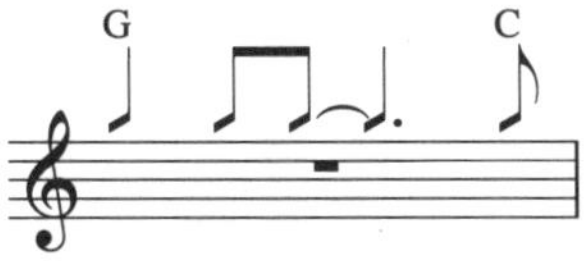

Strum Marks/ Rhythm Slashes: Strum with the indicated rhythm pattern. Strum marks can be located above the staff or within the staff.

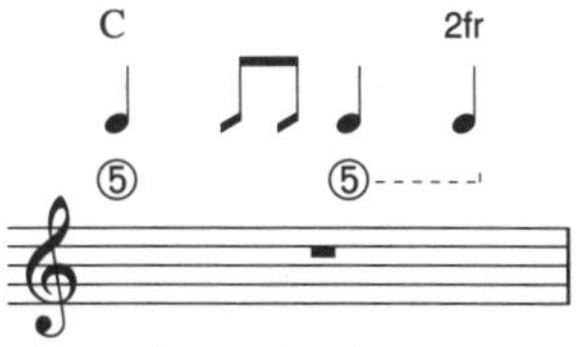

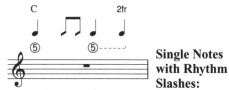

Single Notes with Rhythm Slashes: Sometimes single notes are incorporated into a strum pattern. The circled number below is the string and the fret number is above.

TREMOLO BAR

Specified Interval: The pitch of a note or chord is lowered to the specified interval and then return as indicated. The action of the tremolo bar is graphically represented by the peaks and valleys of the diagram.

Unspecified Interval: The pitch of a note or chord is lowered, usually very dramatically, until the pitch of the string becomes indeterminate.

PICK DIRECTION

Downstrokes and Upstrokes: The downstroke is indicated with this symbol (⊓) and the upstroke is indicated with this (V).

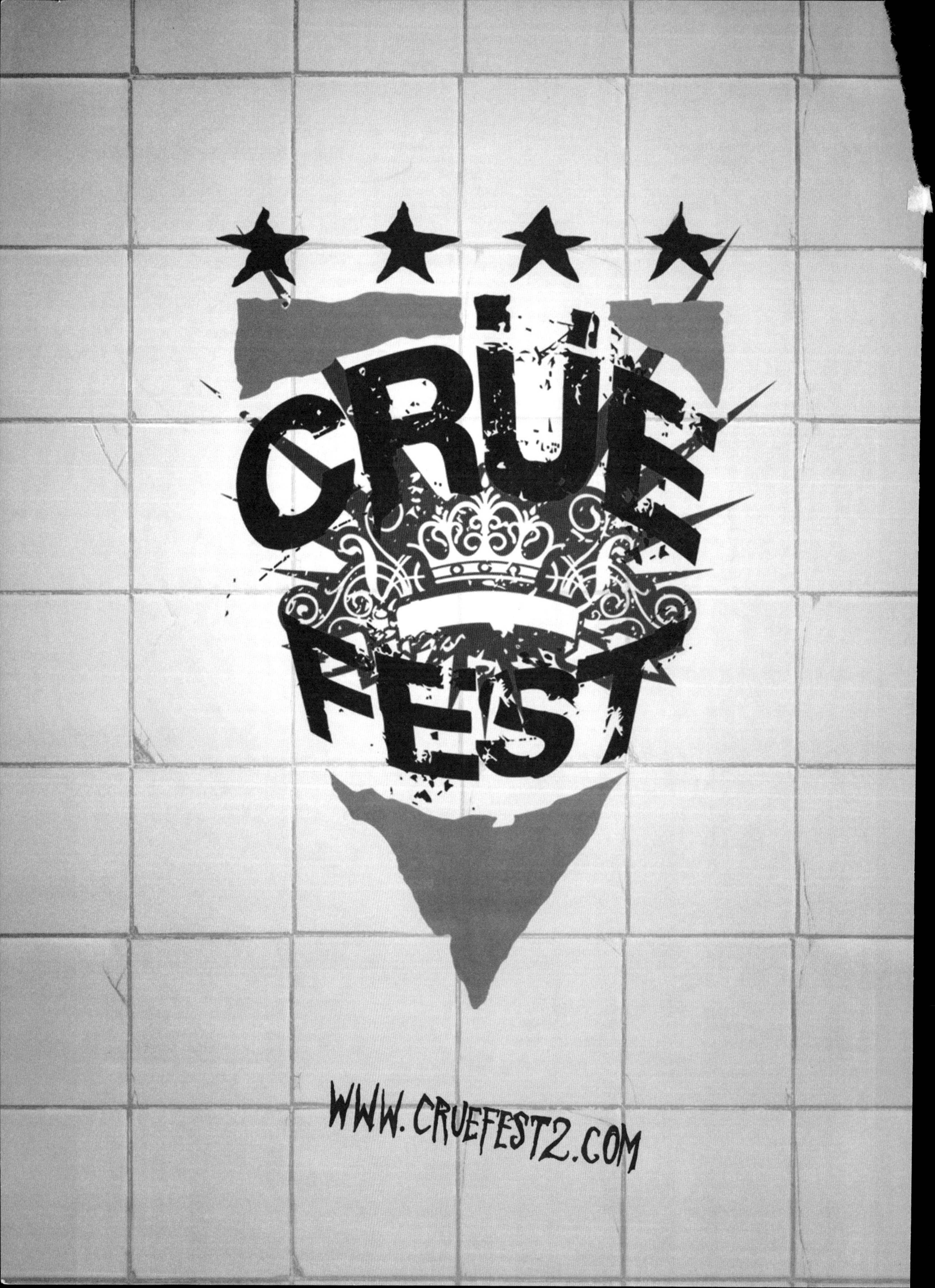
CRÜE
FEST
WWW.CRUEFEST2.COM